J. V. Luce was born in Dublin in 1920. He was educated at Cheltenham College and at Trinity College, Dublin, where he graduated with First Class Honours in Classics and Philosophy in 1942. He was Lecturer in Greek at Glasgow University, 1946–8, and was elected Fellow in Classics at Trinity College, Dublin, in 1948. Appointed Reader in Classics at Trinity College in 1963, he subsequently became Tutor and then Senior Tutor 1964–7. He was Visiting Professor in Classics at Trinity College, Hartford, Connecticut, 1961–2.

Mr Luce has for many years made a close study of the Classical sources relating to the Atlantis legend – in particular of Plato, the originator of the story. He is the author of numerous articles in learned journals.

J. V. Luce

The End of Atlantis

New Light on an Old Legend

Paladin

Granada Publishing Limited
Published in 1970 by Paladin
Frogmore, St Albans, Herts AL2 2NF
Reprinted 1971, 1972, 1973, 1974, 1975

First published by Thames & Hudson Ltd 1969
Copyright © Thames & Hudson 1969
Made and printed in Great Britain by
Hazell Watson & Viney Ltd
Aylesbury, Bucks
Set in Monotype Ehrhardt

Contents

Preface

> The Editors wish to point out that in their opinion the main thesis of this article requires additional support from excavation on selected sites. They hope that such excavations will in due course be carried out.

The 'Editors' in question were those of the English periodical *Antiquity* which in 1939 published a notable article by Professor Spyridon Marinatos, Director of the Greek Archaeological Service, on 'The volcanic destruction of Minoan Crete'. Professor Marinatos maintained with a considerable show of evidence that the recognized and widespread destruction of Knossos and of Cretan civilization generally soon after 1500 BC was the result of ultra-violent volcanic activity on the island of Thera (Santorini) some 110 km. north of Crete.

Now, thirty years later, Professor Marinatos has actually been carrying out excavations at Akrotiri, near the southern end of the main island of the Thera group, and has amplified earlier discoveries of sub-volcanic Minoan (Cretan) walling to an extent which, combined with the great height of the volcanic overburden, may be said to prove much of his thesis of 1939. The whole destructive happening seems to have begun with a shattering earthquake and to have continued in the form of two eruptions of which the second was the more severe and was certainly accompanied by immense tidal waves. Debris and waves alike reached Crete, no doubt with further earthquakes, and the Minoan civilization was in effect blotted out. Only Knossos, relatively sheltered, survived after a fashion, now seemingly under Greek-speaking opportunists from the mainland.

But that is not all. The episode has drawn afresh into the daylight, from nebulous Platonic hearsay and modern peri-lunacy, the old Lost Continent of Atlantis. As long ago as 1909 a young scholar in Belfast had printed the inspired guess that the fabulous

State of Atlantis was in fact a memory of the glittering Minoan Empire which Sir Arthur Evans and other explorers were then beginning to show the world. It remained, as I have recalled, for Professor Marinatos to lend actuality to its legendary destruction, and now, since 1967, to add by excavation some of the basic evidences demanded by his editors in 1939. Others have contributed substantially to the reconstruction of the scene; notably the Greek seismologist Professor Angelos Galanopoulos, who amongst other things took a professional interest in a severe earthquake at Thera in 1956 and obtained a radiocarbon dating for materials from ruins then uncovered beneath the deep volcanic debris. In one way and another, cautious scholarship is increasingly bending towards all this rationalization. The moment seems an appropriate one for the collection and presentation of the problem as it appears at the end of 1968; and this Mr J. V. Luce has here done, after visiting the fieldwork now in progress and receiving the most generous facilities from Professor Marinatos himself.

MORTIMER WHEELER

Introduction

Five cores of sediment from the ocean floor of the Eastern Mediterranean have precipitated a far-reaching reappraisal of Aegean history in the fifteenth century BC. The cores contain volcanic ash from the island of Thera – ash which was deposited over a very wide area by a volcanic eruption of vast explosive power. The evidence was published in 1965 in a remarkable paper by two American scientists, D. Ninkovich and B. C. Heezen. After discussing the distribution of the ash they went on to outline the implications of their findings for Late Bronze Age history. In particular, they suggested that the eruption was a major catastrophe for the island-based empire of Minoan Crete, and that it led directly to a transference of power from the Minoans to the mainland Greeks (Mycenaeans). As long ago as 1939 Professor Marinatos had argued that Minoan Crete was volcanically destroyed, and the work of Ninkovich and Heezen has reinforced his argument with scientific evidence which cannot be ignored, and which demands the fullest consideration.

One of my main aims is to present a picture of Thera and its great Bronze Age eruption based on the principal evidence which has so far accumulated. My general conclusions about the effects of the eruption on Minoan Crete are in agreement with those of Ninkovich and Heezen, but with one important exception: they date the catastrophe to *c.* 1400 BC, whereas I favour a date *c.* 1470 BC. In this earlier dating I am happy to find myself in agreement with Professor Marinatos, and also with M. S. F. Hood, who in his recent book *The Home of the Heroes* has outlined the effects of the Thera disaster (pp. 106–8).

My second main theme is Atlantis. As long ago as 1909 K. T. Frost suggested that the legend of Atlantis was based on a genuine but unrecognized tradition of Minoan Crete. This 'Minoan hypothesis' made little or no impact on learned opinion at the time, but has attracted increasing interest and support since World War II. In the summer of 1967 important archaeological discoveries were made on Thera by Professor Marinatos. In the resulting world-wide publicity, the assertion was often made that 'lost Atlantis' had finally been found. I hope that my account of the Thera excavations (based on a visit to the site and on Professor Marinatos' own report), and also my discussion of

9

the Atlantis legend, will enable my readers to judge in what sense the equation of Atlantis with Minoan Crete in general, or with Thera in particular, is, or could be, true.

I have recalled some former suggestions, and also made what I believe to be some new suggestions about memories of the Thera disaster in Greek literature and mythology, apart from the Atlantis legend. If these suggestions are found convincing, they will go some way to meet Mr Hood's contention that the disaster would have been more clearly remembered by the Greeks if they had been in the Aegean area at the time when it happened. Unlike Mr Hood, I believe that the Mycenaeans were Greeks, and that the Linear B tablets contain an early form of Greek. I therefore conclude that the Thera eruption had a profound effect on early *Greek* history, as well as on the Minoan empire. Some fragmentary traditions about it did survive, I think, particularly in Greek epic, but the Greeks did not realize their significance. Nor did they connect the Atlantis legend with Minoan Crete. With regard to the legend, I follow the view that a genuine tradition of the sudden destruction of Minoan power was preserved in Egypt, and that this tradition was brought back to Greece by Solon about 590 BC, but in a garbled and misunderstood form. Plato later perpetuated the misunderstanding by the literary and artistic form which he imposed on Solon's report.

Even if the equation of Atlantis with Minoan Crete is rejected, the Thera hypothesis can stand on its own, for it rests on a different kind of evidence. The contribution of Ninkovich and Heezen is a significant example of what modern science has to offer to classical archaeology. Further excavations on Thera will doubtless increase our detailed knowledge of Minoan and Cycladic culture, but may not greatly alter our historical perspective. In addition to these excavations, further investigations of the eruption and its effects are urgently needed, if present lines of thought about the fall of Minoan Crete are to be confirmed and extended. Such investigations will call for the closest co-operation between archaeologists, ancient historians, and scientists, especially vulcanologists and submarine geologists.

I wish to express my thanks for the assistance I have received from Trinity College Dublin colleagues in scientific departments: from Professor W. A. Watts in Botany, Professor C. H. Holland in Geology, and Professor J. P. Haughton and Mr F. H. A. Aalen in Geography. I am also much indebted to Professor W. D. Gill and Dr G. Walker of Imperial College, London, for very helpful advice. Dr Walker was kind enough to let me see important data from his as yet unpublished study of ash fall-out in the Azores, and this information helped me to a better understanding of the possible range of effects of the Thera outbreak. I am also grateful to Dr W. T. Stearn of the Botany Department of the British Museum (Natural History) for directing my attention to published material on the import of lichens from Crete and the Cyclades to Egypt. At an early stage of my researches Professor L. J. D. Richardson kindly put at my disposal a useful bibliography which he had compiled. Later, Professor J. Weingreen was good enough to advise me on the complexities of the Exodus problem, and the mentions of Caphtor in the Old Testament. On Thera itself a chance encounter with Mr B. Gill led to a useful exchange of ideas and information. I should also like to thank Mr P. Clayton for his knowledgeable editorial assistance.

The text and bibliography will show how much I owe to the work of Professor Marinatos, and I am also very grateful to him for facilitating my visit to the new excavations on Thera. But my chief obligation is to Sir Mortimer Wheeler. In his capacity as chairman of Swans Hellenic Cruises he has been responsible for most of my visits to Thera and Crete, visits which have fired my interest in Minoan archaeology. And then, in his capacity as General Editor of this series, he very kindly invited me to contribute this assessment of the present state of the Atlantis-Thera question. I am deeply grateful for his support and encouragement.

Finally, I wish to thank my wife for her never-failing interest and encouragement. She has helped me to appreciate the truth of the conclusion of Odysseus' first speech to Nausikaa:

ὁμοφρονέοντε νοήμασιν

Odyssey VI, 183.

Trinity College,
Dublin

J.V.L.

1 Plato's Account of Atlantis

Atlantis: fact or fiction?

We owe to Plato the legend of Atlantis, that haunting story of an ancient island civilization which vanished as the result of a great natural disaster. Ever since Plato first published the story, people have been attracted and puzzled by it, and have tried either to explain it away as a fairy tale or to justify it by locating the remnants of the lost island. These two reactions can be traced back to the generation after Plato's death. Aristotle compared the story of Atlantis with Homer's account of the wall which the Greeks were said to have built round their camp at Troy, and which was later obliterated by divine intervention. His point was that both stories were poetic fictions invented by the authors to help out their narratives. He went on to suggest that just as Homer removed the wall when it had served its purpose, so Plato sank his Atlantis in the depths of the ocean to forestall the critic who might ask for the present location of the island. 'The man who dreamed it up made it vanish,' was Aristotle's curt solution of the Atlantis problem.[1]

But the problem was not to be solved so easily and quickly. Crantor (c. 300 BC), the first editor of the *Timaeus*, went to the opposite extreme. He thought that every point in the narrative was literally and historically true. He even, it seems, went to the length of sending a special enquiry to Egypt to verify the sources of the story, and the priests replied that records of it were still extant 'on pillars'.[2]

Interpretations of Atlantis have hovered between these poles ever since. On medieval maps, that of Toscanelli del Pozzo for example, dated AD 1475 and used by Columbus, many islands, large and small, are marked in the seas west of Europe and Africa. Among them is Antillia (from which the Antilles take their name), and this may preserve in garbled form the name of Plato's Atlantis. The early Spanish and Portuguese navigators were not unwilling to believe that traces of the lost island might still await discovery, and the lure of this quest is a recognizable motive in their explorations. There is more than a grain of truth in J. O. Thomson's epigram: 'In a sense Plato may be said to have invented America.'[3] Even as late as 1882 Gladstone sought (but did not receive) approval from the British Cabinet for expenditure on an Atlantis exploration vessel.

Classical scholars were more sceptical. The distinguished Victorian Platonist Benjamin Jowett dismissed Atlantis as a mere fiction, and so did F. M. Cornford in his commentary on the *Timaeus*. For A. E. Taylor the 'whole tale is Plato's own invention'; for W. W. Hyde 'a geographical fable'; for T. G. Rosenmeyer a *plaisanterie* parodying earlier Utopias.[4]

Undoubted fact, or palpable fiction? Can there be any compromise between these extremes? This book attempts to find and follow a middle way.

The historical element in Greek myths and legends

Developments in the interpretation of Greek mythology and saga over the past hundred years set the pattern for this enquiry. Classical scholars laughed at Schliemann when he set out with Homer in one hand and a spade in the other. But he dug up Troy, and thereby demonstrated that it is rash to underestimate the historical value of folk memory. Sir Arthur Evans did much the same thing when he found the labyrinthine home of the Minotaur at Knossos. As archaeology progressively revealed the remains of the great Mycenaean kingdoms at Mycenae, Tiryns, Orchomenus and Thebes, Nilsson pointed out that the major Greek saga cycles clustered round these very places. In this way he proved that the stories of the house of Atreus, of Heracles, of Oedipus, could no longer be dismissed as mere poetic fancies.[5] On the contrary, they could now be seen as genuine traditions which took shape round the main power centres of the Mycenaean world in the time of its greatest splendour in the Late Bronze Age. What was once regarded as mere myth had now to be treated as historical material, and needed careful sifting to recover the hard core of fact which it contained.

The same trend is still continuing, and in recent years legend after legend has been substantiated by archaeological discoveries in Greek lands. For example, the background of the *Odyssey* has been illuminated by finds on Ithaca. In 1937–8 Miss Benton excavated the remains of a fairly large building and recovered substantial amounts of Mycenaean pottery at Polis Bay on Ithaca. From a nearby cave, sacred to the Nymphs, came pottery ranging from the Bronze Age to the first century AD, thirteen magnificent bronze tripod-cauldrons of the ninth to the eighth centuries BC, and a second-century BC terracotta mask inscribed: 'A prayer to Odysseus'. These discoveries tend to confirm the basic accuracy of Homer's picture of Ithaca as a Mycenaean island kingdom at the time of the siege of Troy.[6]

In the third book of the *Odyssey* Homer tells how Telemachus, son of Odysseus, set out by ship from Ithaca to seek news of his absent father, and sailing south landed at 'sandy Pylos'. There he met king Nestor, and was hospitably entertained in Nestor's great palace nearby. Amongst other details we are told that he was given a bath by Nestor's daughter Polycaste, and that Nestor served him with vintage wine eleven years old.[7]

Homer's picture has received remarkable confirmation in the dramatic discoveries of Professor Carl Blegen at Epano Englianos in south-west Messenia.[8] Thanks to Blegen's excavations from 1952 onwards we can now clearly trace the ground plan of a great Mycenaean palace which was standing in stately splendour in the thirteenth century BC. The marks of fluting can be seen on pillar bases still *in situ* in the 'echoing porticos'. It is even possible to trace successive renewals in the plaster work round the great central hearth of the throne-room (Plate 2), and to make out something of the colour and pattern of the chequered floor. And when one sees a finely moulded and decorated bath-tub still in position in one of the rooms (Plate 1), and when one learns that in a wine magazine behind the palace there were clay sealings with signs presumably indicating vintage and provenance, one has to admit that the convergence of archaeology and Greek literary tradition about this site has become very close and convincing. It is now probably up to the sceptic to disprove, if he can, the identification of the site with Nestor's palace as described by Homer. The palace archives, the famous Linear B tablets of

Pylos, show that this palace was a major administrative centre for western Messenia not far from the time of the Trojan War. Nestor's name has not been found on these records, but it should be remembered that the tablets date from the year of the final destruction of the palace, c. 1200 BC, when a son or grandson would have succeeded to the throne. But Greek epic preserved the memory of Nestor who commanded ninety ships to Troy (the next biggest contingent after Agamemnon's), and bard after bard sang about him until the tale was finally preserved for us in the poems of Homer composed about 500 years later. In view of the details that Homer gives, a modern visitor to Blegen's site cannot be dismissed as excessively credulous if he believes the signpost informing him that he is approaching 'Nestor's palace'.

I have dealt in some detail with the question of the identification of 'Nestor's palace', because it seems to me to be a problem of the same type as the Atlantis problem. In the absence of a certifying inscription, identifications of this sort are based on circumstantial evidence, i.e. 'indirect evidence founded on circumstances which limit the number of admissible hypotheses'. Now it is still, I admit, an 'admissible hypothesis' that what Homer calls the 'illustrious halls' of Nestor await discovery in some other part of the Peloponnese. Recent surveys have shown that a large number of Mycenaean sites remain unexcavated, especially in Messenia. On the other hand, Blegen has unearthed a great palace whose written records show that it had administrative control over a large area. The dates of its construction and destruction, as determined by pottery finds, agree closely with the Greek tradition that there were only four Pylian monarchs: Neleus who acquired the site, Nestor the long-lived, his son Pisistratus, and his grandson. And when one reflects on the Homeric details – the ninety ships, the sandy shore, the name Pylos (common in the vicinity), the wine-stores, and the bathroom – one must wonder whether another palace could possibly turn up to fill all these requirements so aptly.

For a number of reasons the problem of identifying Atlantis is much more complex than the Pylos problem. First, Atlantis stands for a vanished civilization, not just a buried building. Secondly, the legend of Atlantis is much less securely rooted in ancient Greek tradition than the Trojan War saga. Thirdly, if the story does contain a hard core of Aegean history, the events must lie in the early Mycenaean period which was not remembered in much detail by the Greeks. Fourthly, no one in search of Nestor's palace would go outside the Peloponnese, but Atlantis has been sought literally from Ceylon to Mexico, and there are so many false trails that it is hard to know where to begin. But in principle the argument advanced in this book is the same as that used in identifying Agamemnon's Troy or Nestor's palace. It is an argument based on the circumstantial evidence of archaeology, history, and legend, and it tries to use this evidence to limit the number of admissible hypotheses until one emerges as the most credible. It starts from the belief that the legend of Atlantis, like other Greek legends, may embody a hard core of historical fact. It then considers how the legend was transmitted to Plato. Consideration of the transmission route then suggests a time and place for the events which led to the initial formation of the legend. The appropriate space-time location is found in Minoan Crete and its island empire in the Late Bronze Age. Atlantis is thus tentatively identified with Minoan Crete. The details of the Atlantis legend are then compared with what is independently known about the history of Minoan Crete. Finally a decision has to be taken whether the comparison has sufficiently limited the 'admissible hypotheses' for it to be said that the identification is implausible, possible, reasonable, or probable. Certainty is not claimed.

Atlantis apart, the archaeological and scientific evidence set out in subsequent chapters calls for a new look at Aegean history in the Late Bronze Age. One of the main problems here has always been the decline and collapse of Minoan power, in-dependence, and cultural importance, in the fifteenth century BC. Three main reasons have been suggested for this collapse: foreign conquest, internal strife, a major natural catastrophe such as earthquake or drought leading to famine and plague. In recent years, attention has focused more and more on the third possi-bility—namely, that the fall of Minoan Crete was caused, or hastened, by a natural catastrophe or cataclysm. This cataclysm is thought to have consisted of a vast eruption, or series of eruptions, centred on the volcanic island of Thera (Santorin)[9] which lies some 120 km. due north of Knossos.

One of the main purposes of this book is to present the

scientific and archaeological evidence which has been accumulating about Thera over the past hundred years. This evidence has recently been augmented by two very significant investigations: 1) the recovery, in deep-sea cores, of volcanic ash (*tephra*) from the Thera volcano spread over a very wide area of the eastern Mediterranean; 2) the excavation by the Greek Archaeological Service of a site on the south-west coast of Thera which has already yielded evidence of a prosperous Minoan settlement overwhelmed and obliterated by the pumice and ash from a great eruption. The evidence is already strong enough for the date and course of the eruption to be charted within quite narrow time-limits. A reasonable estimate can also be made of its extraordinary violence and destructive power. The effects of the Thera eruption cannot now be disregarded in any historical account of the events of the Late Bronze Age in the eastern Mediterranean, especially in relation to Minoan Crete.

We are again faced with a convergence of archaeology and Greek legend. The legend stems mainly from Plato, and is not at all as deeply rooted in Greek mythology as, say, the story of Troy. But when we read in Plato that the great and ancient civilization of Atlantis 'disappeared in one terrible day and night' we must, I suggest, re-think the old alternatives in the light of the new evidence. Is this the device of a fiction-writer, destroying with a stroke of his pen the edifice of his own imagination? Or does it embody a remote and garbled memory of something which actually happened?

The short account of Atlantis in Plato's *Timaeus*

It is now time to consider in some detail the primary source for the Atlantis legend. Plato outlines the story in his *Timaeus,* and describes Atlantis in more detail in the (unfinished) *Critias.* The relevant passages are quoted in full in the Appendix. To avoid any suggestion that the translation is angled to suit the 'Minoan hypothesis' I present the material in the rendering of the sceptical Jowett. The following quotation comprises the key portion of the statement of the Egyptian priest to Solon, as narrated by Critias in the *Timaeus* (24 d–25 d):

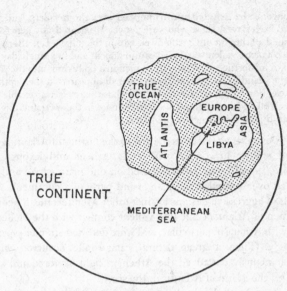

1 Plato's conception of the terrestrial sphere

Many great and wonderful deeds are recorded of your state (*i.e.* Athens) in our histories. But one of them exceeds all the rest in greatness and valour. For these histories tell of a mighty power which unprovoked made an expedition against the whole of Europe and Asia, and to which your city put an end. This power came forth out of the Atlantic Ocean, for in those days the Atlantic was navigable; and there was an island situated in front of the straits which are by you called the pillars of Heracles; the island was larger than Libya and Asia put together, and was the way to other islands, and from these you might pass to the whole of the opposite continent which surrounded the true ocean; for this sea which is within the Straits of Heracles (*i.e.* the Mediterranean) is only a harbour, having a narrow entrance, but that other is a real sea, and the land surrounding it on every side may be most truly called a boundless continent (Fig. 1). Now in this island of Atlantis there was a great and wonderful empire which had rule over the whole island and several others, and over parts of the continent, and, furthermore, the men of Atlantis had subjected the parts of Libya within the columns of Heracles as far as Egypt, and of Europe as far as Tyrrhenia (*i.e.* Etruria in North Italy). This vast power, gathered into one, endeavoured to subdue at a blow our country and yours and the whole of the region within the straits; and then, Solon, your country shone forth, in the excellence of her virtue and strength, among all mankind. She was pre-eminent in courage and military skill, and was the leader of the Hellenes. And when the rest fell off from her, being compelled to stand alone, after having undergone the very extremity of dangers, she defeated and triumphed over the invaders, and preserved from slavery those who were not yet subjugated, and generously liberated all the rest of us who dwelt within the pillars. But afterwards there occurred violent earthquakes and floods; and in a single day and night of misfortune all your warlike men in a body sank into the earth, and the island of Atlantis in like manner disappeared in the depths of the sea. For which reason the sea in those parts is impassable and impenetrable, because there is a shoal of mud in the way; and this was caused by the subsidence of the island.

The above extract contains the gist of the history of Atlantis as an island empire in conflict with early Athens and Egypt. The empire, it will be noted, was based on one main island and extended over several other islands and parts of a continent. As a result of aggressive designs against other Mediterranean peoples the men of Atlantis came into violent conflict with the Hellenes, and with Athens in particular, and were defeated after a desperate struggle. Then a great natural catastrophe occurred which simultaneously destroyed the Athenian fighting force and submerged the island of Atlantis in the sea.

Plato makes Atlantis 'larger than Libya and Asia together'. This is a very vague measure of size, and obviously relative to Plato's own conception of the size of 'Libya' and 'Asia' which we cannot know for certain, but it is likely that he is thinking of a land mass as big as North Africa and Asia Minor put together. He also dates the Atlantis invasion between 8000 and 9000 years before the time of Solon (c. 600 BC). I shall argue later that the large dimensions of Atlantis and the extreme antiquity of her aggression against Greece are distortions and exaggerations imported by Plato himself into a historical tradition which was garbled before it reached him, and which he failed to identify correctly. Here I only emphasize the hard core of the legend as I see it, namely the tradition of a great and highly civilized island empire which had once menaced the autonomy of Greece and Athens in particular, and which came to an end as the result of a natural catastrophe. Plato, I believe, did not invent this tradition. It came to him from his ancestor Solon, as he tells us, and Solon in turn derived it from Egyptian priests.

The sceptic at this point might be excused for quoting the immortal words of Pooh Bah: 'Merely corroborative detail intended to give artistic verisimilitude to an otherwise bald and unconvincing narrative'. But the sceptic must reckon with two undeniable facts: 1) Egyptian records still extant on stone and papyrus go back far into the Bronze Age, and record events of which the ancient Greeks had no knowledge or conception; 2) Solon did visit Egypt. The latter fact is, surprisingly, doubted by Jowett, but we have the evidence of Solon's own poetry to attest it.[10]

Solon in Egypt

Solon's visit to Egypt is usually dated to about 590 BC. He had just completed a series of economic and political reforms in Athens, and he wisely decided to withdraw from the scene for a while to let his measures take full effect in his absence. At this date the Greeks were being well received in Egypt by the Pharaoh Amasis, who was noted for his philhellenic policies. Amasis gave important concessions to the Greek 'treaty port' of Naucratis, which, according to Herodotus, was the only Greek trading post in Egypt at the time. Naucratis had been established perhaps as early as 630 BC, as a result of Milesian penetration into Egypt, and there is abundant archaeological evidence to prove that Greeks from many states were living there at the time of Solon's visit.[11] It was a thriving and expanding place on the Canopic branch of the Nile about 16 km. from Saïs, and Solon's ship would certainly have put into harbour there. From Naucratis Solon could easily have gone to Saïs (as Plato says he did), which was the administrative capital of Egypt at the time. Egyptian antiquarians were at this time taking a lively interest in the history of their own country, and it would have been quite natural for a man of Solon's wide interests to seek contact with such people. There would have been no great problem of communication, for in furtherance of the pro-Hellenic policies of the Saïte dynasty a previous Pharaoh, Psammetichos I, had established a school for interpreters. So it is quite reasonable to picture Solon consulting with Egyptian antiquarians and archivists, possibly the priests of the goddess Neith, as Plato says. And there an old priest spoke the memorable words: 'O Solon, Solon, you Hellenes are never anything but children, and there is not an old man among you.'

The priest meant that the Greeks were young in mind compared with the Egyptians, lacking ancient traditions and sciences. He explained that Egyptian records went back to a remote past of which the Greeks had little or no conception, except through the medium of poetic myths. Greek civilization in comparison with Egyptian lacked continuity. In the past it had suffered catastrophic interruptions from droughts and deluges. In the general decline of their culture the Greeks had lost the art of writing, and consequently they had no continuous records of their history in previous millennia. They had myths like those of Deucalion's flood or Phaethon's disastrous attempt to drive the sun-chariot, but they did not realize that the myths embodied traditions of natural disasters which caused serious retrogressions in Greek civilization. Egypt remained comparatively immune from such catastrophes because of the regular and controllable Nile floods, and so her written records were much more continuous and ancient.

After this very reasonable comparison of Egyptian and Greek traditions, the old priest proceeded to tell the story of Atlantis and Athens quoted above (p. 19). Solon made notes of it, and took the notes back to Athens meaning to compose an epic on the theme of this primeval conflict. Either his political commitments, or advancing years, prevented him from achieving his aim, but he did repeat what he had been told to an ancestor of Plato, and the story was memorized and handed down in the family (possibly accompanied by a Solonian manuscript) until Plato decided to give it to the world.

Plato's attitude to the Atlantis legend

What did Plato himself think of the story? He makes Critias introduce it with the remark: 'Then listen, Socrates, to a tale which, though strange, is certainly true, having been attested by Solon, who was the wisest of the seven sages.' When Critias has finished, Socrates remarks, doubtless not without some irony, that the tale 'has the very great advantage of being a fact and not a fiction.' These comments seem noticeably different in tone from those which frame the myth of Theuth and Thamus in the *Phaedrus* (274 c–275 b). Socrates there introduces his tale: 'I can tell you a story from the men of former times, but only they know whether or not it is true.' And Phaedrus, after listening to the story, comments: 'Socrates, you have no difficulty in composing stories from Egypt or anywhere else you like.' Here it seems clear that Plato is informing his readers that the myth, though not without some Egyptian colouring, is largely his own invention. But it is far from easy to make a similar assessment of how Plato means us to take the Atlantis story. There is irony in his characters' comments, but how much? Those who regard both the story and the setting as Plato's invention will say, I suppose, that Plato is being blatantly ironical like Lucian with his *vera historia*. They will point out that it is common form for composers of historical romances to insist that their stories are really true.

Such an explanation has a certain general plausibility, but I do not find it altogether convincing in the context of the projected trilogy *Timaeus–Critias–Hermocrates*. This was an important philosophical project, and one in which the Atlantis story was clearly designed to play an important part – not to be a mere *divertissement* like the Theuth-Thamus myth in the *Phaedrus*. One notes the elaborate pedigree which Plato gives.[12] The old priest of Neith (with access to the 'house of books' which was a normal adjunct of Egyptian temples) told the story to Solon, who told Dropides, who told Critias senior, who, as an old man of nearly ninety, told it to the Critias who was Plato's cousin. Solon died *c*.560 BC, and the younger Critias was born *c*. 460 BC and died in 403 BC when Plato was twenty-four. To bridge the gap between Solon and Critias junior we have Dropides and the long-lived Critias senior. The oral pedigree is not impossible. Is the transmission route, like the story itself, mere fantasy? Or was there a chain, tenuous and unlikely, but not impossible, by which an Egyptian tradition did come down to Plato?

There is considerable emphasis on the oral character of the transmission. Critias is said to be trusting a boyhood memory of what an old man told him. But there is also an intriguing reference to a manuscript of Solon in which he had set down in Greek form the main proper names in the story, for 'he found that the early Egyptians in writing them down had translated them into their own language.' Critias junior says the manuscript had belonged to his grandfather and was still in his possession.[13] The usual 'family papers', says the sceptic. Did such a manuscript ever exist? Had Plato ever seen it?

It may seem pointless to ask such questions, but at least they remind us that Solon plays a key role in the transmission of the legend as recorded by Plato. At this point the question of Plato's attitude to the legend becomes bound up with the question of his attitude to Solon as a witness. Solon was, to borrow a phrase of Pindar, 'a straight-tongued man', not at all given, so far as we can judge, to irony or gratuitous mystification. Having traced the tradition back to such a man, Plato may then have asked himself whether Solon the Greek 'child' was perhaps the dupe of a wily Egyptian romancer.

At this point Plato, in my opinion, suspended judgment on the truth or falsity of the story which had come into his hands. Posidonius, a leading Hellenistic philosopher and scientist (c. 135–c. 50 BC), records Plato as having said: ' It is possible that the story is *not* an invention.'[14] We have no independent evidence that Plato really made such a comment. The anecdote does not even come from an extant work of Posidonius, but only from Strabo's discussion of the Atlantis problem. But both Strabo and Posidonius are reasonably reliable witnesses, and could have had access to biographical material about Plato not now available to us.

Whether or not Plato made the remark in question, it seems a likely summary of his attitude to the legendary material he was presenting. The Atlantis story was literally far-fetched. It had not come down the usual channels of Greek mythology. There was no obvious way of verifying it. But was there any obvious way of discrediting it without impugning either Solon's veracity or common sense? Plato, I think, adopted an attitude of suspended judgment, deciding to use the Atlantis story more perhaps because he found it useful for his purposes than because he believed in its truth. In saying this I do not want to give the impression that I think he disbelieved it. He felt, I believe, like so many people since, that some dim far-off historical reality lay behind it. His attitude is crystallized for me in the saying, whether genuine or *ben trovato*: 'It is possible that the story is *not* an invention'.

In speaking of Plato's use of 'the story' I have in mind what Aristotle would call the 'essential plot': a great and highly civilized island empire aims at universal domination and is defeated by the courage of the early Greeks, especially the Athenians, and later succumbs to a natural cataclysm. On this framework Plato embroiders a large number of remarkable details.

A summary of the longer account of Atlantis from Plato's *Critias*

The short account of Atlantis in the *Timaeus* is amplified with a considerable wealth of interesting detail in another Platonic dialogue, the *Critias*. The relevant portions are given in full in the Appendix (p. 160). Here I shall merely summarize the main points in the description.

Poseidon was the patron god of Atlantis. Its royal line was descended from five pairs of male twins, the result of a union between Poseidon and a mortal maiden called Cleito. The senior twin was named Atlas, and the whole island and also the surrounding ocean were named after him. Atlantis was apportioned between the ten sons of Poseidon under the overlordship of Atlas. Their descendants ruled in succession for many generations, and their dominion extended over many islands and over portions of the coasts of the Mediterranean as far as Egypt and Italy. They became extremely wealthy, partly from the natural resources of the island, and partly from foreign trade. Atlantis was rich in minerals, metals, and timber, and had a rich and varied fauna and flora including elephants.

The original hill on which the maiden Cleito dwelt had been enclosed by Poseidon with two concentric rings of land and three of water. When this hill became the metropolis of the Atlantean empire (*Fig.* 2), the inhabitants built there a royal palace which was successively adorned and augmented by its kings until it became a 'marvel to behold for size and beauty'. Roads and bridges connected the citadel with its surrounding rings of land, and so with the rest of the island.

In the middle of the inner citadel was a temple dedicated to Poseidon and Cleito, resplendent with silver, gold, ivory and orichalchum. There was a colossal statue of the god driving a team of six winged horses, and surrounded by a hundred nereids on dolphins. The palace was well furnished with hot and cold baths, and there was a race-course for horses on one of the land rings. The whole metropolis was surrounded by a series of walls, and its harbours were always crowded with shipping.

The city was backed by an oblong plain, 3000 by 2000 *stadia*,[15] which was divided into 60,000 lots each ten *stadia* square. An elaborate system of great irrigation ditches surrounded and traversed the plain. The plain faced south and was sheltered from the north by many large and beautiful mountains containing rivers, lakes, meadows and much timber. The coastline of the island was generally steep and precipitous.

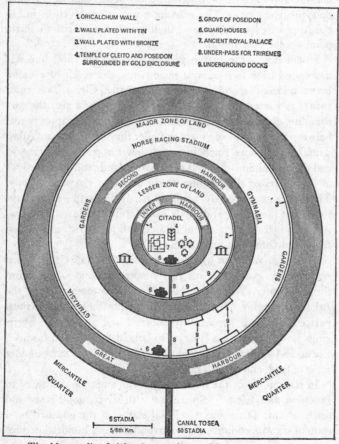

2 *The Metropolis of Atlantis according to Plato*

A code of laws was engraved on a bronze pillar at the temple of Poseidon, and the kings gathered there at the end of four- and five-year periods alternately for general consultation and to conduct assizes. Before administering the laws they were required to hunt bulls which ranged freely in the temple precinct, and to capture one of them for sacrifice using no weapons but only staves and nooses. The bull was sacrificed so that its blood ran down over the sacred inscription on the pillar. After the sacrifice they poured libations, drank and dined, and then, wearing azure robes, conducted their court by night. At dawn they wrote down the sentences imposed on a golden tablet, and dedicated it with their robes for a memorial.

In the course of time the kings fell away from their high standards of justice and became greedy and domineering. Whereupon Zeus, wishing to chastise them, called a council of the gods and spoke as follows . . .

Here the fragmentary *Critias* tantalizingly breaks off in mid-sentence. It is not known why Plato never finished it. Plutarch says he was late in beginning and found the task too much for him.[16]

I have now put before the reader the main features of the legend of Atlantis as told by Plato. In the next chapter I shall consider some current interpretations of it, and in particular the view which finds in it a memory of Minoan Crete.

2 Atlantis and Minoan Crete

The Atlantic location of Atlantis

The quest for lost Atlantis has inspired an immense literature. In 1841 T. H. Martin reviewed scores of serious contributions to the problem.[17] Since then the spate of books has if anything increased. There are said to be over two thousand works dealing with the lost continent. Indeed, the theme of Atlantis amounts to a licence to write on almost anything in pre-history. Evidence for the lost civilization has been sought from the floor of the Atlantic Ocean, and in the art of the Incas. Devotees of the occult have received special information of its whereabouts from the spirit voices of ancient Egypt. Berlioux thought he had found Atlantis in Morocco; Frobenius favoured Nigeria; Spannuth claimed to have seen the walls of its citadel on a submarine reef near Heligoland. Plato's description of the elaborate artificial harbour of the Atlantean metropolis has prompted identification with ancient Tartessus (not yet itself exactly located). And so on.[18]

No review of the full sweep of Atlantis literature can be attempted here. My aim is to review *Plato's story* in the light of recent archaeological discoveries. But Plato does put Atlantis in the Atlantic Ocean west of Gibraltar, so I feel obliged to say something about modern opinion on this particular solution of the problem.

A book which has been very influential in forming modern opinion, particularly in the United States, is Ignatius Donnelly's *Atlantis : The Antediluvian World*. Donnelly's book, first published in New York in 1882, had run through eighteen editions by 1889, was translated into German in 1894, and was still thought worthy of re-issue in 1949. Donnelly was a man of parts—idealist, novelist, Congressman, and assiduous researcher, not merely in pre-history but also in the field of Shakespearean scholarship. His *Atlantis* was an ambitious attempt to set out all that could be known about 'that great, original, broad-eyed, sunken race'. He began with a fine flourish, setting out thirteen propositions whose demonstration would 'solve many of the problems which now perplex mankind'. His basic geographical proposition, taken from Plato, was the former existence of an island remnant of an Atlantic continent opposite the mouth of the Mediterranean. This great island was the cradle of civilization, the original home of sun-worship, the source of bronze and iron technology, the parent of the Phoenician alphabet. It was also the 'original seat' of the Aryans, the Semites, and 'possibly also of the Turanian races'. Its oldest 'colony' was probably Egypt; but its people also populated the shores of the Gulf of Mexico, the Pacific coast of South America, the Baltic, the Black Sea and the Caspian. Nay, more, it was 'the true Antediluvian world; the Garden of Eden; the Garden of the Hesperides; the Elysian Fields; the Gardens of Alcinous; the Mesomphalos; the Olympos; the Asgard of the traditions of the ancient nations.'

One feels that in embarking on such a programme Donnelly could hardly fail to prove something. Indeed he was the first to make the important suggestion that Homer's Phaeacia might be a recollection of Atlantis. But in general his 'Atlantis' reminds one of Plato's 'unhypothetical first beginning' from which everything else can be deduced. Donnelly does not, however, test his preliminary hypotheses as rigorously as Plato would have wished. Having accepted Plato's whole account of Atlantis as true in every detail, he then proceeds to shower on his vast canvas many facts which are undeniable in themselves but whose connection with each other, or with Atlantis, is either tenuous or non-existent. Himself a very uncritical researcher, Donnelly bemuses his readers into a mood of infinite credulity. There was once a land connection between Europe and America: *ergo* Atlantis. Primitive and civilized peoples alike all over the world have Deluge legends: *ergo* Atlantis. Mexican and Peruvian civilizations were as advanced as anything in the Old World: *ergo* Atlantis. Having accepted all this one is in no mood to question such propositions as '*Genesis* contains a history of Atlantis', or 'The Carians of Homer are the same as the Caribs of the West Indies'.

Donnelly abounds in information, but is weak in argument. In its day his book was an interesting, though very uncritical, compilation. One must regard it as fundamentally unsatisfactory nowadays because its account of the origin and diffusion of higher civilization is completely at variance with what is now the accepted outline picture based on the archaeology of the Middle East. Donnelly's time-scale and location of Atlantis are totally incompatible with what we now know of the Mesolithic and Neolithic periods, and the emergence of the great cultures in the river valleys of the Nile, the Tigris-Euphrates, and the Indus. It is a curious reflection on human gullibility that a revised edition, with a puff for Hoerbiger's theory of the moon as a 'captured' planet, should still be offered to the public as a reliable account of how civilization developed.

Donnelly's best-known disciple is probably Lewis Spence, who published three books on Atlantis in the 1920s.[19] Spence tried to put Donnelly's views on a firm scientific footing in two main respects. First, he marshalled some geological support for the notion of a large land mass occupying most of the present North Atlantic Ocean in Late Tertiary times. This Atlantic continent, he argues, first broke down into two island-continents, Atlantis not far west of Spain, and Antillia near the present West Indies. These island-continents with associated smaller islands persisted until Late Pleistocene times. Atlantis was finally submerged about 10000 BC, and Antillia still has a recognizable existence in the West Indian archipelago. This time-scale enables him to link up his island-continents with Old Stone Age cultures in Western Europe, notably the Cro-Magnon, the Magdalenian, and the Azilian. These palaeolithic cultures are well known from the remarkable cave paintings which they produced, and Spence believes that they contributed to the development of civilization within the Mediterranean basin, and especially in Egypt. He also believes that what he calls 'the Atlantis culture-complex' spread to the New World via Antillia, and influenced the development of Mayan civilization.

Spence's views are more moderate and plausible than those of Donnelly. There is, undoubtedly, a mid-Atlantic Ridge running from Iceland to the South Atlantic. This great Ridge lies at an average depth of one mile below the surface, with ocean basins averaging three miles deep to the east and west of it.[20] In a few places it actually comes to the surface, as in the Azores, Ascension Island, and Tristan da Cunha. But modern scientific opinion is against treating it as the remnant of a sunken continent (see below, p. 33). On the contrary, geologists and oceanographers now think that the Ridge has been raised from the floor of the Ocean, probably by volcanic activity. This is obviously a crucial point for Spence's theory. If science finally rejects the notion of a submerged Atlantic 'continent' the main foundation of his theory will have been destroyed. In any case one need not posit a former Atlantic land-bridge to explain cultural similarities between, say, Egyptian and Mayan civilizations. In this connection the evidence of migration into North America via the Bering Strait, and also the possibility that similar cultures may evolve quite independently of one another, must be taken into account.

To return to Plato's Atlantis: no matter what criticisms are made of Donnelly and his school, people who believe in Atlantis will continue, I know, to look for it in the Atlantic Ocean. That is where Plato put it, and that is what the name suggests. But the name 'Atlantis' is a most deceptive guide. Atlantis is *not* derived from Atlantic. Linguistically both names are in the same generation, so to speak, like brother and sister, and both trace their parentage back to Atlas, the giant Titan who held the sky on his shoulders. In Greek they are adjectival forms of Atlas, meaning '(the island) of Atlas' and '(the sea) of Atlas' respectively. They differ in form because the nouns with which they agree differ in gender. So if you decide to use the name of Atlantis as a clue to its location, you must consider what was the original location of the mythical Atlas. Now Atlas may once have been located well inside the Mediterranean before the gradual extension of Greek geographical knowledge pushed him to the west and located him on the High Atlas range in Morocco.[21] You must also consider the possibility that Solon invented the name Atlantis (see below, p. 42).

The name 'Atlantis sea' for a portion at least of what we call the North Atlantic was in use a generation before Plato was born. It first appears in Herodotus in the form 'the so-called Atlantis sea', and seems to have developed without reference to the Atlantis legend. Herodotus was aware that it was possible to circumnavigate Africa and come back via the Red Sea, so he must have regarded the 'Atlantis sea' as very extensive. He also knew of a tribe called the Atlantes who dwelt round an oasis in the desert far to the west of Egypt.[22] They derived their name from a mountain called Atlas which they regarded as a 'pillar of the sky'. It was, as befits such a pillar, 'narrow and completely circular, and so high that its summit could not be seen'. It is clear from Herodotus' whole account of North Africa that the Greeks of the fifth century BC were beginning to acquire a reasonable picture of the whole coastline from Egypt to Morocco.

Plato, writing at least sixty years after Herodotus, would have known all these names and facts, and they probably influenced him to some extent by his location of the island of Atlantis. But his main reason for putting Atlantis outside the Straits of Gibraltar was, I believe, an *a priori* one. He was influenced by an imagined parallel between the Persian invasion of Greece from the east and the antediluvian aggression by Atlantis from the west. In the interests of symmetry the vast land empire had to be balanced by the vast sea empire. He knew all the islands inside the Mediterranean, and considered them far too small to have been capable of mounting an invasion on the required scale. So Atlantis, the island capital of the maritime empire, had to be enlarged to the point where there was no room left for it within the straits. It had to go outside into the boundless ocean which already bore the name of Atlas.

Professor Andrews has recently made the ingenious suggestion that Plato misread Solon's notes on the location of Atlantis. Instead of the true reading '*midway between* Libya and Asia' he read '*larger than* Libya and Asia'. In Greek it is the difference of only one letter – the difference between *mezon* and *meson*.[23] But this clever suggestion is, I suggest, unnecessary. Given his geographical preconceptions, Plato would have put Atlantis outside the Mediterranean in any case. In the *Phaedo* he speaks of the Mediterranean sea as a 'pond', and of the 'true earth' as immensely larger than the inhabited area known to his contemporaries. So in the *Timaeus* he speaks of the Mediterranean as a 'narrow harbour' in contrast with the 'true sea' beyond, and the 'genuine continent' surrounding it.[24] His westward look was conditioned by a sort of expanding perspective, and Atlantis grew as it receded from him. It was the 'true' island in the 'true' ocean.

Plato's Atlantis was thus to some extent an ideal construction. Its location in the Atlantic was partly the result of the westward shift of Atlas, but even more the result of the large size which Plato inferred for it. Plato's placing has seemed the most natural one ever since, but there is now positive geophysical evidence against the possibility of a sunken continent in mid-Atlantic waters. Recent scientific data about the propagation of primary waves after earthquake shock tends to show that ocean floors can never have been continents, because they have a basically different structure. It has also been found that the ocean floors give higher values for gravity measurements. In the case of the Indian Ocean geologists say that the basalts of its bed are of quite different composition from the basalts of the Indian sub-continent. Many scientists now believe that no portion of the Atlantic ocean floor can ever have constituted a land-mass which became submerged as the result of some major disturbance of the earth's crust. If modern scientific opinion is sound on this point – and there seems good reason to think that it is – we must give up the notion of locating Atlantis as a 'lost continent' in the middle of the North Atlantic. I emphasize that this argument applies only to the genuine ocean floor as distinct from the continental shelf. It does not rule out the possibility of quite large subsidences on, or along the edge of, the continental shelf, which extends for quite a long way west of Ireland, for instance, and which reaches out towards Madeira and the Canary Islands. The Azores, however, lie well beyond the range of the continental shelf.

Protagonists of an Atlantic Atlantis have often emphasized the volcanic nature of these island groups. But here they come up against a strong historical argument. Even allowing that there could have been substantial dislocations of land in the Atlantic as recently as, say, the Late Palaeolithic period (which is extremely doubtful), this epoch is still far too early to fit the picture of Atlantis that Plato gives. He describes it as a metal-using literate civilization, well-versed in shipbuilding techniques, and so on. However much we may admire the art of Magdalenian man, no one can seriously suggest that he could have mounted a naval invasion of pre-dynastic Egypt. We are thrown back here to the old dilemma. Either the story of Atlantis is fantasy from start to finish, or else we must look for this highly developed island culture at a point in space and time much closer to Egypt than Plato allows.

The Minoan hypothesis

Minoan civilization was rediscovered only in this century. The ancient Greeks had almost completely forgotten it. They did remember that Minos once ruled the seas, and they could learn some interesting details about Bronze Age Crete from Homer: its ninety cities, the mixed population of the island, the badly sheltered harbour at Amnisos, the dancing floor in broad Knossos (Plates 4, 25). But these were disjointed recollections and beyond that everything shaded off into the vagueness of myth: Theseus and the Minotaur (Plate 3), Ariadne and the Labyrinth, Europa and the Bull, Zeus born in the Dictaean cave, the craft of Daedalus (Plate 9). We can now see that there was historical substance even in the myths, but they would have meant little or nothing to Plato and his contemporaries. For them Crete was a quiet Dorian backwater completely out of the mainstream of history. They remembered nothing of the splendours of the palaces or the glories of Minoan art and technology.

Nothing could have induced Plato, or any other ancient writer, to equate Atlantis with Minoan Crete. Such an identification was impossible until the discoveries of Sir Arthur Evans which began at Knossos in 1900; and now, nearly seventy years later, we can survey the complex architecture of the great palaces at Knossos (Plates 58–62), Phaistos, Mallia and Kato Zakro. We can wander along the little streets of Gournia (Plate 27), or through the villas at Tylissos. In the Herakleion museum we can study the graceful forms and bold swirling decoration of Kamares pottery (Plate 73). The artistry of the frescoes and the craftsmanship of the seal-stones compare most favourably with the ill-formed, ill-executed puerilities of much modern art (Plates 9, 24). In short, as we begin to form an overall picture of Minoan culture, we have to admit that the 'first civilization of Europe' was also one of the most accomplished and inventive that the world has ever known (Plates 5, 6, 65, 66).

Did the memory of this civilization survive in the Atlantis legend? I believe it did. But of course the suggestion is no new one. So far as I can discover, the credit for first making it belongs to a certain K. T. Frost, who was for a time on the staff of Queen's University, Belfast, and who was killed in action in the First World War. Frost published his theory anonymously in an article entitled 'The Lost Continent' in *The Times* of 19 February 1909. He later argued his case in greater detail in an article 'The *Critias* and Minoan Crete'.[25]

Frost's main points are very well made in his 1909 article. In the following quotations I have emphasized his crucial suggestions by the use of italics.

The recent excavations in Crete have made it necessary to reconsider the whole scheme of Mediterranean history before the classical period. Although many questions are still undecided, it has been established beyond any doubt that, during the rule of the 18th Dynasty in Egypt, when Thebes was at the height of its glory, Crete was the centre of a great empire whose trade and influence extended from the North Adriatic to Tel el Amarna and from Sicily to Syria. The whole sea-borne trade between Europe, Asia, and Africa was in Cretan hands, and the legends of Theseus seem to show that the Minoans dominated the Greek islands and the coasts of Attica... The Minoan civilization was essentially Mediterranean, and is most sharply distinguished from any that arose in Egypt or the East. In some respects also it is strikingly modern. The many-storeyed palaces, some of the pottery, even the dresses of the ladies seem to belong to the modern rather than the ancient world [Plates 16, 17, 52, 59]. At the same time the number of Minoan sites and their extraordinary richness far exceed anything that Crete could be expected to produce, and must be due in part to that sea-power which the ancient legends attributed to Minos [Plate 6].

Thus, when the Minoan power was at its greatest, its rulers must have seemed to the other nations to be mighty indeed, and their prestige must have been increased by the mystery of the lands over which they ruled (*which seemed to Syrians and Egyptians to be the far West*), and by their mastery over that element which the ancient world always held in awe. Strange stories, too, must have floated round the Levant of vast bewildering palaces, of sports and dances, and above all of the bull-fight. The Minoan realm, therefore, was a vast and ancient power which was united by the same sea which divided it from other nations, so that *it seemed to be a separate continent with a genius of its own*.

Frost then describes briefly the sudden eclipse of Cretan power (which he attributes to a raid on Knossos) and continues:

As a political and commercial force, therefore, Knossos and its allied

I The cliffs of the Thera caldera rise sheer from the sea to a height of over 270 m. Ships are unable to drop anchor owing to the great depth of the sea at this point, over 200 m., shelving to 400 m. in the centre of the bay. Access to the town is by a steep zig-zag path, over two kilo-metres long, rising in shallow steps. The dark horizontal band seen above the houses on the shore is a lava dyke, the rest of the cliff being largely composed of slag and pumice from former, prehistoric, eruptions

II Just south of Phira town are the Phira quarries from where pumice and ash is exported to Athens for cement manufacture. The cliff face is about 30 m. high, composed of some 20 m. of fine white ash above multi-coloured layers of coarse pumice (see *Fig. 7*). It is below this that the Minoan level is found and can be seen as a thin dark line at the base directly below the highest point of the cliff in the centre foreground. The wall seen in Plate XII is located here

III Detail view of the Minoan level at the base of the Phira quarry cliff seen in Plate II cities were swept away just when they seemed strongest and safest. *It was as if the whole kingdom had sunk in the sea, as if the tale of Atlantis were true*. The parallel is not fortuitous. If the account of Atlantis be compared with the history of Crete and her relationship with Greece and Egypt, it seems almost certain that here we have an echo of the Minoans...The whole description of Atlantis which is given in the *Timaeus* and the *Critias* has features so thoroughly Minoan that even Plato could not have invented so many unsuspected facts. He says of Atlantis: 'The island was the way to other islands, and from these islands you might pass to the whole of the opposite continent which surrounded the true ocean.' It is significant too, that the empire is not described as a single homogeneous Power like Plato's *Republic* and other States in fiction: on the contrary it is a combination of different elements dominated by one city. 'In this island there was a great and wonderful empire which had rule over the whole island and several others, as well as over parts of the continent.' *This sentence describes the political status of Knossos as concisely as the previous sentence describes the geographical position of Crete.*

The above extracts from Frost's original article seem to be to make their case with such conciseness and cogency that it is surprising the learned world did not take more notice of his views. Once the general equation of the Minoan power with Atlantis is established, many of the details fall neatly into place as Frost went on to point out:

The great harbour, for example, with its shipping and its merchants coming from all parts, the elaborate bath rooms, the stadium, and the solemn sacrifice of a bull are all thoroughly, though not exclusively, Minoan; but when we read how the bull is hunted 'in the temple of Poseidon without weapons but with staves and nooses' we have an unmistakable description of the bull-ring at Knossos, the very thing which struck foreigners most and which gave rise to the legend of the Minotaur. Plato's words exactly describe the scenes on the famous Vapheio cups which certainly represent catching wild bulls for the Minoan bull-fight [Plate 68], which, as we know from the palace itself, differed from all others which the world has seen in exactly the point which Plato emphasises—namely that no weapons were used.

Frost's work laid down indispensable guide-lines for the source criticism of the Atlantis legend. Judicious nineteenth-century critics like Martin and Grote had taken the Egyptian origin of the legend seriously, but were unable to round off their argument because they could not trace the legend back to Minoan Crete. Frost started with Evans' discoveries behind him, and re-

37

emphasized the role of Egypt in the transmission of the story. He rightly pointed out that the Atlantis legend makes good historical sense *if its materials are viewed from the Egyptian point of view*. I have already argued that Solon really did acquire information from the Saïte priests (see above, p. 21f.). It therefore seems worth trying to visualize what the priests themselves knew about the period, how they would have presented their knowledge to an intelligent Athenian in the early sixth century BC, and what he would have made of it.

Ancient Egyptian inscriptions are full of praises of the Gods and of the Pharaoh, but manage to contain disappointingly little historical material in proporiton to their bulk. On the whole the Egyptians of the Bronze Age knew little and cared less about foreign countries. They were not great travellers or seafarers, and their geographical horizons were quite restricted. Their world was bounded by Nubia and Punt (Eritrea ?) to the south, by the Euphrates on the east, and by the Libyan desert tribes on the west. They knew something of Cyprus, the south coast of Turkey, and Crete (Plates 71–3), from long-established trading connections. By the first half of the fifteenth century BC they were becoming aware of Mycenaean Greece. But Egypt remained always very much in the centre of their limited universe, and they took note of foreigners only as providers of desirable imports, or as hostile invaders.

Late Bronze Age Egypt left much the same sort of record of itself to the Saïte period as it has to us. I venture to suggest that New Kingdom Egyptian records still extant allow us to reconstruct the sort of information which the priests must have passed on to Solon. From material still available to us we can see how the Atlantis legend could have taken shape, though doubtless the Saïtes had some annalistic information on papyrus which has not survived.

What sort of records, then, would the priests of Saïs have expounded to Solon, knowing that he was interested in the early history of Greece, and in early contacts between Egypt and the Aegean world? These records must have included documents like those still extant which refer to 'Keftiu' and 'the isles which are in the midst of the Great Green [Sea]'. Keftiu is almost certainly Minoan Crete. The identification has been challenged, but is now generally accepted. Keftiu is the same as the Akkadian Kap-ta-ra, a land 'beyond the upper sea', *i.e.* the eastern Mediterranean, and the same as the Biblical Caphtor.[26] Keftiu is first mentioned in an Egyptian document which may go back to the third millennium, and it disappears from reliable records before the end of the fifteenth century BC.[27] The 'isles of the Great Green' are thought to include the islands of the Aegean, or at least the southern part of it, and also some coastlands of the Greek mainland.[28] The 'Great Green' is certainly the Mediterranean. The designation 'isles of the Great Green' first appears in Egyptian records about 1470 BC, and is not found after the middle of the twelfth century. Its use coincides very closely in time with the rise, zenith, and decline of Mycenaean Greece. Vercoutter makes a good case for regarding it as a designation coined by the Egyptian annalists when they first became aware of Mycenaean Greece as an independent power. To Egyptian eyes in the fifteenth century BC Minoans and Mycenaeans must have seemed more alike than different. Mycenaean art and religion, as we now know, were at this time very much in debt to Minoan. Mycenaean traders must have used the same sort of ships and followed the same routes as the Minoans. The Minoan penetration into Greece in the sixteenth century was followed by a Mycenaean penetration of Crete in the fifteenth century. There is evidence that the Egyptian court in the decade 1460–1450 knew of an alteration in the political status of Knossos (see p. 116). Where diplomatic protocol required they could make a distinction between Greeks and Minoans, but for practical purposes such distinctions were perhaps not very firmly drawn. It certainly seems unlikely that Egyptian antiquarians of the Saïte Dynasty could have distinguished at all clearly between the various 'peoples of the sea' (Plates 70, XIV) who either traded or fought with their ancestors in the Late Bronze Age. We may suppose that Solon's informants gave him a composite picture of Aegean–Egyptian relations based on the sort of documents which are still extant, but supplemented by some detailed annals which we do not now possess.

What did Solon make of it all? Let us suppose that the priests took him through a document like the stele of Tuthmosis III from Karnak (Plate 8) with its magnificent Victory Hymn whose phrases were 'borrowed' by three of his successors for their own monuments.[29] In the prelude to the hymn he would have read the following statements:

(A) I [*i.e.*, the God Amun-Re] give thee valour and victory over all foreign countries; I set the glory of thee and the fear of thee in all lands, the terror of thee as far as the four supports [or pillars] of heaven . . .

(B) . . . I have commended to thee the earth in its length and breadth, so that westerners and easterners are under thy oversight . . .

(C) My serpent-diadem which is upon thy head, she consumes them; she makes a speedy prey among *those twisted by nature*[?]; she devours those who are in their islands [or marshes] by her flame . . .

(D) They come bearing tribute upon their backs . . .

Then follows the hymn, which, in eleven stanzas all beginning 'I have come', sets out systematically all the countries of the world known to Egypt and describes their awe and terror before the conquering Pharaoh. The first three stanzas deal with the Phoenician coast, the Palestine-Syria hill-country, and the lands farther to the east, respectively. Stanza 4 deals with Crete and Cyprus as follows:

I have come

That I may cause thee to trample down the western land [*i.e.* the countries at the farthest remove from those of the previous stanza];

Keftiu and Isy are under the awe of thee. [*i.e.* Crete and Cyprus.]

I cause them to see they majesty as a young bull,

Firm of heart, sharp of horns, who cannot be felled.

In other stanzas the Pharaoh is compared to a shooting star, a crocodile, a lion, etc. The appropriateness of the bull simile in relation to Crete needs no labouring. Stanza 6 is also of great interest in so far as it deals with the islands and coastlands of the Aegean other than Crete:

I have come

That I may cause thee to trample down those who are in the islands;

They who are in the midst of the Great Green Sea are under thy battle cry.

I cause them to see thy Majesty as the Avenger

Appearing in glory on the back of his sacrifice [*i.e.* as Horus defeating Seth – an appropriate mythological tilt at the Mycenaeans!]

Other stanzas deal with Mitanni (*i.e.* upper Mesopotamia and North Syria) (5), Libyans (8), 'the ends of the lands … that which the Ocean encircles' (9), 'the front of the land' (*i.e.* desert dwellers near Egypt) (10), and Nubia (11).

The comprehensive and systematic treatment is clear. The writer wants to convey the impression that Tuthmosis III is supreme ruler of the whole world.

Many phrases of this fine panegyric were re-used by later Pharaohs – Amenophis III, Sethos I, and Rameses III. By the time of Rameses III Egypt was very much on the defensive against invaders from Libya to the west of the delta, and also against a grand coalition of 'peoples of the sea' (including Achaeans) (Plate 70) who swept down through Palestine, and were repulsed only after a desperate struggle.

Amenophis III and Rameses II list Keftiu as tributary, but it is thought that these listings are merely repetitive and for propaganda purposes.[27] There is no trustworthy record of Egyptian/Minoan contact after the third quarter of the fifteenth century.

The above references are sufficient to cast Keftiu and the other islands in the role of a great power hostile to Egypt. If Solon had enquired more particularly about Keftiu he would have been told it was an island far away to the west. The Ipuwer papyrus uses the phrase 'as far away as Keftiu'.[30] The priests could have expatiated on the rich 'tribute' of costly vases which it was able to send (Plates 74, XIV), and may perhaps have known something of its influence over the other Aegean islands. They may even have had some record of the domination of Attica by the Keftiu (Plate 7), which would have been particularly interesting to Solon. The possibility of such detailed knowledge is inherent in the religious link between Neith of Saïs and Athena of Athens.[31] If Solon pressed them on the ultimate fate of Keftiu the priests could certainly have told him that it disappeared from their records about the middle of the XVIII Dynasty. Whether they had any information about the Thera catastrophe is conjectural. The Prelude of the Victory Stele (extract C) has an enigmatic phrase about 'those twisted by nature', but this can hardly be pressed in this connection since the translation is uncertain.

In general, one can see how this, and similar, material, expounded from the Egyptian point of view without any clear chronological or geographical framework, could have been worked up by Solon into something like the Atlantis legend as Plato gives it.

We know that Egyptian schoolboys of the XVIII Dynasty, c. 1500 BC, were set the exercise of writing out Egyptian and Cretan names in parallel columns. There is a writing board of this date, now in the British Museum, which is headed: 'How to make names of Keftiu'.[32] We may surely infer from this that Egyptian archives contained Minoan place and personal names together with what the Egyptians conceived to be their equivalents either in sound or sense. Plato tells us that Solon made Greek names by translating what he took to be the sense of the Egyptian names that he was given. If this is true he was only doing the same as Egyptian schoolboys 900 years before.

In the light of this we may put a question which has an important bearing on the origin of the Atlantis story. Is there any semantic connection between the name Atlantis and the name Keftiu? 'Keftiu' means either 'the island of Keft' or 'the people of Keft', depending on what determinative is added in hieroglyphic. The root 'keft' has been connected with *caput* and *capitul*, and it has been pointed out that in the Old Testament 'kaphtor' is used for the capital of a pillar.[33] The ancient Egyptians probably regarded remote and mountainous Crete as one of the four 'pillars of heaven' which supported the sky at the four corners of the world they knew. This must be the meaning of the expression in the third line of the Hymn quoted above. It is even possible that the Egyptian priests had some recorded material about the worship of sacred pillars which was so prevalent in Minoan Crete (Plate 9).[34] Imagine Solon's reaction when confronted with this sort of information about ancient Keftiu. He could not have failed to associate it with the myth of Atlas, who, according to Homer, had a daughter in a remote western island and kept 'the pillars which hold the sky round about'.[35] My suggestion is that Solon translated Keftiu by Atlantis, the island of Atlas, and, since the inhabitants bore the same name, he called them the descendants of Atlas. This must have seemed to him a very reasonable equivalence. The name would scan well in the epic poem he planned, and the 'island of Atlas' would have the right sort of mysterious and western flavour that his plot required.

Frost did not use all the detailed facts and arguments in the preceding paragraphs, but they are all advanced from the point of view which he was the first to suggest as appropriate for source criticism of the Atlantis story. There is, I think, great plausibility in his crucial contention that 'Solon really did hear a tale in Saïs which filled him with wonder and which was really the true but misunderstood Egyptian record of the Minoans.'

Frost's views made little or no impact on learned opinion. His theory sank so much into oblivion that a German scholar in 1951 completed the final draft of a work arguing out a similar conclusion before learning of Frost's priority in the field.[36]

The volcanic destruction of Minoan Crete

Frost's case has subsequently been strengthened in only one major respect. But the additional evidence is so striking and so important that it deserves the fullest consideration. Sole credit for advancing it belongs to Professor S. Marinatos, at present Director-General of the Greek Archaeological Service. His article 'The Volcanic Destruction of Minoan Crete', published in *Antiquity* in 1939, makes a major advance towards the solution of the Atlantis problem. Frost noted the sudden downfall of the Minoan empire, but was brief and vague about the cause of the collapse. Marinatos strengthened the whole hypothesis at this crucial point. His theory had begun to take shape in his mind as early as 1932 when he was excavating at Amnisos.[37] He found there a pit full of pumice stone, and noted great orthostats which had been tilted out of position as though by the powerful suction of a mass of water. And then, as he reflected on the sudden and simultaneous destruction and abandonment of so many Minoan palaces and villas, the conviction grew in his mind that the downfall of Crete was due, not to foreign invaders, but to a natural catastrophe of unparalleled violence and destructive power. The source and focus of this cataclysm was to be sought, he suggested, on the volcanic island of Thera, which lies only 120 km. due north of Knossos.

The editors of *Antiquity* published Marinatos' article with a note saying that they regarded the case as needing further evidence to support it, and expressed the hope that more excavation would be undertaken to solve the problem. Then the Second World War intervened, and no progress was possible for some years. But since the war further work of great relevance and interest has been done by Professor A. Galanopoulos of the Athens Institute of Seismology, by D. Ninkovich and B. C. Heezen of the Lamont Geological Observatory, Columbia University, by Dr N. Platon at the new palace at Kato Zakro in East Crete, and by Marinatos himself on a site on the south-west coast of Thera. It will be the task of the next two chapters to assemble this new evidence. Here I shall remark only that the long north coast of Crete (*Fig. 14*) lay very exposed to the effects of any violent eruption on Thera. If this Bronze Age eruption was as great as is now supposed, it is hardly possible to exaggerate the sudden destruction and loss of life that must have been caused on Crete. Was this the Bull from the Sea that was sent to plague Minos? Have we here the grim historical reality behind Plato's words: 'But afterwards there occurred violent earthquakes and floods; and in a single day and night of misfortune the island of Atlantis disappeared in the depths of the sea'?

3 Thera and its Volcano

The Island of Thera

Thera (Santorin) is the most southerly island in the archipelago of the Cyclades. It was once about ten miles in diameter, and was covered by cone-shaped peaks whose sides were scored by steep ravines. In the centre was a summit of perhaps 1600 metres in height. The deep valleys traversing the ranges would have been covered in vines growing in rich well-weathered volcanic soil. Before it acquired the name of Thera it had been known as Kallistê, the very beautiful island. It was also sometimes called Strongulê, the circular island. These names may preserve a memory of what it once was like, but they are no longer appropriate as descriptions. The eye can no longer view it as a complete circle (Plate 10). It is not even a single island. Thera is in fact three fragments of what was once a single island: Thera proper, the largest portion, crescent-shaped, with four hills between 300 m. and 600 m. and a population of about 5000; Therasia, a much smaller portion to the north-west, with two villages; Aspronisi, the 'white island', to the south-west, a small, stack-like uninhabited fragment with dark cliffs crowned with the thick banks of white ash and pumice which are such a striking feature of the Thera landscape.

When viewed on a map the circular outline of the Thera group of islands is very clear. (*Fig. 3*). One can easily visualize the outer rim of the once united island, and also the inner rim which now surrounds a great central expanse of sea over 80 square kilometres in extent. Everywhere around this inner rim may be seen the shorn-off cliffs (Plates 11, I) which stand as mute reminders of the volcanic violence to which the island has been subjected. And in the centre of the great bay the dark volcanic dome (Plates 20, 21, V) spreads its fretted outlines like the tentacles of

45

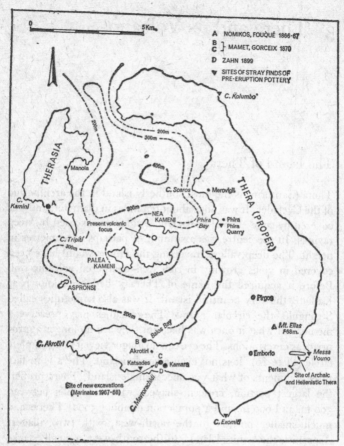

3 *The Thera group of islands showing excavation sites and pre-eruption pottery find-spots*

some giant squid rising from the depths beneath. For Thera is a volcano – the only active volcano in the Aegean. The great bay, with its broken circle of tawny cliffs, is known to science as a *caldera*,[38] which may be roughly defined as a collapsed area above an exhausted magma chamber. In structure, formation, and size it is very similar to Crater Lake in Oregon, U.S.A. (*Fig. 4*). The Thera caldera was formed as a result of a great eruption, or series of eruptions, which wrecked the island between *c.* 1500 and 1470 BC. It was as though some gigantic mine had been detonated deep below the centre of the island. Vast trenches were scooped out in the sea-bed, especially between Thera proper and Therasia. Enormous quantities of fine ash were ejected. The rising force of the explosions in the magma chamber flung masses of debris to the outer perimeter of the island. Finally a large portion of the centre of the island collapsed, leaving the shorn-off cliffs which still look as though they had only recently been split by some Cyclopean hammer.

Today from the terrace of the Hotel Loukas in Phira town (Plate 11) you can look down almost vertically to the little harbour nearly 250 m. below, and beneath the placid water the cliff face continues to plunge down another 200 m. and more. Ships cannot anchor even close to the quay, but have to moor to great buoys secured by long chains to the sea-bed. Within the caldera the water is generally between 200 and 400 m. deep. To the west of Aspronisi, on a line joining the most westerly points of Therasia and Thera proper, the depth is only about 20 m. A detailed chart of the area provides graphic evidence of this steep-sided basin which has been carved out by volcanic action in the floor of the Aegean.

When the great eruption subsided the caldera was an unbroken expanse of water. But on the sea-bed at the centre volcanic vents were still in existence, and intermittent volcanic activity since classical times has built up the dark mass of lava *scoriae* now sprawling menacingly in the centre of the lagoon (Plate 21). There are in fact two distinct island masses which now constitute the dome of the volcano above sea-level. Together they are

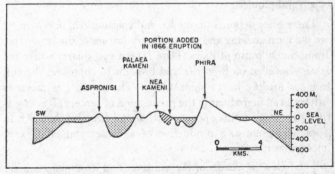

4 *A section through the Thera caldera from SW to NE. Note the shallow stretches on the outer perimeter contrasted with the area 400 m. deep to the west of Palaea Kameni*

known as the Kamenis, the 'burnt islands'. The western one, Palaea Kameni, emerged above the surface in 197–6 BC. The north-west corner of Nea Kameni to the east was formed between AD 1707 and 1711 (*Fig. 4*). Nea Kameni trebled in size during the 1866–7 eruption, extending southwards. Another considerable area, incorporating the previously separate islet of Mikra Kameni, was added to it in the 1925–6 eruption (Plate 20).

Life is not easy on Thera. There was once a lucrative wine trade with Russia, but the Russian revolution put a stop to it. However, the island still produces noted wines, and tomatoes grow well in the grey volcanic soil. Cultivation must have its problems, for the island is completely waterless. The winter rains are stored in deep cisterns. In summer a supply of fresh water is brought once a week in a huge floating plastic container, which is towed behind a lugger from Paros. It takes a whole day to pump its contents up the cliff to the storage tanks of Phira.

There are no olives or cypresses to be seen, and very few trees or bushes of any kind. The vines and tomato plants grow in grey dusty fields thickly strewn with lumps of lava and pumice. The fields are buttressed and terraced with finely built dry-stone walls, some of them 6 m. and more in height. These walls prevent the loose 'soil' from blowing away or eroding in the winter rains. Rising tier upon tier they make cross-country walking extremely laborious, and one is almost forced to follow the line of the winter torrent beds, which are also well walled-in, like little streets, to prevent the stream from cutting too wide a gash in the high banks of ash and pumice.

These huge deposits of pumice and volcanic ash, or *tephra*,[38a] are the most striking and extraordinary feature of the landscape. Immediately south of Phira (Plate II) is a vast quarry where the ash is shovelled on to lorries and brought to chutes on the cliff face for loading on to ships below. The product is taken to Athens as an ingredient in the preparation of cement. It is essentially the same as the 'pozzuolana' found near Naples, rich in silica and lime, and productive of a cement which is very impervious to water.

The following details of the ash layer and its exploitation are taken from a recent excavation report by Professor Marinatos:[39] Many parallel, deep, horizontal tunnels [Plate 13] are opened on the lowest layer of the tephra. Inside the layer these tunnels are crossed by others at right angles so that a grid is formed, which very much weakens the foundations of the tephra-layer. The workmen continue their work quietly for weeks, until their skilled foreman feels rather than observes a light, almost imperceptible tremor in the white mass. Little, almost hair-thin cracks begin to appear. The workmen stop work and come out of the tunnels. They are employed on other jobs, while a day or a week or more is needed, before the mass begins to collapse, after which it is thrown down directly to the ships waiting below the precipices of the crater.

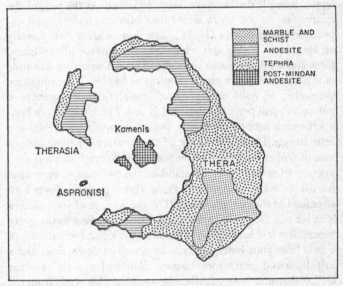

5 Geological map of the Thera group of islands

How and when did these great banks of tephra come to overlay the island with their oppressive bulk (Plate IV)? Not merely in the quarries, but almost everywhere on the island one sees these great gleaming cliffs of white ash. Much must have been eroded down the centuries, but millions of tons remain. As one walks through the ravines and looks up at the strangely eroded cliffs one becomes more and more oppressed by a sense of the utterly overwhelming forces which raised all this material from subterranean depths and deposited it so crushingly on the surface of the once fertile and well-wooded island. And then one realizes that the 'cliff' on which Phira stands is not really a cliff at all in the normal sense. It is not solid rock, but layer upon layer of volcanic debris, of ash and slag criss-crossed with bands of lava – a great multicoloured geological section forcing one to face the fact that the Thera volcano has been active and destructive for thousands of years.

In relation to the Atlantis problem we are concerned only with the great eruption which occurred about 1500 BC, and which led to the formation of the caldera and the deposit of the white tephra mounds that we have been describing. At the base of the quarry face in the Phira mines the 'Minoan' layer is well exposed in places (Plates III, IV). The pumice layer rests directly on the brown loamy soil which was the surface of the island three and a half thousand years ago. You can scoop out handfuls of this earth and let it run through your fingers. Here and there the outline of walls can be seen (Plate XII), and fragments of pottery are still perfectly stratified *in situ*. There must have been a settlement here on the gently sloping floor of a valley beside a little stream. Excavation is out of the question for thousands of tons of tephra are poised above you ready to crash down if even a stone is moved. Even to stand at the cliff-base is somewhat hazardous with bulldozers working above pushing down load after load of the fine white ash. The mechanism of your camera is in serious danger from the fine particles swirling in the gusty breeze. But it is hard to tear yourself away. You have walked half a mile from your hotel, and you have walked down three and a half thousand years into history. You feel a little of what Dr Leakey must have felt when he unearthed his skulls from the lower strata of the Olduvai gorge. You can actually touch the Bronze Age, and hold a little of it in your hand. A workman comes up from some other part of the quarry and holds out a dark fragment in his hand. 'Ancient tree', he says, and smilingly hands it to you for he has noted your interest in the buried past. And so it is – a charred fragment of wood from a tree which was in leaf when Minos ruled the seas, and which was blasted and buried as it stood when the fiery rain of pumice began to fall.

The chronology of the Bronze Age eruption

A severe earthquake on 9 July 1956 disturbed the lower strata in

BC	MAINLAND	CYCLADES	CRETE	EGYPT	BC
2000			MM IB	DYNASTY XII	2000
1900	MIDDLE HELLADIC	PHYLAKOPI II / MIDDLE CYCLADIC	MM IIA	MIDDLE KINGDOM	1900
1800			MM IIB	XIII	1800
1700			MM IIIA	HYKSOS	1700
1600	LATE HELLADIC / SHAFT GRAVES	LATE CYCLADIC / THERA FIRST ERUPTION	MM IIIB / LM IA	XVIII — AMOSIS I, AMENOPHIS I, TUTHMOSIS I, TUTHMOSIS II	1600
1500	MYCENAEAN I, IIA, IIB, IIIA1	THERA EXPLOSION	LM IB — KNOSSOS PALACE PERIOD I, II / PALACES / LINEAR B	TUTHMOSIS III, HATSHEPSUT, AMENOPHIS II, AMENOPHIS III, TUTHMOSIS IV	1500
1400	IIIA2		LM II 'PALACE STYLE' 1 2 / LM IIIA 1 2	NEW KINGDOM — AMENOPHIS III, AMENOPHIS IV, AMARNA EPOCH, TUTANKHAMEN, AY, HAREMHAB	1400
1300	IIIB		LM IIIB	XIX — RAMESSES II, BATTLE OF KADESH, EXODUS?	1300
1200	IIIC	SIEGE OF TROY?	LM IIIC	MERNEPTAH, XX, RAMESSES III, BATTLE WITH SEA PEOPLES	1200
1100	SUB-MYCENAEAN		SUB-MINOAN	XXI	1100
1000	PROTO-GEOMETRIC				1000

6 Chronological table

the large tephra quarry near Phira, and the ruins of what appeared to be an ancient building were noticed under the bottom layer of pumice. Near the ruins some human bones, teeth and charred wood were found, and Professor Galanopoulos arranged for a carbon-14 dating. The results were somewhat inconclusive. Two quite different dates were obtained: 1090 BC ± 150 years, and 1410 BC ± 100 years.[40] The first of these dates may be discounted as the sample is believed to have been contaminated by humic acid. The second date was obtained after the acid had been removed, and is considered to be more reliable.

A more refined dating of similar material has now been published.[39] In 1967 the carbonized trunk of a small tree was found still upright in the lowest pumice layer of the Phira quarry. The upright position of the tree is an important datum because it shows that the tree was still alive when the eruption began. In the case of house timber there is always the possibility that a radio-carbon date for the wood is considerably older than the date at which the house was destroyed, since radio-carbon dates relate to the moment when the material 'died', *i.e.* ceased to absorb carbon from the carbon exchange reservoir of the world. This possibility may be discounted in the case of a tree that was buried as it stood. The 1967 test was carried out by the Physics Department of the University of Pennsylvania, and gave the following results:

| *Half-life* 5568 | *Half-life* 5730 |
| 1456 BC ± 43 years | 1559 BC ± 44 years |

The sample was divided into two parts, and each part was counted for a total of six times.

According to these results the date of the first fall of pumice lies between the limits of 1603 BC and 1413 BC. If we follow the 'preferred' result (based on half-life 5730), the limits narrow to between 1603 and 1516 BC.

The results are an interesting pointer to the date of the beginning of the eruption, but greater precision can probably be obtained by the use of other data, especially that of pottery. Lack of precision is probably inherent in the radio-carbon method. Dr H. Baker has pointed out a number of factors which inevitably introduce uncertainties into radio-carbon dates.[41] These include: 'isotopic fractionation effect' in the case of wood samples, which can cause errors of up to ±80 years; systematic errors due to choice of reference material; the effects of the burning of fossil fuels; atom-bomb tests; long-term fluctuations in the levels of carbon-14 in the atmosphere over the past 1300 years. The existence of this last factor has recently been shown from work on tree rings. It is believed that this factor alone can introduce errors of up to ±1½ per cent in dates. Dr Baker concludes: 'One must accept the fact that the method is not able to resolve age differences of less than several hundred years.'

Fortunately the evidence of pottery enables a more precise dating to be made. At various times in the past hundred years a considerable amount of very interesting pottery (Plates 18, 33–5) has been found at various points on Thera and Therasia. Finds also include a few fresco fragments and an inlaid dagger blade (Plate 31). The various excavations are described in detail in Chapter 4. Almost all the pottery was found sealed in the rooms of buildings directly under the lowest stratum of pumice (Plate XIII). As a group it is remarkably homogeneous in style and decoration, and it must represent the pottery in use on the island at the moment of the first outbreak. Some of it is locally made, some imported, but all of it shows the influence of the Minoan style known (Plate 42) as LM IA. Renaudin was the first to make a systematic study of it in relation to Cretan discoveries, and he classified it as from the end of MM III and the beginning of LM I.[42] Åberg thought the bulk of the material dated from the time of the temple repositories of Knossos, *i.e.* from MM III, but admitted that some of the vases were LM I, *i.e.* post-1550.[43] Before his recent discoveries at Akrotiri, Marinatos had proposed 1520 as the date of the Thera eruption, but now he is prepared to come as low as 1500 on the evidence of the pottery.[44]

The latest datable vase is obviously decisive in this question. Scholes considers this to be the jug Zahn found.[45] He compares its ivy-leaf pattern with a similar motif found on a Mycenaean vase from Lachish (Plates 18, 19), which is assigned by Stubbings to the Mycenaean II style, a style broadly dated between 1500 and 1425.[46]

From this evidence one can infer that the first major fall of pumice on Thera occurred about 1500 BC or possibly even a little later.

It is important to remember that this date, *c.* 1500, is the date of the beginning of the eruption, not of the widespread destruction in Crete. It is the date when the Thera volcano became active again after a long period of quiescence, and ejected the coarser pumice which forms the lowest layer in the tephra deposits. This layer is about four metres thick in the Phira quarry (*Fig. 7*). The effects of this phase of the eruption were probably confined to

IV The Minoan level found during the course of quarrying shows as a much darker layer of loamy soil, small pebbles and rocks. Excavations are carried right down to it because the best quality pumice is immediately above it, seen here as a greyish stratum about four metres high. This is surmounted by a 'colour ribbon' layer of alternate bands of white, grey and pink pumice, the latter colour being caused by the action of sea water penetrating the magma chamber. An exactly similar layer was identified in the deposits on Krakatoa island after the 1883 eruption (see p. 70)

V The cinders and slag (*scoriae*) in the foreground on Nea Kameni is land only recently formed in the 1925–6 eruption (see Plate 20). It contrasts with the white tephra cliffs in the background across the bay on Thera proper

VI The cliffs on the south coast of Therasia provided the Suez Canal Company with their principal source of supply of pozzuolana, prized for its impermeability, in the 1860s. It was at this time that the first discoveries of Minoan-type buildings and pottery (see p. 96) were made along this coast. The dominant colours of red, black and white (pumice, lava and tephra) are a distinctive feature of this area (see p. 144). Early prints show that the tephra came much closer to the edge of the cliff and was much higher. Modern excavation and erosion (notice particularly the channels scored by winter torrents in the soft pumice) have reduced the cliff to a mere two hundred metres

Thera itself. It did not result in the formation of the caldera, but almost certainly all settlements on the island were obliterated, and all the inhabitants either killed or driven away. So few skeletons and valuables have yet been found that it seems as if the inhabitants had enough warning to collect some of their belongings and make a getaway.

Then the volcano entered on a relatively quiescent phase of unknown length. The existence of such a phase is deduced by Reck from the erosion of the pumice layer produced by the first outbreak.[47] An example of such erosion is visible in the V-shaped depressions which may be seen in places in the stratification (Plate 12). Next came some relatively minor outbursts evidenced by the five layers in contrasting colours of white, grey and pink which are also clearly visible in the Phira quarry, running like a coloured ribbon between the coarser pumice and the fine white ash (Plate IV; *Fig. 7*). Then the eruption began again with renewed vigour. Huge boulders were hurled out by the force of explosions in the central vent or vents making considerable dents on landing which are clearly visible in the dip of the strata immediately below them (Plate X). The particular spot illustrated is about 3 km. from the present focus of volcanic activity, and Reck thinks the main Bronze Age crater was even farther away to the north. Far larger 'bombs' have been found in the upper layers of the tephra. The fine white tephra has been measured up to 66 m. thick in parts of the island. There are some horizontal lines of separation in it, but Fouqué thought them not sufficiently marked to enable one to infer considerable time intervals between various phases of the eruption. A light tint of pale yellow at the separation lines indicates, in his view, brief weathering but no more. Above and below the lines there is no difference in the grain size. He concludes:

It is then probable that the beds [of the fine white ash] correspond simply to successive phases of the same volcanic outbreak, which, like later recorded eruptions, could have lasted for some years with alternating periods of relative calm and more violent activity.[48]

We have then a picture of a volcano coming into action about 1500 BC or even a little later, and proceeding by stages to a grand eruptive climax. Unfortunately there seems to be no way of establishing the date of the climax from data on Thera itself. The vulcanological experts agree that there was *some* time-gap between the first outbreak and the culminating paroxysm which produced the caldera, but they cannot say for certain how long this gap was. At this point we must look to Crete for further evidence.

The new stratigraphical data from Knossos helps to provide this. In 1961 an important discovery of a deposit of LM IB vases was made at Knossos by the British School excavation under the direction of Sinclair Hood.[49] This discovery has been described as likely to cause a 'counter-revolution' in an important area of Minoan studies. Evans had always insisted that the pottery period (Plates 14–16) LM IB covered approximately 1500–1450 BC, and that it formed a distinct period between LM IA (Plates 44–7) (sixteenth century BC) and the 'Palace Style' of LM II (1450–1400). A difficulty for his view was that no LM IB vases had been found at Knossos, though they were common enough in other places. Evans explained this by the theory that warrior kings operating from Knossos destroyed the other palaces about 1450, thus sealing in the LM IB pottery, which subsequently went out of use at Knossos and was not preserved there. These views of Evans had come under increasing criticism, and many experts preferred to believe that the LM IB and LM II styles were contemporary and indistinguishable in date, and that all the great sites were destroyed together about 1400 BC.

The new evidence does three things: it confirms that Evans was right in making the styles consecutive and not contemporaneous; it shows that his ingenious hypothesis of aggression from Knossos is unnecessary in so far as we now have LM IB vases from Knossos itself; finally, and most significantly for this study, it shows that there was violent destruction of at least one building at Knossos itself at a time when LM IB pottery was in use there.

The discovery of the LM IB vases was made in a basement room of a building on the north side of the 'royal road' (Plate 4) leading to the palace. The building, dating originally from *c.* 1650, had been much remodelled from time to time, and four distinct floor levels were traceable in the basement room going back to the MM III period. Floor 3 had fragments of classic LM IA pottery resting on it. Immediately above it was Floor 4 with its very significant deposit of LM IB vases. The deposit was

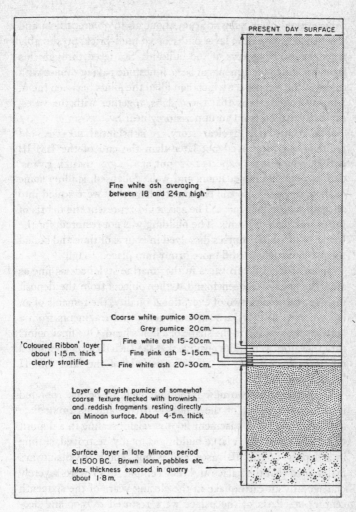

PRESENT DAY SURFACE

Fine white ash averaging
between 18 and 24 m. high

Coarse white pumice 30 cm.
Grey pumice 20 cm.
Fine white ash 15-20 cm.
Fine pink ash 5-15 cm.
Fine white ash 20-30 cm.

'Coloured Ribbon' layer
about 1·15 m. thick
clearly stratified

Layer of greyish pumice of somewhat
coarse texture flecked with brownish
and reddish fragments resting directly
on Minoan surface. About 4·5 m. thick

Surface layer in late Minoan period
c. 1500 BC. Brown loam, pebbles etc.
Max. thickness exposed in quarry
about 1·8 m.

7 Diagrammatic section of the stratification in the Phira quarry concentrated in an ashy stratum about 20 to 30 cm. thick, and was sealed in by a deep layer of dissolved mud-brick, presumably from the upper storeys of the building. Scattered through this layer were many fragments of large limestone paving-stones with traces of the red plaster which had filled the joints between them. The excavators think that these slabs, together with the vases, must have fallen from an upper storey near by.

The record tells a clear story. A substantial 200-year-old building was destroyed not later than the end of the LM IB period, which some experts now put at *c.* 1470, though Evans' date is 1450. Its upper floors and walls collapsed, spilling some of their contents into the basement where they were sealed into an ashy layer a foot thick. The ash could represent the debris of burnt wall or roof beams. The building was not restored, for the bricks of its upper courses dissolved in course of time and sealed the precious deposit still more firmly into place.

Some of the LM IB vases in the 'marine style' are as fine as any that have ever been found. Other objects from the deposit include seal stones, two of exceptional quality, the remains of an ivory comb, an ivory arm of a statuette, and fragments from a large steatite rhyton in the shape of a lion's head. One final point: the excavators were quite positive that the LM IB layer contained no traces of anything at all characteristic of the later LM II 'Palace Style'.

There are thus two new important facts to be incorporated into the chronology of the Knossos palace and its immediate surroundings. (1) A basement floor is relaid, sealing in a deposit of LM IA vases. (2) A large building is totally destroyed, sealing in a deposit of LM IB vases, and is not rebuilt. Evans always maintained that the palace and the Temple tomb were severely damaged by an earthquake in the closing years of the sixteenth century BC. Parts of the palace were restored *c.* 1500 and decorated in the then prevailing LM IB style. Now it has been shown that all major outbreaks of the Thera volcano in historical times have been preceded and followed by serious earthquakes.[50] If the pattern was the same in the Late Bronze Age, then perhaps the Knossos earthquake was the prelude to the first outbreak on Thera, which we have already seen reason to date to *c.* 1500 or even a little later. The earthquake could certainly account for fact (1) above.

What of the implications of fact (2)? A distinctive new style of pottery is developed to a high pitch of excellence at Knossos before at least one large building is totally destroyed there. This LM IB style with its distinctive marine motifs (Plates 14–16) is exported widely through the Minoan world. It seems reasonable to posit at least twenty-five years for the development and expansion of the style, even allowing for the fact that marine motifs are not entirely new in Minoan art and can be traced back to MM times. But at any time after, say, 1475 BC it will not be unreasonable to look for a cause which could reduce a substantial building to the charred and battered condition in which the British excavators found it in 1961.

I suggest that one should look to Thera for such a cause, not this time as the focus of intensified seismic activity, but as the locus of an explosive eruption of unprecedented and devastating violence. It is not merely a question of explaining the destruction of one building at Knossos – which could have been caused by a pirate raid, for example. Destruction at the end of LM IB was not confined to the Knossos area. Widespread devastation with burning occurred throughout most of central and eastern Crete. It was then that the great palaces at Phaistos and Mallia and the villa at Hagia Triada (Plate 26), together with much of their surrounding towns, were destroyed. So was the recently discovered palace at Kato Zakro (Plate 28). But the palaces were not the only buildings to suffer. Large mansions at Tylissos, Nirou Khani, Sklavokambos, Amnisos and Apodoulu were also destroyed. So were the settlements of Gournia (Plate 27), Palaikastro, Pseira and Mochlos. The roof of the sacred cave at Arkalokhori collapsed. A recent field survey has provided further evidence of LM IB period destruction, at Palaiokastro on the coast not far east of Rethymnon, and at Pirgos on the south coast.

The destroyed palaces were not rebuilt, and many of the destroyed sites were not re-occupied. Only the palace at Knossos continued to function as an administrative centre, and there the LM II 'Palace Style' developed out of the LM IB style (Plates 44–6). LM II vases have been found in a tomb near Katsamba, one of the harbour towns of Knossos, in association with an Egyptian alabaster vessel (Plate 78) bearing the name of Tuthmosis III (1490–1436 BC).[51] Matz concludes from this that the 'Palace Style' probably began as early as the second quarter of the fifteenth century.

Pendlebury and others have supposed that the LM IB style persisted at all centres other than Knossos, running simultaneously with the Knossian LM II style until a great destruction which he places *c*. 1400. All the palaces, he thinks, then met their end together. I prefer the view which *separates* the Knossos palace destruction from an earlier destruction at the end of LM IB. The date of the end of Knossos is itself highly controversial, some dating it to *c*. 1400, and others much later, but this destruction is not related to the Thera eruption in my opinion. But not so the widespread destruction of all the other palaces and many sites at the end of LM IB. I follow Professor Marinatos in attributing *this* destruction to the Thera volcano, and I date it to the end of LM IB. Schachermeyr places the end of LM IB at *c*. 1470, and this I would accept as the likely date for the culminating paroxysm of the Thera eruption.

Readers may well wonder whether it is physically possible for one volcano to cause such widespread devastation. Pompeii and Herculaneum were totally overwhelmed, but they were within ten miles of Vesuvius. How could places as far apart as Tylissos and Zakro suffer simultaneously from a volcano as much as 175 km. away? I believe that the next section offers evidence which proves that such a widespread cataclysm is within the bounds of physical possibility.

The nature and intensity of the Thera eruption: the evidence of Krakatoa

The evidence of the great eruption of Krakatoa in AD 1883 is crucial for any attempt to reconstruct what happened on Thera in the Late Bronze Age. Vulcanologists agree that Krakatoa is a volcano of the same type as Thera. The two volcanoes have demonstrably been behaving in a similar way for as far back as we can trace their activity. Krakatoa's violent outburst in 1883 is well documented from many eyewitness accounts and scientific studies. The after-effects were measured and recorded by scientific instruments all over the world. We know what devastation it caused and how many lives were lost.

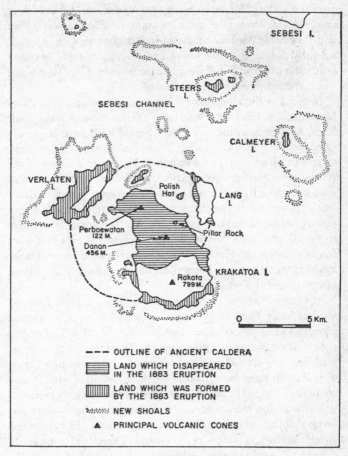

On the map:

SEBESI I.

STEERS I.

SEBESI CHANNEL

CALMEYER I.

VERLATEN I.

Polish Hat

LANG I.

Perboewatan 122 M.

Danan 456 M.

Pillar Rock

KRAKATOA I.

Rakata 799 M.

0   5 Km.

--- OUTLINE OF ANCIENT CALDERA

LAND WHICH DISAPPEARED IN THE 1883 ERUPTION

LAND WHICH WAS FORMED BY THE 1883 ERUPTION

NEW SHOALS

▲ PRINCIPAL VOLCANIC CONES

8 Krakatoa and the surrounding islands from a chart prepared immediately after the eruption

One of the main aims of the present study is to make credible the destructiveness claimed for the Bronze Age Thera eruption. Recent accounts of the volcanic destruction of Crete have emphasized the Krakatoa analogy, but have not, I think, exhausted all the lessons to be learnt from it. I make no apology for going into the Krakatoa eruption in considerable detail.[52]

Krakatoa (*Fig. 8*), like Thera, is a small group of three islands lying roughly in a circle: Krakatoa proper, Lang island and

Verlaten island. The group lies in the Sunda Strait between Java and Sumatra close to a main sea-route joining the China Sea and the Indian Ocean. Before 1883 Krakatoa proper was considerably larger than the other two islands, but the eruption reduced it to about one-third its former size, and Verlaten island was correspondingly increased in area.

In broad outline the volcanic histories of Krakatoa and Thera have much in common. Both lie at the junction of major fault lines. Well back in the quaternary period both were large volcanic cones with the typical 'Vesuvius' outline. Then both suffered violent paroxysmal eruptions leading to collapse of the central cone and massive ejections of tephra. The evidence of deep-sea cores from the eastern Mediterranean (given in detail below, p. 72ff.) indicates that about 23000 BC tephra from Thera was spread by an eruption over a vast area extending from Sicily to the coast of Asia Minor. Similar evidence is expected soon from the area round Krakatoa. It is not known for certain whether a caldera was formed at Thera then, but the outline of an old one can be traced at Krakatoa.

After these ancient cataclysms the Krakatoa caldera *(Fig. 9)* was gradually filled in by materials ejected from new volcanic cones, and this process had gone quite far by 1883. The largest cone, Rakata, was then 790 m. high. At Thera, after 23,000 BC, at least four new cones became active and built up a complex mass of peaks that must have covered much, if not all, of what is now sea in the heart of the island. Thera then entered a long period of quiescence, and the Bronze Age inhabitants probably were unaware that they were living on a dormant volcano. In its renewed violent activity, *c.* 1500–1470, central Thera was completely eviscerated, and the great caldera was formed. Since then the process of re-filling the caldera has gone ahead to the extent which is now to be seen in the Kameni *(Fig. 4)* group with its various small cones. The same process has started at Krakatoa, where Anak Krakatoa emerged in December 1927.

Before the 1883 eruption the Krakatoa group was well-wooded, but uninhabited and little known. No complete geological survey had been made, and the charts of the surrounding waters did not give very full or reliable information. Between May 1680 and November 1681 there had been an eruption, probably from the smallest cone Perboewatan (122 m.), but the island then

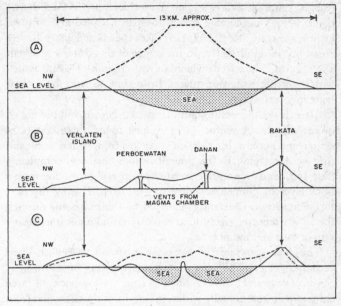

9 *Three phases in the history of the Krakatoa volcano. Section A shows the probable outline of the ancient caldera; the dotted line indicates the conjectured pre-caldera volcanic cone. Section B shows the profile of the Krakatoa group before the 1883 eruption. The ancient caldera has been largely filled in, Rakata enlarged, and two new cones formed. Section C shows the profile after the 1883 eruption. The dotted line indicates material lost in the eruption or added to the flanks of Rakata and Verlaten Island*

became dormant again for nearly two hundred years. The 1883 outbreak was preceded by six or seven years of increasingly severe earthquakes, some of which were felt as far away as Australia. Then, on 20 May 1883, came the start of a moderately severe eruption with booming noises heard up to a hundred miles away. By 22 May a great column of dust and vapour rising to an estimated height of seven miles was clearly visible from the lower parts of the island. Much pumice was ejected, and dust falls were noticed up to 480 km. away.

A week later an excursion party went from Batavia by steamer and landed on the island. They found Krakatoa and all the adjoining islands covered with fine white dust like snow,[53] and the trees stripped of leaves and branches by the falling pumice.

But the eruption debris was no more than a metre thick at any point. With considerable daring the party landed and went to inspect the cone of Perboewatan where they found a large crater about 900 m. in diameter. In the centre of this crater was a vent about 45 m. wide, from which a great column of steam issued with a terrific roar, punctuated from time to time by violent booming explosions.

After this outburst the volcano quietened down, but did not go quite dormant. A visitor on 11 August found three craters in action, and noted at least eleven other foci from which steam and dust were emerging. By this time all the forest had been completely destroyed, and only a few tree trunks were still projecting from a thick layer of pumice and dust 65 cm. deep. During the next fortnight activity constantly increased, and ships passing through the straits reported many loud explosions and a constant heavy rain of dust and pumice.

The great paroxysmal climax came on 26 and 27 August. Vivid accounts are available, not only from survivors on the nearby coasts of Java and Sumatra, but also from the log-books of three ships which were actually within the straits at the time, and from other ships at distances of up to 1840 km. away.

At 2 p.m. a ship 120 km. ENE of Krakatoa saw a black billowing cloud rising up to an estimated height of 25 km. By 3 p.m. explosions were audible up to 240 km. away, and by 5 p.m. they were audible all over Java. The *Charles Bal* was at this time only 16 km. south of the volcano, and her master, Captain Watson, reported a rain of warm pumice in quite large pieces falling on the ship between 5 and 6 p.m. Viewed from a ship 64 km. away to the north-east the cloud at 7 p.m. was like 'an immense pine-tree, with the stem and branches formed with volcanic lightning'.[54]

During the night the *Charles Bal* kept beating about to the east of Krakatoa, and only about 20 km. away. The crew saw 'balls of white fire' (doubtless white-hot fragments of lava) rolling down the south-west rim of the island, and the air was 'hot and choking, sulphurous, with a smell as of burning cinders'. The sky was 'one second intense blackness, the next a blaze of fire'. Krakatoa had now entered a paroxysmal phase of eruption, and was showing phenomena exactly like those witnessed on all such occasions. Small tidal waves were reported from 5.30 p.m. on

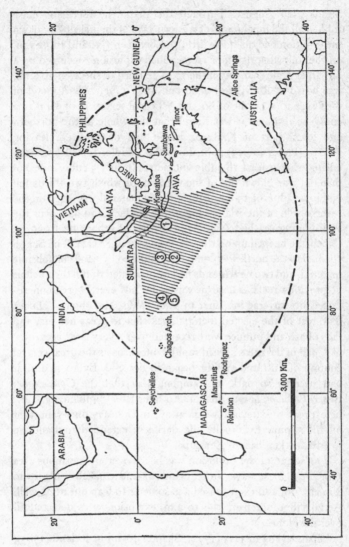

10 *Effects of the Krakatoa eruption in 1883. The shaded area includes localities at which ash is reported to have fallen after the eruption; the dotted line indicates the area over which the explosions were heard (Alice Springs is some 3,500 km. from Krakatoa), and the numbers refer to the sightings of floating pumice described on pp. 67–68*

Sunday, 26 August. Through the night the incessant noise robbed all the inhabitants of western Java of their sleep. By dawn the eruption had quieted a little, but between 5.30 and 10.52 a.m. on the following day four tremendous explosions occurred on a far larger scale than any hitherto. The third of these, at 10 a.m., was heard at Rodriguez, 4800 km. away *(Fig. 10)*. A cloud of dust rose to a height of 80 km. When observation of Krakatoa could be resumed it was found that the whole of the northern and lower part of Krakatoa island had disappeared, leaving Rakata (Plates 22, 23) split down the middle. It had been calculated that at least 18 cubic kilometres (nearly 5 cubic miles) of material was blown out of the volcano, of which two-thirds fell within a radius of 15 km. Much of this material was piled on the reverse side of the islands round the caldera, and also over the surrounding sea-bed *(Fig. 8)*. Deposits of tephra up to 60 m. thick were heaped up on the southern part of Rakata. The Sebesi channel to the north was completely blocked by banks of volcanic material, and two new islands had been formed round the nucleus of previous reefs. These new islands, however, were soon reduced by wave action, first to sand-banks, and then to shoals. The rest of the ejected material was shot to great heights, and falls of ash and pumice were reported over a very large area.

A pall of darkness spread rapidly outwards as the great central column of dust and vapour began to descend. By 10.30 a.m. it had become so dark in Lampong Bay that the *Gouverneur-General Loudon* had to anchor. An hour later complete darkness had spread to Batavia 160 km. away, and a heavy dust-rain went on till 3 p.m. Eventually the darkness extended to Bandong nearly 240 km. east of Krakatoa.

The sound of the explosion was heard over an enormous area *(Fig. 10)*. Blast waves broke windows and cracked walls up to 160 km. off, and even caused a gasometer to leap out of its well. Aerial vibrations from the 10 a.m. explosion were detected all over the globe.

Papandayang in Java (1772), Skaptar Jökull in Iceland (1783), and Tambora in Sumbawa (1815) all ejected more material than Krakatoa. Tambora spread darkness twice as far. But in recorded eruptions Krakatoa has no rival in the extreme violence of its culminating paroxysms, and in the catastrophic air- and sea-waves to which it gave rise.

The tidal waves were extremely destructive *(Fig. 11)*. Nearly 300 towns and villages bordering the Sunda Strait were devastated, and 36,380 people lost their lives. The extent of the flooded areas was immense. The town of Tyringen, 48 km. from Krakatoa, was the first to suffer. Many houses near the sea were destroyed in a wave which swept in between 6 and 7 p.m. on 26 August. The same wave damaged Telok Betong in Sumatra 72 km. away from the volcano. At 1 a.m. on 27 August the village of Sirik was submerged. At 6.30 a.m. Anjer was almost completely devastated, and simultaneously the lower part of Telok Betong was overwhelmed. The causation of the waves has been much discussed. The main originating factors are thought to have been the formation of submarine trenches by the explosions, and the avalanching of material from submarine slopes or from the land into the sea. It is at any rate certain that the largest wave was associated with the loudest explosion. Not long after 10 a.m. an enormous wave flooded all the shores bordering on the straits, and carried away what was left of the towns of Tyringen, Merak and Telok Betong, as well as many villages. Owing to the darkness and terror, reliable observation of the height of the waves was almost impossible. They are thought to have reached 36 m. in places. The lighthouse-keepers at Vlakke Hoek, 88 km. away, recorded them at 15 m. high. Another quite reliable estimate is from Telok Betong where the water washed to within 2 m. of the top of a hill 23 m. high. It was at this port that the gun-boat *Berouw*, which had been moored in the harbour, was carried nearly 3 km. inland and left at nine metres above sea-level. In general it may safely be reckoned that at distances of between 50 and 80 km. from the volcano the waves averaged 15 m. high, and that they tended to pile up much higher at the head of bays. Undulations travelled westwards across the Indian Ocean and were measured up to 2·5 m. in Ceylon and about 65 cm. in Mauritius. They were picked up at Cape Horn, and a final faint undulation may even have reached the English Channel where tide-gauges in Britain and France simultaneously recorded slight rises.

At no time was the fall-out of ash and pumice disastrously heavy in the straits, but it was recorded up to immense distances. Large amounts of floating pumice were noted by ships all over the Indian Ocean for many months afterwards *(Fig. 10)*. I give some typical extracts from log-books; the position of each ship is given by the appropriate number on the map on p. 65.

1 Barque *Actaea* 2 p.m. 20 May – 9 a.m. 21 May, a continuous fall of very fine dust.

2 Barque *County of Flint* 28 August, noon: Great quantity of dust falling; supposed to be coral dust.

3 Brig *Brani* 28 August: De minuit à 11 heures du matin une très grande quantité de sable très blanc et très fin a couvert toutes les parties accessibles.
29 August: Il tombe continuellement du sable très fin au point d'obscurir l'atmosphère.

The *Brani* observations were made at a point 1600 km. west of Krakatoa.

4 Barque *Gipsy* 9 September: Grand banc flottant de pierreponce [pumice] pendant toute la journée.

5 Barque *Ta Lee* 2 December: Passed a bank of pumice extending about 25 miles; some pieces about two feet square.

The floating pumice was still causing interest and excitement in April of the following year as may be seen from my final extract:

6 Brig *Flora* Le capitaine tombe à la mer en pêchant des pierres-ponces.

The after-effects of the great 1883 eruption finally faded away in sunsets and after-glows of striking beauty which were noted all over Europe and America during the winter months.

I have described the Krakatoa eruption in considerable detail because it provides one of our main yardsticks for estimating the probable after-effects of the Bronze Age Thera eruption. Leading authorities agree that calderas of these two similar volcanoes were formed in the same way by engulfment following explosions of extreme violence. Their history over the last 30,000 years or so seems to have followed the same pattern – a recurrent pattern of

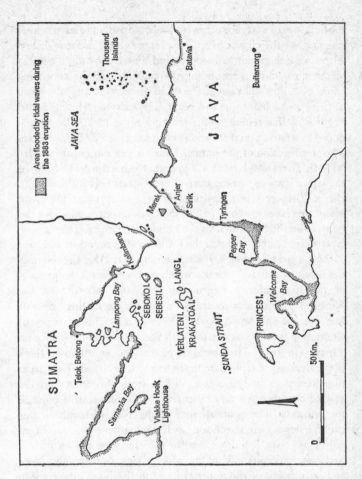

11 The Sunda Strait and portions of Java and Sumatra. The shaded areas were flooded by tidal waves following the 1883 eruption. Note the large areas flooded at the head of the four main bays facing Krakatoa, the absence of flooding on the leeshores of some islands, and the erratic incidence of flooding on the south coast of Java

the build-up of a cone or cones leading eventually to a paroxysmal eruption, at the climax of which a large caldera is formed. For Thera we lack eyewitness reports, but we have the mute witness of the sheer cliffs surrounding the caldera, and the enormous banks of tephra still rising to 66 m. in places even after the lapse of three and a half thousand years. The extreme whiteness and fineness of this tephra points strongly to its having been produced by a paroxysmal eruption after a long period of quiescence. The stratification of the pumice banks is extraordinarily similar on both Thera and Krakatoa. On both, the horizontal bedding of the layers is more marked in the lowest strata (Plate IV; *Fig. 7*). On both, there is a thinnish layer of pink pumice. On Lang island this layer is about 10 cm. thick and about 7 m. above the base of the 1883 deposits. In the Phira quarry there is also a pink layer *(Fig. 7)* about 10 cm. thick and about 4 m. above the base of the *c.* 1500 BC deposits. It has been suggested that the colour is the result of contact with sea water, and represents the product of the first submarine eruption. Williams' account of the Krakatoa pumice also mentions 'a quickly alternating series of fine pumice and lapilli layers'.[55] An exactly similar series of alternating layers is associated with the bank of pink pumice on Thera. On both Thera and Krakatoa the enormously thick upper deposits of tephra are much less well stratified. They seem to represent an enormous mass of lava-froth blown out from the magma chamber in a very short time at the culminating point of the eruption. The proportions of older rock materials in this massive deposit are significant; at Krakatoa 5 per cent; at Thera only 1 per cent. It follows that the calderas were not formed by 'explosive decapitation' of the older cones, but by subsidence and engulfment of the upper crust of the islands. Subterranean explosions exhausted the magma chambers below and the 'roof' fell in.

We know that this happened at Krakatoa within twenty-four hours, and there is every reason to suppose that the Thera eruption culminated in the same way. A study of the trenches *(graben)* in both calderas reveals a very similar pattern with deep fissures running out at right-angles and following major fault lines. Each caldera is roughly divided by a ridge into two basins, and the underwater contours are not dissimilar, but Thera reaches a greater maximum depth (400 m. to 279 m.). Also, the area enclosed by the caldera walls at Thera is four times as large as the surface area of the lost portion of Krakatoa (83 sq. km. to 22·8 sq. km.). It does not follow, as has sometimes been suggested, that the Thera explosion was four times as powerful. The morphology of the caldera, however, and the extent of the pumice deposits indicate that it was at least as powerful, and it may well have been more powerful, judging from the greater depth of the *graben*. We do know that fine Thera tephra was scattered over an area of 300,000 sq. km., mainly in a south-easterly direction. There is also some indication of a tidal wave over 200 m. high on nearby Anaphi. More research is needed here, but in the light of what is already known it is reasonable to consider the probable effects of the eruption on the neighbouring islands and in particular on Crete. Personally I do not doubt that they were extremely devastating. If walls were cracked by aerial vibrations up to 160 km. from Krakatoa, the mudbrick upper storeys of tall Cretan palaces and mansions could have suffered very severely from the same cause. None of the major centres of central Crete is even as far as 160 km. from Thera. If waves of between 15 and 30 m. height lashed the shores of the Sunda Strait, what must they have been like along the north coast of Crete when roughly four times the area of lost Krakatoa collapsed into the sea at Thera? Upwards of 36,000 people perished within twenty-four hours on Java and Sumatra, and 290 towns and villages were destroyed. We do not know what happened on Crete and on the islands and coasts of the Aegean, but I consider it a safe guess that the loss of life and damage to property were no less. They may well have been many times as great. We can say with reasonable assurance that Crete had ceased to be a great maritime power after the middle of the fifteenth century BC. Is it not reasonable to suppose that the Thera eruption was a major factor in her downfall?

In addition to the effects of blast and tidal waves, the effect of a heavy fall-out of ash must be considered in this connection. This factor will be discussed in more detail below, p. 80 ff. Here I shall merely state that there is good ground for supposing that the hills and valleys of eastern Crete were covered with a considerable depth of ash fall-out. It has been found that a deposit of 10 cm. can put fields out of action for ten years. A deposit of about a metre can kill trees and destroy buildings. We can envisage that the Minoans of central and eastern Crete who escaped the waves may well have found much of their land uncultivable, their orchards destroyed or stripped of leaves, and their buildings flattened. This factor of fall-out could be the explanation for the widespread devastation of sites well away from the north coast, and for the westward migration which is clear from the archaeological evidence (see p. 133).

The evidence of deep-sea cores

Fortunately we are not entirely dependent on the analogy with Krakatoa for estimating the nature and force of the Thera eruption. Since the Second World War some very valuable direct evidence about the volcanic activities of Thera has resulted from the analysis of cores of sediment taken from the bed of the eastern Mediterranean. This evidence has been assembled by D. Ninkovich and B. C. Heezen of the Lamont Geological Observatory of Columbia University.[56] Ninkovich and Heezen tell a fascinating story of how deposits of tephra from Thera have been identified in 21 cores taken from the sea-bed at depths of over 2000 fathoms in many cases. Seven of these cores were obtained by the Swedish Deep Sea Expedition of 1947–8 on the *Albatross*. During cruises 10 and 14 of the Lamont vessel *Vema*, in 1956 and 1958, 14 more cores were secured with the tell-tale ash. More than 95 per cent of the ash consists of very fine particles of colourless volcanic glass. Identification with the same material on Thera is secured by analysis of the mineral content of the samples. Two distinct falls of tephra can be distinguished. Ninkovich and Heezen call them the 'upper' tephra and the 'lower' tephra. They have different refractive indexes (n. 1.509 and n. 1.521). Analysis of the cores indicates that the 'lower' tephra comes from an eruption in the Würm period about 25,000 years ago *(Figs. 12, 13)*. The 'upper' tephra is from the Late Bronze Age eruption, and is interbedded with post-Pleistocene carbonate sediment.

Distribution maps of the tephra fall-out have been made on the basis of the find-spots of the various cones, and of the tapering off in thickness of the deposit as the distance from the volcano increases. It seems definite that the ash was transported

1 The stately palace of Nestor is described by Homer in the third book of the *Odyssey* when Telemachus visits it in search of news of his absent father Odysseus. Homer locates it in the western Peloponnese; a palace answering in many respects to his description was discovered at Pylos by Professor Carl Blegen in 1939 and subsequently excavated. *Above*, the so-called bath of Telemachus *in situ* in a room of the palace

2 *Above*, the great central hearth of the throne room, over 4 m. in diameter, which still shows some of its flame-coloured decoration on the stucco

3 Theseus' exploit in slaying the Minotaur in the labyrinth at Knossos
was preserved by Athenian traditions, and the anti-Cretan bias of the
Athenian writers probably reflects actual tension between Athens and
Crete in the fifteenth century BC. This exploit, the most popular of
Theseus' 'labours', is found widely depicted in Greek art. The tondo
of a red-figure kylix shows (surrounded by Theseus' other exploits) the
hero dragging the slain Minotaur from the labyrinth, here symbolized
by a maeander pattern. There may even be a hint of the typical, down
tapering, Cretan column (see Plate 51) in the one shown in the
background

4 The fine quality of Minoan masonry is well illustrated in the approach road from the west leading to the so-called Theatral Area at the palace of Knossos. The road has been called the 'oldest road in Europe', and it has been suggested that the Theatral Area was used for displays of ceremonial dancing. Homer may be referring to it when he talks of the 'dancing floor which Daedalus made for Ariadne in broad Knossos'

5 The sophisticated nature of Minoan society may be seen in this object which has been interpreted as a royal gaming board. Measuring 105 x 58 cm., it is made of ivory inlaid with gold, silver, lapis lazuli and rock crystal. The pieces associated with it, also of ivory, were 8 cm. in height

6 A selection of jewellery from the fifteenth-century tomb of a queen or princess at Arkhanes, south of Knossos. The jewellery was found with the burial in an undisturbed, gable-lidded chest (*larnax*) which even preserved some remains of the lady's clothing

7 Evidence of the Egyptian schoolboy's enforced interest in Keftiu is provided by this wooden writing-board which tabulates in hieratic script Egyptian equivalents for names of people from the land of Keftiu. The board is dated to the XVIII Dynasty, probably before the reign of Tuthmosis III

8 The great Victory Stele of Tuthmosis III from the temple at Karnak. It records his conquests in all foreign countries and specifically mentions that 'I have come that I may cause thee to trample down the western land; Keftiu and Isy are under the awe of thee' (line 16), and in line 18, 'I have come that I may cause thee to trample down those that are in the islands; they who are in the midst of the Great Green are under thy battle cry.' Highly personal as this inscription is, later Pharaohs, Amenophis III, Sethos I and Ramesses III (see Plate 69), have no compunction in 'borrowing' large extracts for repetition on their own monuments. The stele is headed by two scenes of worship in which Tuthmosis makes offerings to Ammon attended by the goddess of the Theban necropolis who, on the left, carries his bow and arrows and mace whilst he proffers incense in two small vases

9 A cult of sacred pillars was widely prevalent in Minoan Crete. Pillar-crypts with lustral areas are a common feature of the palaces. In the crypts the heavy pillars do not in fact serve any architectural purpose in supporting the roof. *Left*, an enlargement of the bezel of a gold ring. It shows a figure descending through the air beside a tall pillar standing before a shrine. The figure on the right in a flounced skirt, a priestess or votary, stands in the typical Minoan attitude of worship with her hand raised to her brow

10 An aerial view of the island of Thera. *Below*, the whole island group seen from the west. The largest portion is Thera proper, to the left is Therasia, and the very small fragment at the entrance to the caldera is Aspronisi. In the centre of the bay is the volcanic dome consisting of the smaller island of Palaea Kameni and the larger island of Nea Kameni which is the present focus of volcanic activity (see Plate 21)

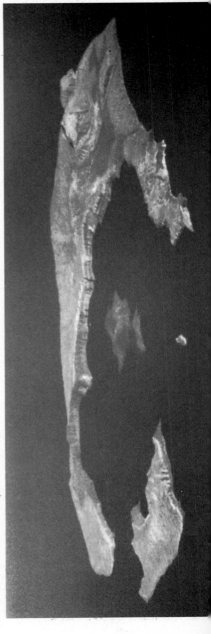

11 The line of the caldera cliff from Cape Scaros, which is topped by an old Venetian fortress, through Merovigli to Phira

12 The surface of the lower pumice (see Fig. 7) was at one time eroded to form a *V*-shaped run-off channel about 5 m. wide. Subsequent falls of pumice, constituting the 'coloured ribbon' layer, filled in the depression and the various bands can be seen following the contours of the gulley

13 Mining methods in the Phira quarries are here illustrated by the dark openings of tunnels which are driven into the base of the soft but elastic ash deposit. Cross passages join the tunnels to form a grid undermining the mass which in due course collapses and is then loaded on to lorries, tipped down the cliff face, and shipped to Athens

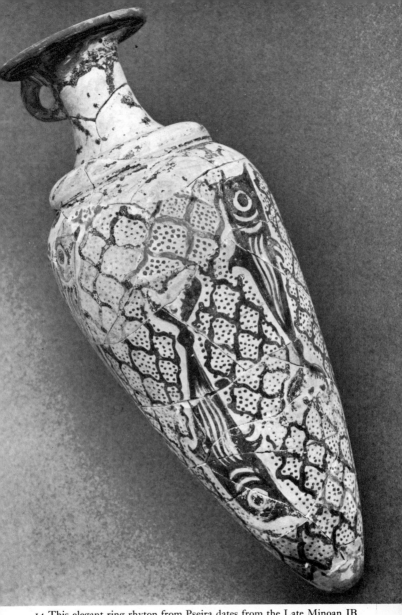

14 This elegant ring rhyton from Pseira dates from the Late Minoan IB
period (*c.* 1500-1470 BC). It illustrates the uniformity and excellence of
the 'marine style' pottery of this period.
This type of rhyton is depicted as part of the
tribute brought by the people of Keftiu to Egypt (see Plates XIV and 74)

15 The adaptation of the octopus to the spherical surface of this small 'pilgrim-flask' from Palaikastro shows the easy mastery of design achieved by the potters of the Late Minoan period. This type of composition is in sharp contrast to the formal banded designs of the later Mycenaean-influenced 'Palace Style' pottery (see Plates 44-46). The octopus continued as a favourite motif but became stylized beyond recognition

16 Nautilus shells are a common feature on the 'marine style' vases.
This libation vase comes from Phaistos. This motif subsequently travelled
to the Greek mainland and occurs, for example, inlaid on the blade of a
dagger from Pylos

17 This beautiful jug is a fine example of the 'plant style' motif of the first half of the fifteenth century. It was found in the palace at Phaistos. The shape, a typical water ewer, is traditional but the decoration of grass or reeds is characteristically Late Minoan

18, 19 A most important piece of dating evidence for the first outbreak of the Thera volcano is this jug (*top*) found by Zahn in 1899 on the Akrotiri peninsula. It is dated to *c.* 1500 and its main decorative motif, ivy leaves and tendrils, is also found on an Early Mycenaean fifteenth century goblet from the Fosse Temple at Lachish in Palestine (*above*)

20, 21 The Thera volcano has been active in recent years; quite serious eruptions occurred in 1925-6 (*left*) and 1938-41. Sporadic activity occurs without causing major damage (*right*) but the water round the Kamenis is frequently discoloured as a prelude to and during such outbreaks. Milky discolouration can be seen to the north and west (right of the photograph) of the island. In the 1925-6 eruption a substantial portion was added to the north-east corner of Nea Kameni

22,23 Two views of the cone of Rakata on Krakatoa island after the 1883 eruption. *Above*, seen from the south-east the cone is blanketed with a heavy deposit of tephra. The torrential rains so often associated with violent eruptions have already scored the surface with a diverging pattern of rain-water channels. The sea has begun to erode the base of the deposit to form sizeable cliffs. *Below*, the collapse of the north-west portion of the island has split the mountain, forming a striking and nearly vertical natural section about 800 m. high. White tephra deposits are clearly visible on both flanks of the peak itself and many lava dykes branch off laterally from the central vent

24, 25 Amnisos was a sea-port of Knossos and is mentioned in Homer as an indifferently sheltered harbour. A Minoan villa excavated here in the 1930s yielded some fine frescoes (*above right*) in which madonna lilies are shown in a setting perhaps meant to indicate a formal garden. They are painted in white against a red background. This fresco may date from c. 1600 BC. *Left*, among the waves on the seashore at Amnisos may be seen the remains of walls of Minoan houses. The site is clearly very vulnerable to a tidal wave from the north despite the protection of the off-shore island of Dia on the distant sky-line. Marinatos reported in his 1932 excavations, large building blocks prised out of position apparently by water-suction and a pit full of volcanic pumice

26 Two sites on the coast of Crete which were destroyed simultaneously in the first half of the fifteenth century BC are shown on this and the following page. *Above*, the villa of Hagia Triada, near Phaistos, and not too distant from the sea

27 The town of Gournia on the north-east coast is the only fully excavated Bronze Age town in the Aegean. The walls in the foreground formed the basements of small two-storeyed houses (see Plate VII)

28 The site (*opposite page*) of the newly discovered and excavated palace at Kato Zakro in Crete lies on a small plain where a deep limestone gorge, known as the 'Valley of the Dead', debouches on the sea. Kato Zakro was an important naval base and port, and was destroyed at the same time as the palaces at Mallia and Phaistos and other sites in Crete

29 Alone of all the great Minoan palaces, Kato Zakro was not plundered after its destruction and one of the rooms in it has yielded a rich series of finds. Here is a beautiful chalice made of speckled obsidian, a particularly hard volcanic rock perhaps imported from the little volcanic island of Yiali near Kos

30 Found in the Temple Repositories along with the famous goddesses, this small jug, perhaps for wine, was imported from Melos. Crete had close connections with Melos from the Middle Minoan period on and Melos, in turn, is thought to have influenced the culture of Thera. The bird motif also appears on pottery from Thera

31 Bronze weapon found on Thera in the nineteenth century excavations. The dagger blade (*above*) has a centre panel on which gold axes have been inlaid by a distinctive technique, familiar from similar finds at Mycenae and Pylos, which may derive from Minoan craftsmen

32, 33 Pottery from the earlier excavations on Thera (see also Plate 34). The terracotta chalice (*top*) has close parallels for its form from Kato Zakro (Plate 29). The jug (*bottom*) is in the 'plant style' familiar from Crete (*cf.* Plates 17, 25)

34 This tall jug with its stylized spiral anticipates a motif on the 'Palace Style' pithos from Pseira

35 In the same room as a row of storage jars (Plate XIII), this pithos was found lying on its side on a bed of pumice about a metre deep near a window. It must therefore have fallen from an upper storey after the eruption had been in process for some time

36 The site of the new Thera excavation near Akrotiri is typical of the location of many Minoan settlements on or near the sea (see Plates 26–28). The sea may once have come almost up to the settlement, forming a narrow sheltered bay which was later filled in by the volcanic debris. *Above*, the view south down the valley towards Crete, 110 km. away

37 The most enigmatic structure on the Akrotiri site is a monumental ashlar masonry wall of which about 5 m. has been exposed. Its eastern end disappears under a field above the ravine. The wall appears to be resting on soft ash and the stones are severely damaged, possibly by extreme heat. Perhaps this wall was built between the first and final outbreaks of volcanic activity, a period of some 25 to 30 years

38 Some idea of the appearance of houses in the Minoan settlement
on Thera is given by these faience and ivory (far right) plaques from
Knossos. The faience plaques formed part of a 'town' mosaic and it is
interesting to note that some of them have three storeys and a roof
penthouse. The dark horizontal lines may represent timber tie-beams,
traces of which have been found in the pumice overlay at Akrotiri (see
Plate IX).

39 Present-day inhabitants of Thera find that the deep layers of
pumice can be easily hollowed out to form stables and boat-houses such
as this, which opens on the south beach of the island. The freshly
excavated walls of such caves can be quickly cemented by passing a damp
cloth over them

by high altitude winds because of its fine grain quality. The tephra from the Bronze Age eruption covers an area of approximately 300,000 sq. km., and is detectable up to 700 km. away from Thera – a good indication of the force of the explosion which flung it into the upper atmosphere. It is suggested that the differing pattern of fall-out is due to the fact that the Würm eruption occurred in winter while the Bronze Age eruption occurred in summer. In the former case the tephra was carried westwards by the winter high altitude winds; in the latter case the summer Etesians were blowing, and so the distribution was mainly to the south-east of Thera. The summer dating (June to August) is confirmed by plotting distance against grain size. The resulting figures indicate that the ash was carried by relatively low velocity winds – a fact which suits the Etesian pattern.

The 'upper' tephra from cores 50 and 58 are the thickest tephra layers from deep-sea sediments so far recorded, 212 cm. and 78 cm. thick respectively. Core 50 is particularly interesting because it has an alternating pattern of coarse- and fine-grained ash indicating three distinct deposits with sharp contrasts between each layer. Ninkovich and Heezen infer that the three graded deposits are related to three successive eruptions of Thera. If they are correct, this is possibly good evidence for an extended time-scale in the eruptive process. It does not, however, seem possible to be sure that the deposit was not the result of secondary accumulation due to turbidity currents. One may also point out that the evidence is not easily squared with the view of vulcanologists that the Thera eruption proceeded by stages to a grand climax and then ceased altogether. In core 50 the *lowest, i.e.* the earliest, graded segment is also by far the thickest. Core 50 came from the abyssal plain about 12 km. west of the most northerly point of Karpathos and about 145 km. from Thera. It is greatly to be hoped that the problems raised by core 50 *(Fig. 13)* will be solved by further samples taken from this area. If it can be established that a direct fall-out of over 2 m. occurred at that distance from the volcano, this fact will have a most important bearing on the destruction of sites in Crete (see above, pp. 71-2, and below, p. 8off.).

Further exploration of islands in the Cyclades might well reveal tephra deposits which would confirm the distribution pattern indicated by the deep-sea cores. In 1924–5 Sonder

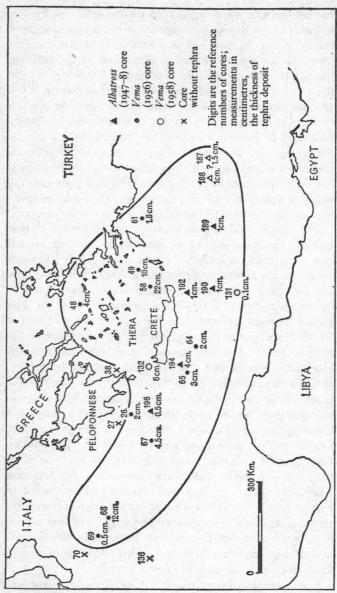

Legend:
- ◄ *Albatross* (1947–8) core
- ● *Vema* (1956) core
- ○ *Vema* (1958) core
- × Core without tephra

Digits are the reference numbers of cores; measurements in centimetres, the thickness of tephra deposit

TURKEY

EGYPT

188 △
1cm.
187 △
? 1.5 cm.

189 ◄
1cm.

61 ●
1.8cm.

49 ●
10cm.

58 ●
22cm.

48 ●
4cm.

THERA

192 ◄
1cm.

190 ◄
1cm.

CRETE

131 ○
0.1cm.

LIBYA

132 ○
6cm.
194 ●

64 ●
2cm.

65 ◄
3cm.

64 ◄
4cm.

38 ×

196 ◄
0.5cm.

27 ×
26 ×

2cm.

PELOPONNESE

67 ●
4.5cm.

GREECE

ITALY

69 ●
0.5cm.
68 ●
12cm.

70 ×

136 ×

0   300 Km.

12 *Distribution pattern of the lower tephra layer originating from a major Thera eruption of approximately 23000 BC. The evidence derives from deep-sea cores*

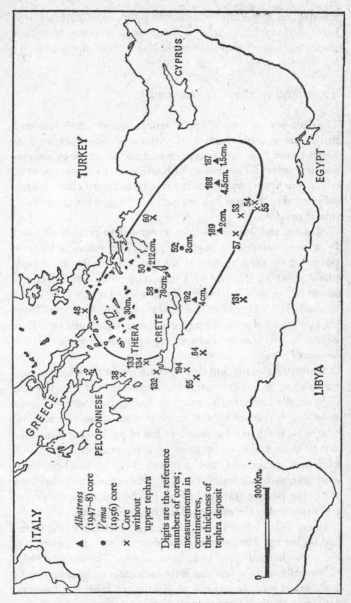

13 *Distribution pattern of the upper tephra layer, based on deep-sea cores, originating from the Late Bronze Age eruption of Thera*

reported on a volcanic ash covering the recent limestone in Paros, but practically no systematic work seems to have been attempted in this field which could be of major importance.

Thera and tidal waves (*tsunamis*)

The deep-sea cores with 'upper' tephra provide strong evidence that a paroxysmal eruption of extreme violence occurred on Thera in the Late Bronze Age. Was it accompanied by destructive tidal waves? The analogy of Krakatoa strongly suggests that it was (see above, 67f.), but it must be admitted that scientific evidence of such waves is, if not totally lacking, at least regrettably thin at present.

Marinos and Melidonis have attempted to remedy this lack by a very interesting suggestion.[57] They found a layer of pumice 5 m. thick resting at the head of a valley on Anaphi island about 24 km. east of Thera. The pumice bank lies at a height of 250 m. They believe it was washed up there by one of the vast tidal waves after the Thera eruption. Professor Platon has also reported piles of pumice on parts of the coast near Kato Zakro in east Crete. Further research along these lines is obviously needed.

Marinatos also thought that he could detect the effects of tidal waves when he was excavating at Amnisos in 1932. In a building right on the seashore (Plate 25) he found that the lower levels were deeply buried by masses of pumice stone and sand. A square pit inside the building was full of pumice pebbles of the sort that can be picked up today on many beaches in the Greek islands. It seemed clear to him that the building had been swept away almost to its foundations by tidal waves, and that later sea-borne pumice was washed over it by normal wave action, and deposited in the cavities of the ruined structure.

In the Villa of the Frescoes (Plate 24), which lies a little inland and higher up, Marinatos noticed that the walls and corners of the rooms had collapsed in an unusual way. The outward bulge of the walls, and the fact that huge orthostats up to 2 m. long by 1 m. broad were prised out of position or missing altogether, made him think of the sucking action of a huge mass of receding water. The villa also showed evidence of extensive fire damage

– a point which at first sight seems inconsistent with the tidal wave theory. However, as Marinatos has pointed out, exactly the same thing was observed after the Krakatoa eruption. He quotes a report of Verbeek about houses at Tyringen which were over-turned by the waves and then set on fire by the lamps which the inmates had lit to counteract the pall of darkness from the eruption.[58]

It may be objected that such reasoning applied to a site like Amnisos is mere guess-work and not evidence. Clearly it would be very difficult to find objective certification of the explanations of Marinatos in this case. Nevertheless I feel they should not be dismissed out of hand. An excavator often knows more about his site than he can put into words or justify by argument, and his considered 'hunches' should be allowed to carry some weight.

So far as I know, these observations of Marinos, Melidonis, and Marinatos are the nearest approach we have to direct evidence of destructive *tsunamis* associated with the Thera eruption in the fifteenth century BC. The case has to be made out with the help of indirect evidence and analogy. But I suggest that it is a strong case.[59]

In AD 365 Knossos, Gortyn and eight other places in Crete were destroyed by an earthquake, and destructive associated *tsunamis* were reported from Crete and from as far away as Alexandria. At Alexandria ships were carried over buildings and left among the streets of the city.

In 1672 the Cyclades, and especially Thera, were shaken by an earthquake. The island of Kos was reported 'swallowed up', presumably by a *tsunami* associated with the shock. Such an association is almost invariably found with submarine earthquakes.

On 29 September 1650 there was a destructive earthquake on Thera followed by a submarine explosion from the Kolumbo volcano whose crater lies in the sea off the north-east flank of the island. There was also a devastating *tsunami* preceded by a large withdrawal of the sea, particularly on the east coast. On Ios waves up to 16 m. high were reported. In Crete rowing boats were sunk in Herakleion harbour.

One could be excused for being a little sceptical about all the facts and figures in the above reports. But the details of the 1956 earthquake centred near the south-east coast of Amorgos are well documented. The shock was very severe (7·8 magnitude), and was followed by three large *tsunamis* which caused much damage on Amorgos itself, and on the following islands, all of which, except Ios, lie to the east: Ios, Astypalaea, Kalymnos, Leros, Nisyros, Kos, and Karpathos. Minor damage was reported from Patmos, Crete, Tinos, Melos, and Seriphos. More than eighty small ships and rowing boats were wrecked or lost. Very surprisingly only one person was reported drowned. The height of the waves varied greatly: on the coasts of Amorgos and Astypalaea facing the epicentre they were from 25 to 40 m. high; on the opposite coasts of the same island, only between 2 and 4 m. high.

As destructive tidal waves have been associated with the above-mentioned seismic activity centred in or near Thera, and as they were certainly associated with the analogous Krakatoa eruption, it seems reasonable to suppose that they accompanied the great Bronze Age eruption, especially in its final caldera-forming stage.

How destructive were the *tsunamis*? The effect of such waves depends on their height and speed, and also on the configuration of the surrounding coasts. Tidal waves over 200 m. high are *possible*, and have been observed. In the case of the postulated Thera waves the height is unknown, unless the datum given above on p. 76 is accepted as a guide. But we do know that the *speed* of such waves is a function of the depth of the sea through which they are propagated. The deeper the sea, the swifter the wave. The waters round Krakatoa are quite shallow (between 50 and 150 m.), but, even so, speeds of up to 41 m. per second were calculated for the *tsunamis* associated with the eruption. Between Thera and Crete the sea averages 1000 m. deep – a depth which would propagate the waves with enormously high speeds. Even close to the Cretan coast the depth is still 500 m. Then the bottom shelves up rapidly, and this would exert some braking force on the waves, but it would also make them rear up with great curling crests, and we must suppose that if they came they struck the coast with devastating velocity. A glance at the map on p. 81 *(Fig. 14)* will show how exposed the whole northern coast of Crete is to waves coming from Thera. Large *tsunamis* could have spread devastation over all the coastal plains and off-shore islands, and at the heads of bays like the gulf of Mirabello and Siteia bay. The great palace of Mallia lay only about 600 m. from the coast, and, with its surrounding town, was very little above sea-level. Harbour towns like Amnisos and Katsamba and Nirou Khani could have been as totally destroyed as Tyringen and Anjer on the Java coast. Gournia was within easy reach of the sea, and so were the Siteia valley and Pisko-kephalo. On the east coast a great wave travelling past could have inundated Itanos, Palaiokastro, and Kato Zakro (Plate 28), all of which are low-lying and close to the sea. The newly dis-covered palace at Kato Zakro is only about 100 m. from the present shore, and the sea may have come even closer to it in antiquity.

Knossos alone, of all the great palaces and settlements on the north and east coasts, would have had a chance to escape annihilation. It lies between 5 and 6 km. inland and is sheltered from the sea by a low range of hills. Also, the long ridge of the island of Dia lies like a protecting screen off the coast directly between it and Thera. Very large waves could have washed around it, but it could have escaped total destruction.

The fate of Phaistos and Hagia Triada is not at all clear. They certainly suffered much damage at the same time as the other sites. But they are on the south coast protected from the north by mountains over which no wave could possibly have travelled. Hagia Triada (Plate 26) is quite close to the sea, but Phaistos is at least as far inland as Knossos, and stands 70 m. above sea-level. The damage can hardly be attributed to waves, at least in the case of Phaistos. Other possibilities are: earthquakes pre-ceding or following the eruption; blast damage to upper storeys combined with the breaking down of roofs and upper floors by a heavy fall-out of ash; pillaging by the starving survivors of the disaster.

Central and eastern Crete in the early fifteenth century BC was covered by a thick network of settlements, villas, and roads *(Fig. 14)*. To judge from the remains it was densely populated, especially in the coastal regions. A large population was at risk, and casualties must have been heavy if the disaster took the form that I have outlined. It is easy to imagine that far more lives than the Krakatoa total of 36,380 were lost. In general, a large *tsunami* hitting a stretch of coast is likely to be much more destructive of life and property than all but the most exceptional earthquakes. Figures for eighteen really severe Japanese earthquakes between 1703 and 1927 show that only one caused more loss of life than the Krakatoa *tsunamis*, and only one other even approached them in this respect. One has to go to the really great earthquakes – such as Lisbon 1755 (50,000 killed) or Messina 1908 (100,000 killed) – to find larger casualty lists than that of Krakatoa.

Effects of the ash fall-out

After the eruption, Crete, especially in its eastern half, must have been overlaid with a layer of volcanic ash. Ninkovich and Heezen were the first to note this fact, and to discuss some of the implications of it. If, as seems probable, the eruption took place in the period June–August, all vegetation in central and eastern Crete would have suffered severe damage. Crops still in the fields are likely to have been completely destroyed. Olives and vines would have been defoliated, and so on.

Some interesting data bearing on this point is available from more recent eruptions. The 1815 eruption of Tambora in the East Indies took place in summer, and 80,000 people died from disease and starvation caused by the disruptive effect of the ash fall-out on agriculture.

The effects of such fall-out have also been closely studied in Iceland. There, thanks to close collaboration between archaeologists and geologists, the investigation of tephra layers has been placed on a scientific footing during the last twenty-five years. A new word, tephrochronology, has been coined by Dr S. Thorarinsson, one of the leading experts in this field.[60] Tephrochronology is the science which identifies the various layers of volcanic ash that are such a marked feature of soil profiles in Iceland, and assigns absolute dates to them, either by correlating them with annalistic records, or by carbon-14 methods. White layers of ash are particularly important in this study for a number of reasons: they are more easily identifiable, they are usually thicker than other layers, and they are thought to derive from explosive eruptions which take place after a long period of quiescence. They are also more acid (rhyolitic) than darker tephra.

Iceland has a large number of volcanoes, and more than 120

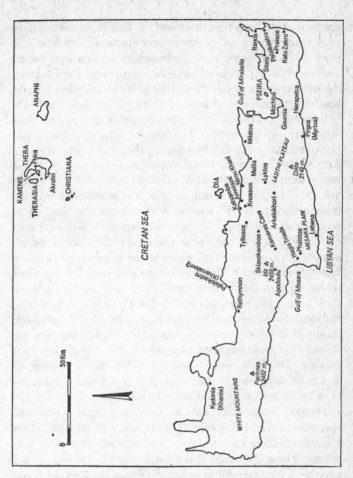

14 *Crete and Thera showing sites mentioned in the text*

eruptions have been recorded since the first settlements nearly 1100 years ago. Some interesting results have been obtained from the excavations of early medieval farms which were buried under tephra deposits by some of these eruptions. For example, the farm at Stöng in the Pjórárdalur valley in southern Iceland was buried under a thick layer of white pumice from the Hekla eruption of AD 1104. This eruption occurred after several hundred years of quiescence. The pumice filled the house and preserved the walls virtually intact to their full height. Another farm at Gröf in the south-east was excavated in 1955–7. It was buried during the disastrous eruption of Öraefajökull, the largest volcano in Iceland (2119 m.), in 1362. The pumice debris in the ruins included 'bomb' fragments of considerable size, up to 60 cm. long. The eruption was purely explosive; it did not produce any lava, but only what the report calls 'an enormous amount of rhyolitic tephra', which lay up to 40 cm. thick at the foot of the mountain. This must seem a very small fall-out when compared with the deposits on Thera, which are up to 66 m. thick after 3,500 years, but it wiped out an entire community, and extended in a noticeable layer over quite a lot of the island, mainly in an easterly direction. The whole surrounding area was deserted for about ten years after the eruption. From data such as these Dr Thorarinsson has concluded that a fall-out of 10 cm. or more leads to the desertion of farms until the ash has been blown away or leached from the soil.

The destructive effect of the ash depends on its thickness, and also on its chemical composition. It has been noted that the Thera volcano produces more sulphate and chloride than most volcanoes. These chemicals, if present in the ash fall-out, would have been very harmful to soils and vegetation. Ninkovich and Heezen estimate that the ash layer over central and eastern Crete must have been 'over 10 cm. thick'. On the analogy of Iceland this must have led to the abandonment of much farm land for a considerable period. The average rainfall on a Mediterranean island will not leach the soil very quickly. Labour for clearance work was probably in short supply because of the loss of life from the tidal waves. It seems very possible that the whole economy of Crete was seriously crippled and disrupted in the decade after the final Thera eruption. Much of her productive land may have been put out of action for years. The same argument applies to other islands in the area of the fall-out, many of which had Minoan colonies.

The fall-out layer may have been considerably thicker than the minimum of 10 cm. postulated by Ninkovich and Heezen. Core 58 was obtained at a point 110 km. from the volcano, and 40 km. due north of Itanos. It contained a single deposit of ash 78 cm. thick. Knossos and Mallia are only 120 km. from Thera. They could have been buried by between half and three-quarters of a metre of ash. Even at Kato Zakro (165 km.) the fall-out could have averaged 30 to 40 cm. in thickness. Platon has suggested that lithic ejecta reached Kato Zakro,[61] but this claim has not yet been proved by scientific analysis of the site materials. Pumice and lithic particles of between 0·5 and 1 cm. have been recorded at distances of about 115 km. from Crater Lake and two or three other volcanoes, but these are the greatest distances yet recorded anywhere in the world.[62] Pending further evidence, Kato Zakro must be regarded as outside the range of direct bombardment by 'bombs' from Thera, but not, of course, immune from fine ash fall-out carried by high-altitude winds.

The historical consequences of the eruption will be considered in more detail in Chapter 5. Here I merely note that there is archaeological evidence for a considerable displacement of population from eastern to western Crete in the fifteenth century BC. Such a westwards movement would result from a heavy ash fall-out as postulated.

Some subsequent Thera eruptions

Strabo records the sudden formation of a volcanic island at Thera as a striking example of violent natural change. Writing about the 197–6 BC eruption he says:[63]

Midway between Thera and Therasia flames came bursting up from the sea for four days, causing the water to seethe and flare up. Gradually an island emerged and was built up, as though it had been forged by implements out of a red hot mass, until it reached a circumference of 12 *stadia* [2 km.].

This island still remains as Palaea Kameni.

Continued links between natural phenomena in Crete and Thera are attested by a passage in Philostratus describing a journey of Apollonius in Crete.[64] Apollonius was paying a visit to the temple of Asclepius at Lebena near Phaistos when an earthquake struck Crete. A thunderous noise came from the ground, and the sea retreated nearly a mile from the shore. Many in the crowd were afraid that the water would return and wash them away, but Apollonius cried: 'Do not be afraid; the sea has given birth to land.' They failed to understand what he meant. But a few days later news came that, at noon on the day when the portent occurred, an island was cast up in the strait between Thera and Crete.

Writing of the eruption of AD 726 Theophanes, a Byzantine historian, records that pumice reached the shores of Asia Minor and Macedonia. The explosion of the AD 1650 eruption was heard at the Dardanelles, 500 km. away. This outbreak ended with the upheaval of an island to the north-east of Thera which has since sunk and now forms a reef below sea-level. In 1707 Nea Kameni emerged above the surface, and in the 1866 eruption it extended southwards and was enlarged threefold. In this outbreak pumice covered all the beaches of Thera and was carried by the waves as far as Crete.

The story of Thera eruptions continues into the present century. The same phenomena recur. *Tsunamis* have been associated with all the eruptions, and have often caused great damage on surrounding coasts. Conditions have sometimes been most unpleasant for the inhabitants of Thera and the neighbouring islands. 'Bombs' and blocks have been hurled at them from the vent of the volcano. Gaseous vapours have provoked fainting, headaches, vomiting, and even led to suffocation. The white walls of houses in contact with the vapours have turned green or rust-red. Submarine exhalations have poisoned large quantities of fish. Vegetation has been badly affected, acid-laden dust has induced conjunctivitis, and sulfurated hydrogen vapour has been responsible for angina and bronchitis. In certain wind conditions suffering has been caused as far away as Ios, Anaphi and Sikinos.

Let me end this chapter of disasters on a lighter note with some personal reminiscences of the proprietor of the Hotel Loukas in Phira. He told me some interesting facts about a warning signal which indicates that an eruption is imminent. Two or three days before the outbreak, the water in the bay around the Kamenis becomes curiously discoloured in patches of sulphurous yellow, crimson, black and white (Plate 21). As the eruption develops, these patches of colour become quite bright, and swirl and change in kaleidoscopic patterns. This information agrees quite well with an eyewitness account from the previous century. P. Dekigalla recorded that on the evening of 20 January 1866, the sea round Kameni was white and milky. On the next day it turned green and violet.[65]

The eruption which began on 28 October 1938 lasted, my informant said, until 10 August 1941. The volcano made booming noises every day during this period, and the sea was constantly steaming as hot boulders fell into it. An amusing incident occurred on 18 September 1940. Early that day an Italian plane flew over the island and swooped down to bomb a ship lying near the Kameni islands. It was a ship used for conveying the products of the Phira quarry to Athens. The plane unloaded all its bombs but failed to score a hit. These detonations, however, seemed to stimulate the volcano into more intense activity. It poured out a dense cloud of smoke which soon covered the ship, enabling it to escape from danger. The crew of the bomber were quite happy when they saw the smoke for they felt sure it came from the burning ship. They reported to base that their mission had been accomplished, and the 'success' was duly reported that evening on Rome radio, much to the amusement of the locals who had seen the ship get away unscathed.

The volcano is rarely so co-operative with the islanders. Strong barrel-vaulted roofs on many houses remind one that the island is very subject to earthquakes. A severe shock on 9 July 1956 killed 53 people and destroyed 2400 houses. Many emigrated after this disaster, but the rest remained and tenaciously rebuilt their shattered churches and homes. And again today a long white line of houses from Cape Scaros to Phira Bay defiantly confronts the dark spreading mass of lava across the blue water of the great caldera bay (Plates 11, V).

4 Excavations on Thera

The old excavations

The first clear evidence of Bronze Age settlements on Thera came to light in the 1860s as a result of quarrying operations occasioned by the building of the Suez Canal. New harbour installations were required at Port Said, and it was found that pumice dust mixed with lime in the proportion 3 to 1 made a very durable cement which was also very resistant to seawater. Thera provided an inexhaustible supply of pumice, and vast quantities of it were removed by the Suez Canal Company from points on the interior of the bay north of Akrotiri, near Cape Tinos on north-east Therasia, and over almost all the extent of the cliffs on the south of Therasia. In some places on the south face of Therasia the lower limit of the pumice was indicated by numerous stone blocks which hindered the quarrying operations. They were in fact the tops of ancient walls, and those in charge knew this quite well. The violent eruption which began in January 1866 attracted the attention of the scientific world to Thera. M. Christomanos, Professor of Chemistry at Athens University, was a member of the scientific mission sent by the Greek government to study the eruption. He was the first to draw attention to the Therasia walls, and to assert that they were anterior to the formation of the pumice layer, though many believed they were later tombs. This is, perhaps, the first recorded instance in the history of modern archaeology in which the interests of a commercial undertaking are seen in sharp conflict with the need for the careful scientific investigation of a site. Much valuable material was doubtless destroyed as the extraction of the pozzuolana continued. However, Alafousos, proprietor of the site, and Nomicos, a Theran doctor, managed to get an excavation started, and uncovered a multi-roomed house with associated pottery.

Fortunately a French *savant*, M. Fouqué, was also on the island with a French mission studying the eruption. Though primarily a vulcanologist he saw the historical importance of what was being uncovered. Fouqué prosecuted the excavations further, called in others to help him, and recorded and described much of the material found.[66] He describes a pillar crypt with a central pillar of two great squared blocks of lava each a metre high and 50 cm. broad. He also mentions the finding of the skeleton of an old man of medium build. This excavation of Fouqué's took place in 1867.

Fouqué also enquired about antiquities at Akrotiri, and a peasant conducted him to a nearby ravine. Then followed what must surely be the first recorded field survey of a Minoan settlement. From Fouqué's description, the ravine is almost certainly that in which Professor Marinatos is now conducting his excavations. He was shown the remains of walls standing in the pumice and recognized them as similar to those on Therasia. He was anxious to uncover them, but a 'misunderstanding' with the owner of the site prevented him from doing so, However, he continued his survey in the neighbourhood, and later, in the same ravine, under a bank of pebbles 3 to 4 m. thick, he spotted a layer about 30 cm. thick 'formed almost entirely of vase fragments'. After digging for some hours he recovered a considerable number of sherds out of which he later assembled more or less complete vases. In another ravine farther to the east he was shown two small vaulted tombs which had been plundered. Nearby he found more sherds, and obsidian blades, and his conductor produced two gold rings which had been discovered in the same layer.

These discoveries of Fouqué led to a more formal excavation conducted by Mamet and Gorceix of the French School of Archaeology at Athens in April and May 1870. Mamet published his findings in an elegant Latin thesis *De Insula Thera* (1874), and Fouqué also gives a full description and plans of the buildings found. Apart from Akrotiri, Mamet does not record a single place name or owner's name, but from his carefully drawn and contoured map one can see that the most exciting finds were made on the east side of the ravine where Marinatos is now working. This is confirmed by some topographical indications in Fouqué.

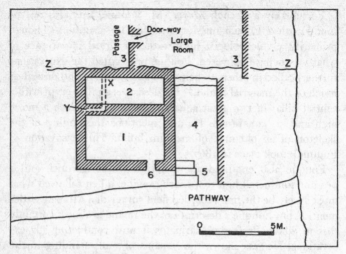

15 Plan of the 'House of Frescoes' excavated by Mamet and Gorceix near Akrotiri in 1870. 1 Rain-water cistern(?). 2 Room of pitchers. 3 Frescoed walls. 4 Cellar with slab roof. 5 Staircase. 6 Blocks missing. XY Water conduit. ZZ Line of steep bank on east side of ravine

The plan of one of the buildings found is shown above (*Fig. 15*). The excavators took Room 1 to be a cistern, as a water conduit runs from x to y, presumably draining water from roofs at a higher level. Many pitchers were found in Room 2, but the highlight of the excavation came when the diggers broke through the wall at the back of Room 2 and found an open pumice-vaulted passage. This opening went through and under a steep bank about 3 to 4m. high on top of which was a vineyard. A bank of gravel was poised precariously overhead (*cf.* Plate 39), but the excavators ventured in, and became the first moderns to see a Minoan fresco. The surface of the passage wall, and also of a wall in the larger room beyond, was covered with fine white plaster. The plaster was painted with frescoes in bright colours: blood-red, pale yellow, dark brown, and a brilliant blue which faded almost immediately on contact with the air. The lower part of the wall was decorated with alternate bands of the four colours. Above, on a white ground, flowers 'with stamens longer than corollas' were painted in red. From numerous glazed fragments on the floor it was concluded that the rooms had had painted ceilings. The party was afraid to open up any more of the building because of the danger that the overlying banks of pumice and gravel would collapse, and in fact this disaster happened soon after they had suspended work. They had secured, however, about a hundred vases, some of them finely painted (Plates 32–4), and specimens of these now form the bulk of the collection of Thera pottery in the French School of Archaeology in Athens.

Mamet and Gorceix next excavated a smaller house 60 m. down the ravine, and a house on the cliffs north of Akrotiri near Balos Bay. In the latter place they found two rooms about 4 m. sq. with walls of squared limestone blocks, and more pottery. Some of the house walls had been cut off short by the collapse of the caldera. Two very large *pithoi* had remains of carbonized straw and barley. Smaller jars contained barley, lentils and peas. One had 'a twist of crude rope passing through the lid'. The rope 'seemed to be woven from tree bark', but as soon as Mamet touched it, it crumbled into dust. A copper saw was found, and the bole of a large olive tree in a courtyard.

The reader can appreciate something of the problems, and also the opportunities, facing further excavation on sites like Akrotiri. Precious and delicate objects such as textiles, frescoed walls, and wooden furniture may well be sealed in rooms under the pumice layer. Professor Emily Vermeule found fragments of painted plaster in 1967. Professor Marinatos is well aware that full exploration of the site is going to take a long time. Rooms will have to be opened up, possibly by tunnelling, with the utmost care and patience. It will obviously be desirable to have the best possible scientific equipment for recording, and if possible preserving, any delicate and perishable objects that may be found.

Fouqué and Mamet concluded that the inhabitants of their sites were civilized and artistic people, but they did not get very far with the problem of their date, origin and nationality.

After the 1870 excavations no further work was carried out on Thera until 1899. In that year R. Zahn dug at Kamara in the valley of Potamos some distance to the east of the present Akrotiri site. Apart from a short report on Hiller von Gaertringen's monumental *Thera*,[67] Zahn never published his excavations. Some information based on Zahn's diaries, and some fine pictures of vases (Plates 32–4), is given by Åberg.[68]

16 This pithos found on Thera and published in 1866 must be one of the earliest Minoan-type pots illustrated in the literature. It was naturally not recognized as such prior to the re-discovery of Minoan civilization in 1900 with Sir Arthur Evans' excavations at Knossos, but it was realized that the pot was pre-classical

Hiller von Gaertringen's own work, though extremely important, is not relevant to the present study. It was carried out on the promontory of Mesavouno at the south-east corner of the island. The remains found are chiefly from the Hellenistic period when Thera was used as a naval base by the Ptolemies of Egypt. There are also some very important archaic inscriptions on the rocks near the extreme end of the promontory – among the earliest examples of Greek alphabetic writing that we possess. Hiller von Gaertringen's researches greatly clarified our picture of Thera in the classical and Hellenistic periods, but contributed little or nothing to the history of the island in the Bronze Age.

As a result of these various excavations the Thera museum had come to possess a representative and fairly homogeneous collection of Cycladic pottery of the Late Bronze Age (Plate 43). In 1956 K. Scholes characterized it as follows: 'On the whole the pottery seems to have been inspired by contemporary Minoan types, but some of it has a distinctly Melian flavour about it, which suggests there was a certain amount of influence exerted from the larger island.' He suggested that the Melians of Phylakopi might earlier have planted a colony or colonies in Thera to cultivate vines in its rich and well-weathered volcanic soil.[69]

Fouqué had acquired his two gold rings. There was also a fine bronze dagger from Thera with the blade inlaid with gold axes (Plate 31).[70] But apart from the frescoes there was not a great deal in the earlier finds to suggest that the Late Bronze Age settlements were at all wealthy or luxurious. The extent of the Minoan connections had not been fully appreciated.

The new excavations

After Zahn's short campaign nothing was done to increase our knowledge of Bronze Age Thera until 1967. In that year Professor Marinatos initiated a most important new excavation at Akrotiri. The account which follows is greatly indebted to his full and prompt report of the 1967 season.[71]

The excavator of Bronze Age sites on Thera must look for a place where the pumice layers have been thinned to a manageable depth. Walls buried under 20 to 30 m., as in the Phira quarry (Plates III, XII), are tantalizingly inaccessible. In the broad plain which slopes gently to the sea to the south and east of Akrotiri village erosion has proceeded quite far (Plate 36). The pre-eruption surface has even been exposed in places in the beds of winter torrents. It was this which enabled Fouqué and the other nineteenth-century excavators to discover what they did. Marinatos re-surveyed the area between 1962 and 1964 and decided that further exploration was called for. And so the 1967 campaign was set on foot.

The first trial trench (Bronos I) was opened on 25 May 1967 in a field belonging to Madame Calliope Bronos at a spot called

Favata *(Fig. 17)*. Encouraging results were obtained on the very first day. The upper part of intersecting walls was cleared, and a lamp was found with the marks of soot still visible on its rim. This first 'dig' lasted only a week, but it produced Minoan sherds (Plate 42) dating from between 1550 and 1500 BC, and revealed a constructional feature of Minoan type – a 'door jamb' with corners formed by wooden beams (no longer in position). This latter feature was found in trench Arvanitis I.

Digging was resumed on 21 June, and the 'door-jamb' was found to be part of a broad window. What had been thought to be a 'threshold' turned out to be a window sill about a metre above floor level. The window opened on a room where the most spectacular finds were made. Still standing in a row along the south side of the room were six large jars (Plate XIII), some painted and some decorated in rope-relief pattern. Marinatos has called the room a store-room, but it may well have functioned as a kitchen also, for on its west side a low square hearth was found with beakers, a stone mortar and a large three-legged cooking pot *in situ*. Possibly the jars served as storage bins for corn, oil, vegetables, etc. Three broken jars to the north of the hearth contained a 'black fatty organic substance' not yet identified. A kidney-shaped stone bowl sunk in the floor near the hearth may have been a seething pit.

The row of jars was buried in pumice which had preserved them so well that they were ready for photographing as soon as they had been cleared. Further dramatic evidence of volcanic destruction was provided by a nicely painted jar which was found lying on its side near the window (Plate 35), and almost level with the sill. It had apparently fallen from the floor above the store-room on to a layer of pumice, and, though cracked, had not broken. When pieces of it were removed it was found to contain loom weights and volcanic stones.

The story of the disaster begins to take shape. As the eruption begins pumice rains down. The inhabitants leave, taking what they can carry with them. There is no time to move the storage jars, or even the pots and pans. Debris pours in through the open window covering the floor to a depth of about a metre. Then the eruption becomes more violent. Lava bombs crash through the roof and land in the room above the store-room. Two of them actually land in the jar where loom weights are stored. It heels

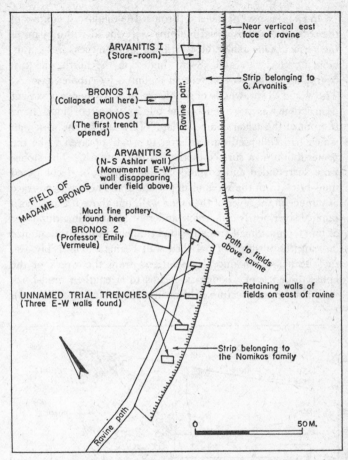

ARVANITIS I
(Store-room)

BRONOS IA
(Collapsed wall here)

BRONOS I
(The first trench
opened)

ARVANITIS 2
(N-S Ashlar wall)
(Monumental E-W
wall disappearing
under field above)

Much fine pottery
found here

BRONOS 2
(Professor Emily
Vermeule)

UNNAMED TRIAL TRENCHES
(Three E-W walls found)

FIELD OF
MADAME BRONOS

Ravine path

Ravine path

← Near vertical east
face of ravine

← Strip belonging to
G. Arvanitis

Path to fields
above ravine

Retaining walls of
fields on east of ravine

Strip belonging to
the Nomikos family

0   50 M.

*17 Sketch plan of the 1967 Thera excavations at Favata in the
ravine near Akrotiri*

over on its side. Then the roof gives way under the accumulated
weight of pumice and brings down the upper floors with it. The
jar falls down to the store-room below. So does the loom. The
ash and pumice continue to pour down until the whole building
is completely covered and sealed in. The heat of the debris cracks
the jars, but does not destroy them. They remain in position
until the groping hand of archaeology gently restores them to
view nearly three and a half millennia later.

On another part of the site (Bronos IA) the lowest courses of
the corner of a substantial building were found within 3 m. of
the surface. One ashlar block still in position measures 1·4 m.
long, 65 cm. wide and 38 cm. high. On the north wall two
courses of ashlar blocks were surmounted by rubble masonry.
The west wall was wholly of rubble masonry. Evidence of violent
destruction was provided by the pile of scattered blocks lying
in front of the ashlar courses (Plate VIII), and by the west wall
which had collapsed outwards on to what appeared to be the
pre-eruption lava surface of the island (Plate IX). The stones
were surrounded and covered by the remains of decomposed
mud-brick from the walls of upper storeys. There was no trace
of pumice in the layer of the fallen wall, but above it there was a
pumice layer nearly 2 m. thick, and above that again a thin layer
of fine tephra. Small straight-sided tunnels through the pumice
indicate the position of perished wall beams and possibly also
roof beams which once lay scattered from the wreck of the
house. The use of wooden tie-beams to strengthen mud-brick
walls is a common feature of Minoan-style architecture (Plate 38).

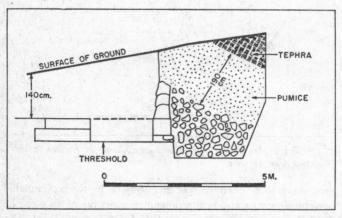

*18 Section of trench Bronos IA showing collapsed upper portion of a
house wall with superimposed pumice and tephra (see Plate IX)*

From the fact that the pumice layer lies on top of the fallen
masonry Marinatos concluded that 'one or more serious earthquakes destroyed first the buildings and only then began the rain

of pumice which accompanied the eruption.' In the present state of the evidence it would seem safer to say 'destroyed *this* building'. The fallen jar in the store-room was resting on nearly a metre of debris (including presumably pumice) which must have accumulated before the upper parts of its building gave way. Destruction of buildings must have taken place in various ways and at various stages of the eruption. The possibility of destruction by shock waves from violent explosions, and also by the sheer weight of accumulated tephra on flat roofs, must be borne in mind.

From trench Bronos 2 (Professor Emily Vermeule's work) appeared confused remains of ashlar masonry, parts of plastered walls, and large patches of decayed mud-brick. Occasionally the bricks were preserved sufficiently for them to be measured. One was 56 × 30 × 9 cm. Holes which once held timber supports, and a pillar, possibly *in situ*, were recognized. Some of the plaster was coloured and patterned. 'The normal design seems to be speckled sponge-prints in brown on a buff ground or in black on a white ground.' Some pieces combined pink and red with a green wash on top, some were plain background pieces in yellow or white. One feature in the trench, which is not yet fully cleared, may turn out to be a complex arrangement of wooden doors. A Minoan-type threshold of stone was found. The door was 'hinged from the right as you entered from the east, opening inward.' It gave access to a room whose slabbed floor – and it is the floor of an upper storey – is still preserved in position. The excavators think it may be a shrine. This discovery of an upper room still reasonably intact should throw a lot of light on constructional details of Minoan-type architecture. The room contained a fine imported Minoan clay bowl. Unfortunately the Bronos 2 building has been quite badly eroded by the winter torrent which has deposited grey gravel and boulders diagonally across it.

In Arvanitis 2 a north-south wall of fine ashlar masonry (Plates 37, 40) was found. A puzzle is also posed by a large wall, 'the most important and yet the most curious structure yet discovered', whose 'large stones are extremely brittle, as if an intense fire had damaged them'. The wall rises to a height of 2 m., but rests on the soft ash of a characteristic tephra layer. Was it built like this, or did an earthquake unseat it from its proper foundations? Further excavation is needed to solve this problem, and this may be difficult and expensive as the wall disappears under the cultivated vineyards to the east of the ravine. At present Marinatos is at least considering the possibility that after the first outbreak people either remained on the island, or returned to it, and began to build in this imposing way.

If this suggestion proves well-founded, we will have good evidence for a considerable time-gap between the first outbreak and the final cataclysm. There is further evidence for such a gap in another significant datum pointed out by Marinatos. In parts of the settlement mud-brick walls seem to have protruded above the upper limit of the pumice layer produced by the first outbreak. These walls then decayed, leaving brown patches on the surface of the pumice which were later covered up by further falls of fine tephra.

The 1967 excavations at Akrotiri have yielded very significant results, but clearly they are only a foretaste of what is to come from this site. It is not yet clear, for instance, whether the buildings so far found are separate buildings or linked parts of one complex. If the latter turns out to be the case obviously Marinatos is right to call it a 'remarkable palatial establishment'. The riddle of the great wall on the ash layer is most intriguing. Further exploration here may throw important light on the blank period between the first and final eruptions. Enough evidence has been accumulated for us to say with some assurance that the settlement has distinctly Minoan features, and was clearly in close contact with Crete. It is likely to have been a Minoan colony or dependency, possibly the seat of the Minoan ruler of the island. Before the eruption the sea may have come nearly up to the excavated buildings. It is clear that the massive debris from the final eruption has spilled over the Akrotiri peninsula and greatly extended the shore line at this point. One may picture a river entering the sea at the head of a sheltered little bay, and the shore covered with the houses of a prosperous port strategically placed on the part of the island nearest to Knossos. Great hopes must be entertained for future campaigns at the Akrotiri site.

I The cliffs of the Thera caldera rise sheer from the sea to a height of over 270 m. Ships are unable to drop anchor owing to the great depth of the sea at this point, over 200 m., shelving to 400 m. in the centre of the bay. Access to the town is by a steep zig-zag path, over two kilometres long, rising in shallow steps. The dark horizontal band seen here is a lava dyke, the rest of the cliff being largely composed of slag and pumice from former, prehistoric, eruptions

II Just south of Phira town are the Phira quarries from where pumice and ash is exported to Athens for cement manufacture. The cliff face is about 30 m. high, composed of some 20 m. of fine white ash above multi-coloured layers of coarse pumice (see Fig. 7). It is below this that the Minoan level is found and can be seen as a thin dark line at the base directly below the highest point of the cliff in the centre foreground. The wall seen in Plate XII is located here

III Detail view of the Minoan level at the base of the Phira quarry cliff seen in Plate II

IV The Minoan level found during the course of quarrying shows as a much darker layer of loamy soil, small pebbles and rocks. Excavations are carried right down to it because the best quality pumice is immediately above it, seen here as a greyish stratum about four metres high. This is surmounted by a 'colour ribbon' layer of alternate bands of white, grey and pink pumice, the latter colour being caused by the action of the sea water penetrating the magma chamber. An exactly similar layer was identified in the deposits on Krakatoa Island after the 1883 eruption (see p. 70)

V The cinders and slag *(scoriae)* in the foreground on Nea Kameni is
land only recently formed in the 1925-6 eruption (see Plate 20). It
contrasts with the white tephra cliffs in the background across the bay
on Thera proper

VI The cliffs on the south coast of Therasia provided the Suez Canal
Company with their principal source of supply of pozzuolana, prized for
its impermeability, in the 1860s. It was at this time that the first
discoveries of Minoan-type buildings and pottery (see p. 86) were made
along this coast. The dominant colours of red, black and white (pumice,
lava and tephra) are a distinctive feature of this area (see p. 144). Early
prints show that the tephra came much closer to the edge of the cliff
and was much higher. Modern excavation and erosion (notice particularly
the channels scored by winter torrents in the soft pumice) have reduced
the cliff to a mere two hundred metres

VII Evidence for at least two-storeyed Theran houses at Akrotiri (cf. Plate 38) is seen in this small interior staircase with a right-angled turn leading to an upper floor. Mamet and Fouqué also reported finding traces of stairs in the building they excavated on the east side of the ravine in 1870 (see Fig. 15)

VIII Evidence of the destruction in the early stages of the eruption is provided by the fallen blocks lying in front of the lower course of ashlar masonry of the north wall of the building in trench Bronos IA (see Fig. 18)

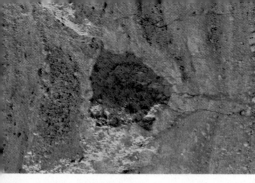

IX The collapsed portion of the west wall in trench Bronos IA consisting of rubble masonry which has fallen outwards and rests on the pre-eruption surface. The collapse took place before the fall of pumice and ash which covered some wooden beams fallen from an upper storey. When the beams decayed they left cavities in the pumice which are here visible as dark openings (see Fig. 18)

X The rim of a large Minoan-type storage jar or pithos here shows in the side wall of an excavation trench at Akrotiri. It appears to have fallen on its side in the course of the eruption and was deeply buried in layers of pumice. Pithoi fallen from upper storeys have been found on other parts of this site and in the Minoan settlement on Keos (see Plate 56)

XI Startling evidence of the explosive phase of the eruption is seen here in the bending of the strata of 'coloured ribbons' by a large boulder, or 'bomb', projected from the vent of the volcano at least three kilometres distant. The fallen boulder was subsequently covered by layers of the fine tephra

XII A substantial wall, 1.5 m. wide, of the pre-eruption period emerging from the typical dark Minoan layer buried under a cliff of ash approximately thirty metres high (see Plates II and III). A fragment of an obsidian blade and sherds of coarse domestic pottery were found in association with this wall. A sample of 'soil' from above the wall was pollen-free and could be the remains of decayed mud brick

XIII Found *in situ* in the remains of a storeroom in trench Arvanitis I were these pithoi decorated with typical Late Minoan 'whirl' designs. Cracks in the pottery could be heat cracks caused by the warm pumice which buried them. The small heap of pumice on the right has been left in position by the excavators because it contains a vertical hole left by a decayed wooden post, possibly part of a supporting framework for the jars

XIV Copy of a wall-painting showing men of Keftiu in the tomb of the Vizier Rekhmire at Thebes (see Plate 74). The figure on the left carries an ox-hide ingot of copper on his shoulder and a typical Minoan rhyton and his companion bears an ornamental bowl decorated with rosettes

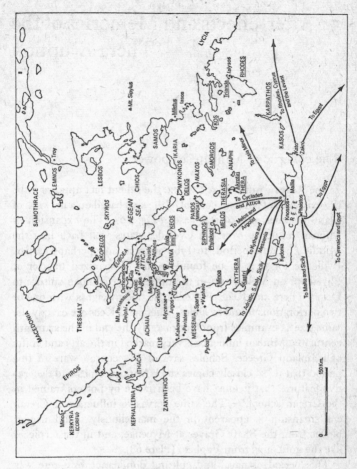

19 Greece, Crete and the Aegean showing main Minoan trade routes and overseas bases. There are indications of Minoan settlement at places underlined and of Minoan influence at places marked with a cross

5 After-effects and Memories of the Thera Eruption

The collapse of Minoan sea power

In the Aegean world of *c.* 1500 BC the salient fact appears to be the existence of Minoan control of the seas based on a network of island colonies and coastal bases *(Fig. 19)*. The expansion of Minoan influence over the Cyclades dates well back into the Middle Cycladic period, to 1700 at least, and perhaps earlier. Evidence for it is to be found in the Minoanized quarter at Phylakopi on Melos, and in the diffusion of Minoan culture to Delos, Thera and Keos. For example, loomweights with one or two perforations found in Delos, Thera and Keos are exactly the same size as examples from Gournia. By the end of the sixteenth century BC Minoan influence is very marked in the arts and crafts of mainland Greece. Scholes says of Mycenaean ware of this period that it 'so closely copies stock Minoan types and decorative features that it must have been made by potters trained in the Cretan school.'[72] The same pervasive influence of Cretan craftsmanship is apparent in the marvellously inlaid dagger blades from the Shaft Graves at Mycenae, and in masterpieces like the gold cups from Vapheio (Plate 68).

This period of naval and cultural dominance by Crete was remembered by the Greeks as the 'thalassocracy' of Minos. Thucydides records it as an undoubted historical fact:[73]

For Minos, the oldest bearer of the traditional name, acquired a fleet and dominated most of what is now the Greek sea. He ruled over the Cyclades and was the first to plant colonies in most of them, after expelling the Carians and installing his own sons as rulers. As one might expect, he also cleared the sea of pirates so far as he could, so that more revenue might come in to him.

The progress of archaeology in the Aegean is continually providing fresh confirmation of this passage of Thucydides.

VII Evidence for at least two-storeyed Theran houses at Akrotiri (*cf.* Plate 42) is seen in this small interior staircase with a right-angled turn leading to an upper floor. Mamet and Fouqué also reported finding traces of stairs in the building they excavated on the east side of the ravine in 1870 (see *Fig. 15*)

VIII Evidence of the destruction in the early stages of the eruption is provided by the fallen blocks lying in front of the lower course of ashlar masonry of the north wall of the building in trench Bronos IA (see *Fig. 18*)

IX The collapsed portion of the west wall in trench Bronos IA consisting of rubble masonry which has fallen outwards and rests on the pre-eruption surface. The collapse took place before the fall of pumice and ash which covered some wooden beams fallen from an upper storey. When the beams decayed they left cavities in the pumice which are here visible as dark openings (see *Fig. 18*)

X Startling evidence of the explosive phase of the eruption is seen here in the bending of the strata of 'coloured ribbons' by a large boulder, or 'bomb', projected from the vent of the volcano at least three kilometres distant. The fallen boulder was subsequently covered by layers of the fine tephra

XI The rim of a large Minoan-type storage jar or pithos here shows in the side wall of an excavation trench at Akrotiri. It appears to have fallen on its side in the course of the eruption and was deeply buried in layers of pumice. Pithoi fallen from upper storeys have been found on other parts of this site and in the Minoan settlement on Keos (see Plate 56)

XII A substantial wall, 1·5 m. wide, of the pre-eruption period emerging from the typical dark Minoan layer buried under a cliff of ash approximately thirty metres high (see Plates II and III). A fragment of an obsidian blade and sherds of coarse domestic pottery were found in association with this wall. A sample of 'soil' from above the wall was pollen-free and could be the remains of decayed mud brick

XIII Found *in situ* in the remains of a storeroom in trench Arvanitis I were these pithoi decorated with typical Late Minoan 'whirl' designs. The example on the far right has a rope pattern. Cracks in the pottery could be heat cracks caused by the warm pumice which buried them. The small heap of pumice on the right has been left in position by the excavators because it contains a vertical hole left by a decayed wooden post, possibly part of a supporting framework for the jars

XIV Copy of a wall-painting showing men of Keftiu in the tomb of the Vizier Rekhmire at Thebes (see Plate 74). The figure on the left carries an ox-hide ingot of copper on his shoulder and a typical Minoan rhyton and his companion bears an ornamental bowl decorated with rosettes

The excavations of the British School on Kythera revealed that the Minoans established themselves there soon after 2000 BC.[74] The recent campaigns of the American School on Keos have shown that there was a flourishing and well-fortified town with strong Minoan connections at Ayia Irini in the sixteenth century BC (see below, p. 106). Firm evidence of Minoan trade and occupation is available for a number of other islands in the Cyclades: Melos, Amorgos, Thera, Siphnos, Delos. It can only be a matter of time before this list is extended by new finds, and Thucydides' statement that Minos 'ruled over the Cyclades' will be fully justified. But the lines of Minoan expansion did not end with the Cyclades and the Peloponnese. There is some evidence that Minoan naval power made itself felt as far north as Euboea, Skopelos and Skyros – an interesting confirmation of the obscure reference in Homer to an expedition of Rhadamanthys to Euboea.[75] The strong tradition that Minos exacted tribute from Attica looks very plausible when one sees the ring of Minoan bases from Keos round to Aegina and Minoa off Megara. To the east the Minoans settled in Karpathos and Rhodes, and their trading posts extended up the Asia Minor coast to Kis, Iasos, Samos and Miletus. Finally we must not forget their penetration of the western seas as far as southern Italy and Sicily.

The Minoans were the first people, so far as we know, to 'rule the waves' and build up an empire on the basis of long-established marine trade routes. Apart from the pirate menace – and we may believe Thucydides that Minos kept this firmly under control – there seems to have been no threat to this great and novel Minoan supremacy in the eastern Mediterranean. The older empires of the east were land-based. The Greeks had not yet found themselves as a nation, and were in no position to challenge Crete on the sea.

The archaeological record shows that from 1600 BC onwards Crete became more prosperous than ever before. The great palace at Knossos (Plates 58–9, 62), badly damaged by an earthquake about 1570, was rebuilt in increased splendour. The other palaces flourished (Plates 17, 29). A network of opulent villas, possibly the seats of provincial governors, covered the land. Records were kept in the Linear A script. There were brilliant achievements in the arts of fresco painting, gem engraving, and pottery (Plates 14–16).

And then, quite suddenly, while the art of the LM IB period was at its peak, Crete suffered a widespread disaster. All the great palaces except Knossos were destroyed. So were their surrounding towns, as well as many smaller towns and villas. From then on the brilliant and intricate Minoan civilization went into a sharp decline. Minoan trading posts and settlements overseas were abandoned or destroyed. Minoan arts and crafts lost their creative pre-eminence. The balance of power in the Aegean tilted sharply away from Crete to mainland Greece.

The palace at Knossos lasted until about 1400 BC, or possibly a little later. Some fine pottery was produced there in the style called the 'Palace Style' or LM II (Plates 44–6). The shapes and the decoration are still recognizably Minoan, but the underlying spirit of the art has undergone a subtle transformation. The old creative exuberance has been placed under the restraint of a new formalism. The former effortless mastery degenerates into a striving after the grandiose. New masters now rule in Knossos. The palace records are kept in Greek, and the 'warrior graves' bespeak a new spirit of militarism (Plates 47–9). With the destruction of Knossos itself at the end of the fifteenth century, 600 years of palace-centred Minoan culture came finally to an end.

If we take a wide look over the eastern Mediterranean at this time we find significant signs of Mycenaean expansion and dominance. The record of Mycenaean pottery found in the Cyclades from c. 1600 to 1200 BC tells a significant story. In the first half of this period the bulk of imported Mycenaean ware comes from Melos and Naxos, with a certain amount from Keos and Delos. Elsewhere Minoan ware is dominant. But between 1400 and 1200 Mycenaean pottery is found on sites in twelve Cycladic islands: Amorgos, Andros, Delos, Keos, Kimolos, Kythnos, Melos, Naxos, Paros, Scriphos, Siphnos, Tinos.[76] The lord of Mycenae now, in Homer's phrase, 'rules over many islands and all Argos'.[77] In Melos, the best-documented site, the amounts of Mycenaean and Minoan pottery seem to have been about equal during the Late Cycladic I and II periods, but subsequently Mycenaean almost completely ousts Minoan.

After 1400 Crete still maintained a distinctive style of pottery within her borders. It spread from the Knossos area all through the island, but it was very little exported. LM III ware has been found in Kimolos, Melos and Amorgos, but only in very small

amounts. The remarkably uniform Mycenaean ware is per-
vasively dominant everywhere outside Crete itself. Crete did
recover something of its former prosperity towards the end of
the Mycenaean period. She sent an important contingent to fight
for Agamemnon at Troy, but it is quite clear that she was never
again an imperial power as she had been in the days of the
'eldest Minos'.

What caused the collapse?

Historians have noted this sudden change in the fortunes of
Crete in the fifteenth century BC, but have not always produced
very convincing explanations for it. There has been some uncertainty as to whether the widespread destruction occurred
c. 1450 BC or c. 1400 BC. Matz and Pendlebury put all the destruction at the later date. Evans and Furumark put it all, except
Knossos, at c. 1450.[78] There has also been uncertainty whether
or not the LM I pottery style overlaps with the LM II 'Palace
Style'.

Evans thought that the Minoan decline was caused partly by
earthquakes and partly by the aggression of Knossos against the
other palaces. But earthquake damage is usually quite localized.
Besides, the Minoans were used to earthquakes. They had been
badly hit by them before, but had always recovered and pro-
gressed to greater heights. But this time there was no come-back.
Evans inevitably adopted a Knosso-centric viewpoint. A wider
hypothesis is required to account for the breakdown of Minoan
commercial power and overseas connections.

Pendlebury thought that the evidence pointed to a 'deliberate
sacking of the chief cities of Crete'.[79] He viewed the 'relentless
destruction' as due either to a massive foreign invasion, or to a
popular uprising against foreign garrisons, and dates it to
c. 1400 BC. Now the palace of Knossos was destroyed about then,
and the dynasty there, almost certainly Greek, could have been
ousted either by a local revolution or by rivals from the Greek
mainland. But the archaeological evidence for Crete as a whole
indicates that the really widespread devastation occurred about
two generations earlier. If we go back to 1450 or earlier there is
no reason to suppose that the Cretan populace was ready to rise

against its rulers even if supported and encouraged by an outside aggressor. And where could this aggressor have come from? The Greek mainland? How, then, did his fleet break through the protective screen of naval bases which ringed Crete to the north? How could his ships have crossed the waters which had been for so long a Cretan lake? The islanders of the Aegean had been seafarers for hundreds of years, but it seems impossible to suppose that they could have formed a coalition powerful enough to mount an invasion of Crete. The complete absence of fortifications on Crete down to the end of LM I is proof that the Minoans did not feel in any danger of invasion. Even an isolated pirate raid, though possible, seems unlikely, and certainly could not have caused the almost universal destruction that we find.

In the first half of the fifteenth century the Hittites were dominant in Asia Minor, but were not a naval power. The Egyptians under Tuthmosis III had extended their empire over Palestine, Syria, and up to the Euphrates (Plate 8), but they had no naval force capable of challenging the Cretans. Only the mainland Greeks can be even supposed to have had the sea power and the inclination to attack Crete. There is certainly a strong Greek tradition of friction between Attica and Minoan Crete. Philochorus records that Athens and Attica were subject to Minos and paid tribute to him in the time of King Cecrops. Traditionally the tribute took the form of youths and maidens for the bull-ring at Knossos, and was said to have been imposed as a punishment for the killing of Minos' son Androgeos on Attic territory.[80] With Minoans settled in force at Keos, only 24 km. from Sunium, and also occupying Minoa to the west of Salamis, there was not much that the Athenians could do. The mainland Greeks of the early fifteenth century could not have been much of a threat to Crete unless her power was in serious decline at the time. And there is no evidence that it was. On the contrary, the evidence of material remains from Minoan sites in the first quarter of the fifteenth century shows that Crete was as rich and powerful and progressive as she had ever been.

Professor Matz, in the revised *Cambridge Ancient History*, writes:[81]

The peaceful transfer of power in Crete from the Minoans to the Mycenaeans is difficult to explain. Since all other hypotheses do violence to the archaeological evidence in one way or another, we may be justified in suggesting that a passive renunciation of power was in accord with Minoan character.

'Passive renunciation of power' does not seem a very plausible solution to the problem. In my opinion the volcanic destruction theory is more convincing. Historians, trained to look for human causes for human events, will naturally be reluctant to entertain such a hypothesis. There is certainly no parallel since then for the destruction of a powerful empire by a natural cataclysm. We cannot say that it has ever happened, especially if we take into account Woolley's evidence for a great flood in Mesopotamia in the fourth millennium. But we must, I suggest, seriously consider the possibility that it did happen in the fifteenth century BC. Thera lay right in the centre of the network of Minoan bases in the Aegean. It is the nearest Cycladic island to Crete. On a clear day one can still see Mount Ida from its highest point. The evidence of the previous chapters shows that its volcano erupted with vast and devastating violence between about 1500 and 1470 BC. The first outbreak obliterated a rich Minoan settlement on Thera itself. The culminating paroxysm, with its tidal waves and fall-out of ash, was like a dagger plunged into the heart of Crete. We must suppose it likely that the waves destroyed her naval power, and the ash disrupted her agricultural economy. Overnight she lay crippled and defenceless, her protective shield of bases swept away, thousands of her citizens drowned, the rest panic-stricken and starving. It was a knock-out blow. Minoan Crete was battered to her knees by the brute forces of nature, and never rose again.

The only palace to survive into the second half of the fifteenth century was Knossos, which appears to have been sufficiently far inland to escape the full force of the tidal waves. For Knossos the archaeological record after *c*. 1460 is quite detailed and very significant. The throne-room block is reconstructed, and the throne-room itself decorated with a frieze of griffins (Plate 50) – a motif found later in the Mycenaean palace at Pylos. An uncharacteristic note of militarism is struck in the Fresco of the Negroes under the command of a white officer. Are they the bodyguard of a new dynasty? The 'warrior graves' are well stored with rapiers and helmets (Plates 47–9). The palace records are now kept in Greek. Knossos, it seems, has become a Mycenaean-type citadel.

It is a reasonable assumption that some of the mainland Greeks took advantage of Crete's extremity, and moved in to occupy the capital of the stricken land. Did a memory of this survive in the legend of Theseus, who slew the Minotaur and gained from Amphitrite the ring of Minos, a symbol of naval supremacy perhaps? Greece must also have been affected by the cataclysm, but her power centres were not nearly so exposed as Crete and its island dependencies. They were much farther from the volcano, and also farther inland. Low-lying areas round the bay of Argos and the Saronic gulf were probably inundated (see below, p. 118 f.), but the cataclysm was not a mortal blow to Greece. If Theseus ruled Attica at this time he would soon have been in a position to turn the tables on the oppressor. He could have mustered a fleet and sailed unopposed to Crete, where his bronze-clad warriors would have found unfortified Knossos an easy prey.[82]

Over Crete as a whole the record is also clear and informative. The LM II style of pottery is virtually confined to Knossos itself (Plates 44–6). Only three excavated sites have yielded it in central Crete and four in eastern Crete – a marked contrast to the copiousness and ubiquity of LM I pottery (Plates 14–17). The ruined palaces are not rebuilt. Some of the former town sites are deserted. A dispersal of population is evident. Pendlebury, though not accepting the eruption theory, describes the post-disaster situation as follows: 'It seems to have been the ruling classes and the cities which suffered, and small communities replace larger ones.'[83] Villages grow up on the higher ground (Plate 57) away from the sea, and there is a noticeable influx of people into the western part of the island. Kydonia develops into an important centre, and it is hoped that excavations now planned for this area will throw more light on the course of events after the disaster.

These facts may be explained as follows. After the eruption the dispirited remnant of the Cretan population retired from the coastal sites where they suffered so severely, and sought the shelter of the uplands away from the sea which had so suddenly turned against them. Inland they would also be less exposed to pirate raids from the islands or the Greek mainland. Any attempt at rebuilding the palaces would have been stopped by the new Greek overlords of Knossos. In any case the fertile plains round

Mallia and Phaistos, and the hinterland of Kato Zakro, were now covered in tephra, and agriculture, art and commerce were at a standstill. The fall-out map shows that the western third of Crete escaped relatively lightly. Hence the westward migration, and the sudden rise to importance of Kydonia.

In the next section I shall try to interpret events in one of the Minoan overseas bases.

The convergence of archaeology and tradition at Keos

The island of Keos (also called Kea) lies about 24 km. east of the Sunium promontory of Attica. Since 1960 the University of Cincinnati, in collaboration with the American School at Athens, has been conducting an important series of excavations there under the directorship of Professor John L. Caskey.[84] In particular an important site has been uncovered at Ayia Irini on a promontory of the bay of Ayios Nikolaos opposite Vourkari. The site was inhabited at least as early as the Middle Bronze Age, and had developed into an important place in the early part of the Late Bronze Age, when it had connections with Minoan Crete, the other islands, and the mainland. A large number of vases, either made in Crete or made under very strong Cretan influence, have been found and dated to LM IB – LH II. Some Linear A signs have also been discovered. The settlement was violently destroyed in the fifteenth century – Caskey says by earthquakes – and later rebuilt.

There was at least one large 'establishment' (22 × 17 m.) with a courtyard, staircase, corridors and cellars. Most of the cellars were choked with debris, including large quantities of pottery, fresco fragments and miscellaneous objects (Plate 56), which apparently fell from upper rooms when the building was destroyed. Caskey attributes this destruction to 'the final great earthquake', but the whole site is very close to the sea, and the possibility of inundation by tidal waves should not be overlooked. One room cleared in 1963 yielded 'an exceptionally fine array of imported pottery along with the usual quantity of plain local wares'. Five pots illustrated in Caskey's 1964 report make an interesting study. Two are fragments of alabaster of Cretan origin, one in the marine style of LM IB, the other with a pattern of ferns and rosettes. The fresco fragments are reminiscent of Minoan MM III – LM I work with bands of plain colours interspersed with leaves, blossoms, reeds and grasses. A large jar 'may have been made in the Argolid'. Two other pieces are 'Minoan or Mycenaean'. The excavators believe that the whole deposit was sealed in at the same time. As such it provides good evidence of a prosperous Minoan colony in close touch with Mycenaean Greece, and suddenly destroyed by natural forces at the end of LM IB.

This picture is confirmed by the evidence of the adjoining temple, a very interesting multi-roomed building with a cult history extending from the Middle Bronze Age to Greco-Roman times. The temple also suffered severe damage at the same time as the adjoining 'establishment'. Deposits included an imported Minoan bronze statuette, and pottery 'not later than LM IB and LH II'. But the most sensational find was that of fragments of at least nineteen terracotta statues, some 1·5 m. or more in height (Plate 53). All were female, with flared skirts reaching to the ground, heavy bands at the top of the skirts, narrow waists, close-fitting collars and open-type bodices. There is no need to labour their close resemblance to the famous snake goddess from Knossos (Plates 52, 54-5). Some of the largest statues may have been cult images, with others representing attendants or votaries. They are of local workmanship, yet represent a Minoan cult with Peloponnesian connections. They were found badly broken and heaped in great confusion as though they had fallen heavily from a height, possibly from a wooden bench or an upper storey. Many fragments of the group were widely scattered through the rest of the building, suggesting perhaps that inundation accompanied the destruction. Interestingly enough, one head was salvaged by later inhabitants of the site and apparently venerated in the twelfth century. Another head received similar treatment in the eighth century!

The evidence all points to a sudden destruction of the site at the end of LM IB, followed later by re-occupation and rebuilding under Mycenaean rule. In this Keos site we have yet another example of detailed convergence between archaeology and Greek literary tradition. The poet Bacchylides (fifth century BC) wrote a victory ode for a certain Argeius of Keos who had won at the

Isthmian Games. In the fashion of such compositions he detailed some of the legendary history of the island, and in particular told how its ancient ruler Euxantius came to be born. The poem is fragmentary, but the opening stanzas (as printed and translated by Jebb) tell a clear enough story:[85]

On the third day thereafter came warlike Minos, bringing a Cretan host, in fifty ships with gleaming sterns. And by the favour of Zeus 'Eukleius' he wedded the deep-girdled maiden Dexithea; and left with her the half of his folk, warriors, to whom he gave the rocky land, ere he sailed away to Knossos, lovely city. And in the tenth month the maiden with beautiful locks bore Euxantius to be the lord of the glorious isle.

In sober historical terms we have here a tradition of Minoan military occupation strengthened by dynastic intermarriage. In the light of the American finds it is hard to resist the conclusion that a genuine tradition of the Minoan colony was actually preserved on the island down to the time of Bacchylides.

This conclusion can further be supported by a passage from the Paean which Pindar composed in honour of Delos, at the request of the people of Keos.[85a] Here too Euxantius is introduced, and made to speak on the theme of security in a small island as preferable to grief and strife in a richer kingdom. Pindar tells how the sons of Pasiphae, presumably the Knossians, offered Euxantius the 'seventh part' of Crete, but he declined, reminding them about his 'portent'. The start of his speech seems so significant for my general thesis that I quote it in full:

I tremble at the heavy-sounding war between Zeus and Poseidon. Once with thunderbolt and trident they sent a land and a whole fighting force down to Tartarus, leaving my mother and all the well-fenced house.

Euxantius interprets this disaster as an omen discouraging him from leaving his native Keos, and so he continues: 'Let go, my heart, the cypress, let go the pastures about Ida.'

The Thera disaster seems a key well fitted to unlock the secrets of this passage. The eruption must indeed have been 'heavy-sounding', and accompanied by electrical storms and tidal waves ('thunderbolt' and 'trident'). It certainly resulted in massive subsidence on Thera, which could well be the 'land' which was sent down to Tartarus. The 'fighting force' which was totally destroyed could be a reference to the breaking of

Minoan naval power by the catastrophe. Pindar's noun could refer to a navy just as well as an army. It is even just conceivable that the Minoan navy could have started to use Thera again as a base after the first eruption (see p. 95f.), and that a whole squadron was engulfed there at the time of the final outbreak. Keos certainly suffered damage also, but at least it did not subside into the sea like Thera. The 'well-fenced house' survived, and continued to be a place of some importance in the Mycenaean and later periods.

I suggest that a genuine historical tradition of the Thera disaster survived also, and is embodied in this passage of Pindar. Temptation to speculate further about the passage is probably to be resisted, but I cannot refrain from pointing out that the historical situation envisaged by the poem is not at all inconceivable. There may well have been a vacant governorship, if not a kingdom, in Crete after the disaster, which could have been offered to, and declined by, a cadet son of Minos on Keos. The struggle or quarrel between Zeus and Poseidon is not a common motif in Greek mythology, but it is mentioned in one of Pindar's Odes,[85b] and also in the Orphic *Argonautica*. Interestingly enough, the latter passage refers to the devastation of a land which is probably Crete, as one result of the struggle (see below, p. 130). In Pindar the gods quarrel over who is to wed Thetis the Nereid – a reflection, perhaps, of maritime tension between Crete and Greece at the time of the Thera cataclysm.

The evidence of Trianda

The transition from Minoan to Mycenaean supremacy is clearly illustrated at the Minoan settlement of Trianda on Rhodes.[86] Three phases are distinguished on this site. In the first, Trianda I, which goes back into the sixteenth century BC, the better pottery is of fairly advanced LM IA type, and the plain domestic ware also of Minoan type. In the second phase, Trianda IIA, the chief pottery is of a type which Furumark calls Sub-LM IA. It is contemporary with LM IB at Knossos, and indeed many sherds of *imported* LM IB type have also been found. This dates this phase to *c.* 1500–1450 BC. In addition, there are many imported sherds of *Mycenaean* type IIA (1500–1450 according to

Furumark), showing that the colony had trade relations with mainland Greece as well as Knossos. Then the houses of the settlement are severely damaged, by an earthquake it is thought, and there is a reconstruction leading on to the third and last phase of the colony, Trianda IIB. The pottery of this phase is of both Minoan and Mycenaean types alike in the superior ware and also in the plain domestic ware. Most of the Minoan ware is contemporary with LM II at Knossos, and the Mycenaean is mainly dated to 1425–1400, but there is some imported Mycenaean IIB pottery (1450–1425) and also some sherds of LM IA–B. Much of the Mycenaean ware was made on Rhodes itself, and we seem to have here evidence of a short period of friendly intercourse between the older Minoan settlement and a new Mycenaean colony, probably that of Ialysos close by. But quite soon, about 1410 BC, Trianda is devastated, and the manufacture of Minoan ware in Rhodes comes to an end. Furumark connected the end of Trianda with the final destruction of the palace at Knossos and both with 'the fall of the Minoan central power'. But, as we have seen, the fall of Minoan power is probably to be dated earlier to the end of LM IB when the almost total devastation of Crete occurred. I therefore suggest that the Trianda evidence should be interpreted rather differently. The earthquake damage between phases IIA and IIB should be associated with the Thera cataclysm and the end of Minoan power overseas. Trianda was far enough away from the volcano for it to escape the full destructive power of the waves, but there was probably some inundation (see below, p. 121). The colonists continued on the site and were soon co-operating with the newly arrived Mycenaean colonists of Ialysos, and interchanging pottery with them. They also continued to use, and perhaps to manufacture, some of the older pottery from LM IB which had escaped destruction. But this period of 'peaceful co-existence' was brought to an abrupt end when Mycenae tightened its hold on Crete by destroying the last remaining palace there, and simultaneously meted out the same treatment to the surviving Minoan outpost on Rhodes.

The Praisian tradition
of the depopulation of Crete

There is an isolated tradition in Herodotus which may well preserve a genuine folk memory of the great disaster.[87] Herodotus reports it on the authority of the people of Praisos (Plate 57), a city where Eteo-Cretans ('genuine' Cretans) speaking a non-Greek language maintained themselves as an independent community until about 140 BC. The tradition seems to me so significant that I quote it in context:

It is said that Minos went in search of Daedalus to Sicania which is now called Sicily and met his death through violence. Some time later at the instigation of the god all the Cretans except the Polichnitans and Praisians came with a great armada to Sicania and besieged the city of Kamikos for five years – a city now inhabited by the Akragantines. In the end they were not able to capture it, and shortage of food compelled them to disperse, so they departed for home. On their voyage they had got as far as Iapygia [*i.e.* the 'heel' of Italy], when a great storm struck them and flung them ashore. Their ships were smashed to pieces, and since there seemed no available means for returning to Crete they remained where they were and founded the city of Hyria. They changed from Cretans into Messapians of Iapygia, and from islanders into mainlanders. *In Crete itself, bereft of its inhabitants, as the Praisians say, other people settled, and especially Greeks.* The Trojan War occurred in the third generation after the death of Minos, in which the Cretans distinguished themselves as avengers for Menelaus. Their reward was to return from Troy to find plague and famine among themselves and their flocks. Crete was then depopulated for the second time, and received a third wave of immigrants, the present Cretans [*i.e.* the Dorians] who inhabit it with the remnants of previous inhabitants.

The general historical framework here is sound: Minoans first, then Mycenaean Greeks occupying the country, and finally the Dorian colonization. What of the details? Undoubtedly the Minoan sphere of influence extended as far as southern Italy and Sicily, and a Minos may well have been operating with a fleet in that area when he met his death. Diodorus describes his tomb in Sicily (of which there is now no trace) in terms very reminiscent of the Temple Tomb (Plate 61) near Knossos.[88] Perhaps Minos was trying to strengthen and extend his western trade routes. Perhaps he was actually seeking the extradition of a rebellious subject. There is a strong tradition that Daedalus was an

Athenian, and he may have fled from Minos' court in annoyance at Minoan oppression in Attica. From the fourteenth century we have a contemporary record – the well-known Tawagalawas Letter – of a Hittite king seeking the extradition of a trouble-some subject who had fled by ship from Miletus to territory controlled by the King of Ahhiyawa (almost certainly Achaean Greece).[89] There is nothing inherently improbable in Minos' doing the same sort of thing in Sicily. Nor is it unlikely that the Minoans should have sent a punitive expedition to avenge his death. After failing in its purpose the Minoan armada starts for home and is 'flung ashore' on the south-east coast of Italy. It could, of course, have been an ordinary storm, but it is just con-ceivable that the Thera *tsunamis* could have been destructive even at that distance. At any rate the survivors despair of ever reaching home. Why? If Crete still ruled the seas they could have been fetched back by another convoy. But if Crete had simul-taneously been devastated and her naval power broken, it may well have seemed better to the survivors to stay put and establish a new settlement where they were. And so with characteristic versatility they become 'mainlanders instead of islanders'. Per-haps refugees sailing west from Crete joined them, and this could help to explain their success, as Herodotus tells it, in colonizing from Hyria quite a large area of the south coast of Italy. Far to the east of them lay Crete, 'bereft of its inhabitants', as the Praisians say, and there was no future for them in the old setting.

It seems that the Praisians did not know the reason for the first 'depopulation' of Crete. Herodotus implies that it was the result of the failure of the Sicilian armada to return, but this does not seem an adequate explanation. Herodotus dates the disaster 'three generations before the Trojan War', and this dating will have to be greatly stretched to take us as far back as *c.* 1470. But this is not a very serious objection to associating the 'depopu-lation' with the aftermath of the Thera eruption. Greek dates before the Trojan War are very unreliable, and any date to do with 'Minos' is easily corrupted by association with a later bearer of the name. On the whole it seems credible that the secluded Praisians may really have preserved a memory of the great loss of life which followed the Thera eruption.

I went to Praisos recently. The site consists of a fine acropolis flanked by two other limestone outcrops (Plate 57). It lies in a fertile valley ringed round with hills about 20 km. south of Siteia. It is obviously a secluded 'pocket' where remnants of the old Minoan population could have lingered on. The soil is rich and well-watered. The acropolis hill forms a natural redoubt. The site is well removed from the sea, and there is no clear outlet through the mountains to the south. I took a little footpath that wound down a hill below the village of Nea Praisos. It was well paved in places, and it was easy to fancy that one was treading on Minoan cobblestones as one followed the natural contours of the ground down through orchards of apple, pomegranate and fig, past well-cultivated plots of onion and tomato, across a small ravine, and up past vineyards where the sultana grapes were already browning on their drying floors. I thought of the gardens of Alcinous with tidy vegetable beds, orchards where the fruit ripened month by generous month, and a drying floor in a level spot baked by the sun.[90] When I returned to the village I was taken to a coffee-shop, and the villagers insisted on standing me a drink. I had to answer the usual questions, of course, and my replies were interpreted by a stout Cretan who had just returned for a holiday in his native village after twenty years – in Melbourne. When they heard I was interested in antiquities one of them (the local schoolmaster, perhaps) slipped out and soon returned with Professor Platon's latest excavation report on Kato Zakro. And when it was time to go, they loaded me with bunches of grapes and ripe figs, and I returned to Siteia convinced that the fabled hospitality of Phaeacia was no myth. In my imagination that secluded valley still breeds Eteo-Cretans.

Egyptian records and the Thera disaster

So far in this chapter I have been outlining a general picture of the Minoan empire and its sudden collapse in the first half of the fifteenth century BC as a direct result of the Thera eruption. I have suggested that there may be a genuine memory of this disaster in the Praisian tradition recorded by Herodotus. I will now consider whether there are any other records of the Minoan collapse, apart, of course, from the Atlantis legend which I take to contain a faint memory of it filtered through Egyptian sources.

There does not seem to be any clear reference to it in the Egyptian documents which are still extant from the fifteenth century. But this is not very surprising. As already noted, Egyptian inscriptions are, on the whole, rather disappointing in the amount of solid history that they contain. They are full of extravagant eulogies of the Pharaoh and poetic protestations of the divine favour which graces his throne, but they tend to be short on hard facts. They also record very little of what was going on in other countries. Egypt always tended to be a self-centred, self-contained place. If invaders actually menaced Egypt they were recorded in some detail, as in the famous inscriptions of Merenptah and Rameses III (Plate 69).[91] But generally speaking, foreign affairs were of little concern to the average Egyptian of the Bronze Age.

Foreign trade, however, was a different matter. The Egyptian economy was very dependent on imported timber, and there was another less obvious product of trees whose loss is perhaps deplored in a well-known passage of the Ipuwer papyrus, *Admonitions of an Egyptian Sage*.[92] Traces of the 'sprout lichen' (*Evernia furfuracea*) have been found in ancient Egyptian tombs. The plant does not grow in Egypt today, and botanists believe that it must have been imported from Crete or the Cyclades.[93] It is common in Crete. Oak moss resin, an important base in modern perfume manufacture, is extracted from it. The ancient Egyptians used it to pack the body cavity of mummies, either as a preservative or simply as an aromatic filling. They also used it in bread-making. Among other funerary requisites which had to be imported were pine-wood resin and cedar-wood for coffins. Crete could have been a source for these as well as the Lebanon. These facts go far to explain one of the laments in the *Admonitions*:

No one really sails north to Byblos today. What shall we do for cedar for our mummies? Priests were buried with their produce [*i.e.* with the produce of foreign trade], and [nobles] were embalmed with the oil thereof as far away as Keftiu, [but] they come no [longer]. Gold is lacking ... How important it [now] seems when the oasis-people come carrying their festival provisions: reed-mats, ... fresh redmet-plants.

The last sentence contrasts the insignificant local trade with the former foreign commerce. Keftiu is Crete, so the passage is evidence of an interruption of trade with Crete, possibly in the lichens mentioned above. But the passage can only be referred to the fifteenth century on the supposition that it is a later interpolation. The *Admonitions* is a Middle Kingdom document and almost certainly refers to the breakdown of law and order in the period after the Old Kingdom. The confusions of that period would be sufficient to account for the interruption of foreign trade. On this supposition this is much the earliest reference to Crete in Egyptian documents. The case for the reference being an interpolation rests on the fact that the text as we have it is a XIX or XX Dynasty copy of the original, and also on doubt whether a third-millennium reference to Keftiu is acceptable. But it is not a strong case. On the whole it seems safer to refer the passage to the First Intermediary Period, and not to the 'disappearance' of Crete after the Thera eruption.[94]

Egyptian art from the fifteenth century is more obviously and closely relevant to our problem. A well-known series of tomb paintings depicts men of Keftiu bringing 'tribute' to Egypt.[95] They carry copper ingots, metal cups and vases (Plates 74, XIV). Among the vases we can recognize distinctively Minoan types such as bull-headed rhytons, and 'Vapheio' cups. After some hesitation, scholarly opinion has now on the whole come to accept the equation of Keftiu with Minoan Crete. It had been suggested that Keftiu was really in Cilicia, but the indications favouring this location are probably to be explained by the fact that much Minoan trade with Egypt went via North Syrian ports. We know that the Minoans had trading posts at Alalakh and Ugarit, and we also know that between *c.* 1480 and 1450 Tuthmosis III was campaigning vigorously in this area. He used the Syrian ports as bases for his army, and it would have been diplomatically appropriate for the rulers of Crete to secure their entrée into these ports by sending, as nominal 'tribute', the presents which we see depicted on the wall-paintings in the tombs of Tuthmosis' chief ministers.

The Keftiu appear in four successive paintings. The first of these is in the tomb of Senmut, *c.* 1492 BC. Here they carry among other offerings a Vapheio-type cup ornamented with two bulls' heads. They are dressed in cut-away kilts with codpieces. There is no inscription in Senmut's tomb. They next appear in the tomb of Useramon, *c.* 1476, one carrying a bull's-head rhyton and all again wearing codpieces. An inscription mentions

20 Detail of the kilt of one of the men of Keftiu in the tomb of Rekhmire at Thebes. It shows the overpainting of the earlier style Minoan codpiece to turn it into the later Mycenaean style of longer wrap-over kilt

gifts from the 'islands of the Great Green'. The third series in the tomb of Rekhmire, *c.* 1470, is the most important. There are three panels, in the first of which Minoan 'tribute' is shown piled on three shelves with an Egyptian scribe making a list of the offerings which include a typical LM IB collared rhyton and a bull's-head rhyton. The other two panels show fourteen men carrying offerings (Plates 74, XIV), including copper ingots and an elephant's tusk. They were depicted first with the codpiece familiar from the earlier representations *(Fig. 20)*. But later, *c.* 1460 to 1450, the figures were overpainted to show a more decorous patterned kilt drawn into a long point in front. This type of kilt is recognizable at Mycenae from about 1560 BC. Schachermeyr thinks it probable that, by ordering this over-painting, Rekhmire was giving diplomatic recognition to a change of regime at Knossos.[96] Rekhmire, as Vizier, had the duty of receiving vassal princes and their offerings; he could be regarded as Egypt's 'Foreign Minister'. The change in his tomb decoration can hardly be discounted as a mere artistic whim. It must surely have political significance. As such, it seems very good evidence for dynastic change at Knossos in the decade or so before 1450 BC. I have argued earlier (p. 104) that the Greek take-over at Knossos was facilitated by the prostration of Crete after the Thera eruption. The 'overpainting', dated c. 1460–1450, will then tend to confirm that the volcanic destruction of Crete occurred somewhat before the middle of the fifteenth century, and probably not far from 1470. The inscriptions in the tomb appear to corroborate the political interpretation of the overpainting. There is a general introductory inscription covering all the tributary peoples depicted, including Punt, Retenu and Keftiu. Then, over the Keftiu section, the inscription reads: 'Coming in peace of the Princes of the country of Keftiu and the Isles which are in the midst of the sea ...' If the second part of this formula is a later addition, it could be taken as an indication that Crete and the Mycenaean world are now presenting a united tribute with Knossos under the overlordship of a Greek ruler.

The last appearance of Keftiu bearing Minoan objects is in the tomb of Menkheperresoneb which goes down to the time of Amenophis II, 1444–1412. Here the men of Keftiu are unambiguously shown wearing a more decorous form of skirted kilt. A prince of Keftiu, with his name clearly depicted, does obeisance (Plate 75).

So much for fifteenth-century records of Keftiu and its people. Mention must also be made of an interesting piece of information preserved in a late extract from Manetho. Manetho's work still forms the basis of Egyptian chronology. He was high priest in Heliopolis about 280 BC, and dedicated a *History of Egypt* to Ptolemy II. Unfortunately Manetho's *History* survives only in extracts quoted by later historians and chronographers, notably Josephus, Eusebius and Syncellus. His work became the subject of much discussion and criticism, controversy developing especially round his account of the Jewish Exodus. Consequently the problem of the transmission of Manetho's text is complicated and difficult. It is generally agreed, however, that Manetho had access to very good sources, and wherever we can be reasonably sure that we have a genuine extract from him, his information deserves great respect. Since he was writing for Greeks he was interested in synchronisms between Greek and Egyptian history, and so there is no *a priori* reason not to accept the following fragment as genuine. It comes from a list of XVIII Dynasty Pharaohs, and is recorded by Syncellus (c. AD 800): 'The sixth, Misphragmuthosis, for 26 years: in his reign the flood of Deucalion's time occurred.'[97]

Breasted held that Misphragmuthosis is a corruption of Menkheperre Tuthmosis, the two cartouche names of Tuthmosis III, and this has been generally accepted. Tuthmosis III reigned from 1490 to 1436 BC, and it is an interesting fact, as Marinatos has recently pointed out, that a mythical event like Deucalion's flood should here be associated with a firmly dated period in the fifteenth century. This period, of course, is that in which independent lines of enquiry place the Thera disaster. The fragment, therefore, at least suggests the possibility that the tradition of Deucalion's flood may have something to do with the great tidal waves that were almost certainly associated with the Thera eruption.

Deucalion's flood and ancient tidal waves in Greek tradition

The story of Deucalion and the flood probably originated in Boeotia, for Deucalion's original landing in his 'ark' was placed on Mt Parnassus.[98] Sir John Forsdyke explains it as the memory of a 'local catastrophe in Boeotia where inundation was frequent and the formation of the huge Copaic lake had followed the destruction of a Minoan drainage system.'[99] The Copaic basin is an elevated limestone plain largely dependent for drainage on natural 'swallow-holes'. If natural or artificial channels were blocked by an earthquake, serious flooding could easily have resulted. The flood which was remembered as Deucalion's could have resulted from earthquake damage associated with the Thera eruption. The Parian Marble definitely dates the flood to 1529 BC, which is reasonably close to the Thera eruption dates. It should also be remembered that torrential rain often accompanies a major eruption. Apollodorus is quite positive that the flood lasted for nine days only, which sounds like a serious but localized disaster. When the waters subsided Deucalion came to Athens and founded the temple of Olympian Zeus. His grave at Athens, and a hole where the flood waters had run away, were still being pointed out in the second century AD. By the time of Ovid the story of Deucalion had been given a much wider currency, and also a moral context. Like Noah's flood, it was viewed as a punishment inflicted by Zeus for the wickedness of the men of the Bronze Age. Perhaps the best guide to its date as a real event is the fact that Deucalion was the father of Hellen who in turn became ancestor of the Hellens.[100] In terms of myth-history the event therefore stands right at the beginning of the development of Greek national consciousness, that is to say, in the early part of the Late Bronze Age.

I do not, however, wish to press the possible connection of Deucalion's flood with Thera. Excessive rain is one thing; tidal waves are another. If one is looking for memories of the Thera cataclysm, one is on safer ground with local traditions of ancient coastal inundations. Such traditions are quite widespread in Greek legend, and come from both sides of the Aegean. I give a summary list of them with some comments:[101]

1) *Attica*
Cape Sunium is the nearest point on the Greek mainland to Thera. One would therefore expect to find a tradition of a cataclysmic inundation in Attica, if anywhere. And expectation is not disappointed. The tradition forms a pendant to the legendary contest for the possession of Attica between Athena and Poseidon – a tale which may itself reflect Minoan-Mycenaean tension in Attica *c.* 1500 BC. According to the story, Athena produced an olive tree, and Poseidon a spring, and Athena's 'invention' was judged more useful. Poseidon proved a bad loser and, in his anger, flooded the country. Apollodorus says: 'Poseidon was very wrathful, and flooded the Thriasian plain [round Eleusis], and submerged Attica under sea-water.'[102]

2) *The Argolid*
A similar story is told about Argos. Poseidon is said to have disputed possession of it with Hera, and, on losing the contest, to have flooded the Argive plain.[103]

It is tempting to regard these traditions as embodying a memory of the Thera *tsunamis*. The coasts of Attica and the shores of the Bay of Argos are two of the most likely regions to have suffered from waves spreading from Thera.

3) *Troezen and the Saronic Gulf*
Poseidon is said to have contested possession of this land too with Athena, and to have flooded it and made it unfruitful for a

time.[103a]; There is also a tradition of a remarkable tidal wave in this region – the wave sent by Poseidon to overwhelm Hippolytus. Euripides' description of this event is most graphic. It comes in the messenger speech in the *Hippolytus*:[104]

> And when we struck into a desolate place –
> There lies beyond the frontier of this land
> A shore that faces the Saronic Sea –
> There came a sound, as if within the earth
> Zeus' hollow thunder boomed, awful to hear.
> The horses lifted heads towards the sky
> And pricked their ears; while strange fear fell on us,
> Whence came the voice. To the sea-beaten shore
> We looked, and saw a monstrous wave that soared
> Into the sky, so lofty that my eyes
> Were robbed of seeing the Scironian cliffs.
> It hid the isthmus and Asclepius' rock.
> Then seething up and bubbling all about
> With foaming flood and breath from the deep sea,
> Shoreward it came to where the chariot stood.

The details here are very much what one would expect for a wave of submarine origin. Such waves would appear to swell up and blot out the view across the bay without showing any visible crest. Only when they came close to the shore would they appear to seethe and foam as the breaking effect of the shallow water caused them to rear up and curl over.

4) *Lycia*

Plutarch records that Bellerophon, on being badly treated by a certain Iobates, prayed to Poseidon to make the land 'fruitless and forgotten'. Poseidon thereupon sent 'a wave which reared up and flooded the land – a terrible sight as the sea came in at a high level and covered all the plain'.[105]

5) *The Troad*

Strabo reports 'a great earthquake which occurred long ago in Lydia and Ionia as far as the Troad. Villages were swallowed up and Mt Sipylus laid waste. It happened in the reign of Tantalus. Marshes turned into lakes, and a tidal wave flooded the region round Troy.'[106]

The unusual detail that marshes turned into lakes might embody a remote memory of the torrential rain which often follows large eruptions. A similar detail occurs in the next tradition.

40 A solid wall of ashlar masonry, which appears to be the outer wall of a substantial building, runs for about 14 m. along trench Arvanitis 2. Recesses at regular intervals occur along the wall. In a room to the west side of the wall was found a floor made of tiny sea-pebbles trampled into the ground surface

41, 42, 43 One of the first finds in trench Bronos I was the stone lamp (*below*) whose nozzle still showed the traces of burning from the wick. Most of the pottery found on Thera was made locally but shows the influence of Minoan decorative designs, as in this pithos, recovered in earlier excavations. A few sherds from trench Bronos I are of Late Minoan IA pottery imported from Crete between 1550 and 1500 BC (*above right*)

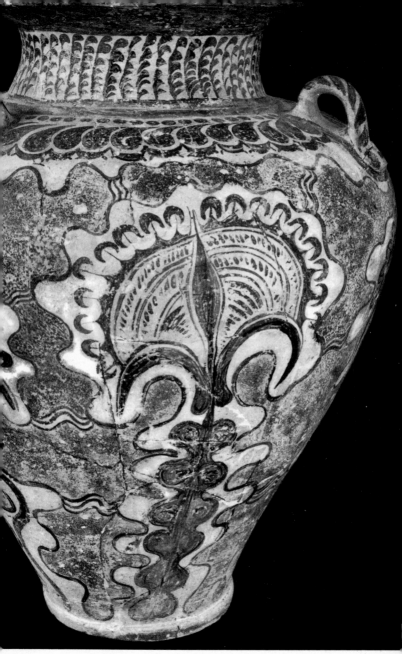

44 'Palace Style' pithos from Knossos. Its decoration illustrates the typical rigidity of this style and is here a stylized papyrus plant

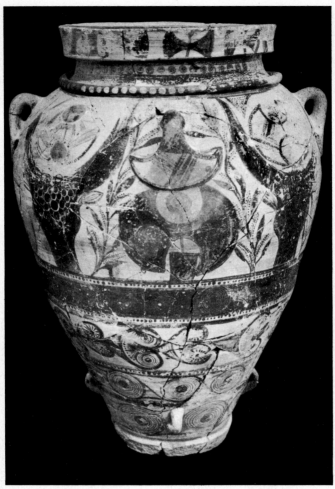

45 An example of 'Palace Style' pottery, LM II, *c.* 1470-1425 BC. The style is formal by comparison with the 'marine' and 'plant' style vases and may well reflect mainland influence arising from the Greek occupation of Knossos. All are products of the palace workshop at Knossos, but these two examples (*above and on opposite page*) were found on the island of Pseira. The bulls' heads and double-axes are familiar earlier Minoan motifs and the olive sprays are reminiscent of the 'plant' style. The running spiral at the base becomes entirely dominant on the other example shown (*opposite page*)

46 Another example of 'Palace Style' pottery. On this one the running spiral at the base of the vase on the preceding page becomes entirely dominant

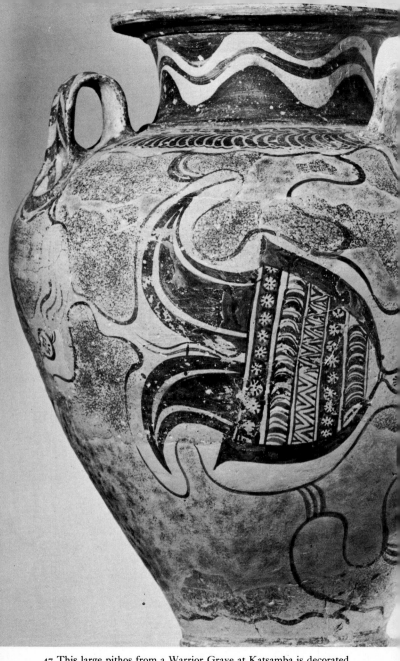

47 This large pithos from a Warrior Grave at Katsamba is decorated with boar's tusk helmets of a type known to Homer. Such helmets were probably imports from the mainland as there are thought to have been no wild boars in Crete at this date

48, 49 A note of unaccustomed militarism appears at Knossos from about 1460 BC onwards, particularly with objects found in the so-called Warrior Graves. The conical helmet with cheek pieces and plume holder is made of bronze, and came from the same Warrior Grave at Knossos as the collection of swords, spear and arrowheads (*below*)

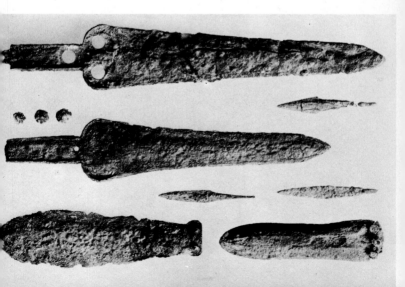

50 The throne room (*above*) was reconstructed in the closing phase of the palace of Knossos and may be associated with the intrusive Greek dynasty, *c.* 1460 BC. The throne and benches are original and the frescoes of the remains found *in situ*, now in the Herakleion Museum. They show a heraldic frieze of griffins and lilies, the former reappearing on a gold bead found in the palace at Pylas and on ivories from Delphias

51 Off the Grand Staircase which descends from the Central Court of the palace at Knossos, is a lobby known as the 'Guard Room'. The frescoes show a series of figure-of-eight shields of the type known to Homer, and elsewhere associated with the Mycenaeans. The columns are typically Minoan with their thickened capitals and downward tapering shafts

52 One of the best known of Minoan statuettes is the little faience figure
of a goddess from the Temple Repositories at Knossos. Her long
flounced skirt, apron, narrow waist, open bodice and elbow-length sleeves
are typical of the dress of Minoan ladies as seen in the companion pieces
from this find and the frescoes. The snakes which she holds in her hands
are symbols of the protector of the household

53 Another terracotta statue found with the fragments on the next page. This statue stands almost a metre high. Her flared skirt and narrow waist are very Minoan in style

54,55 A large number of broken female terracotta statues were found in the temple at Ayia Irini on Keos. These fragments show the typical open bodice and short sleeves. It is suggested that the group comprised a goddess or goddesses with attendant votaries

56 The large storage jar seen here wedged in a basement corridor fell from an upper storey of a complex Minoan-type building at Ayia Irini on Keos which was violently destroyed in the LM IB period. Apparently during an earthquake the walls buckled, allowing the jar to drop through into the narrow space, and then closed above it

57 Praisos lies in a secluded valley in eastern Crete about 20 km. from
the sea. It was occupied in Minoan times and people called Eteo-Cretans
speaking a non-Greek language maintained an independent existence here
until about 140 BC. At this time they occupied the natural limestone
acropolis seen in the near middle distance

58 The Kephala mound at Knossos was inhabited in Neolithic times, and about 2000 BC the great palace complex began to develop on the site, lasting until the fifteenth century BC when it was violently destroyed. Sir Arthur Evans began excavations in 1900 and carried out extensive restorations which enable the visitor to appreciate the complex architecture of this extensive and many storied building (Plates 50, 51, 60, 62, 65, 66). It is seen here from the east

59 An imaginative reconstruction of the palace at Knossos, concentrated around a great central courtyard, covering in all more than 20,000 square metres. The flat roofs, light wells and decorative schemes give it a very modern appearance

60 A four-storeyed mansion below the south-west corner of the great palace at Knossos. Often referred to as the 'priest's house', it has its own small pillar crypt, and must have had close connections with the palace to be allowed a site abutting on the main palace mound

61 The Temple Tomb at Knossos lies just south of the palace. Built on two levels, it is reminiscent of the tomb of Minos in Sicily (as described by Diodorus) in which the tomb was below and a mortuary chapel above. It is built into the hillside and an open paved court (*above*) gives access to an inner hall followed by a pillar crypt, giving on to the sepulchral chamber. Another pillared room stood above the pillar crypt

62 One of the main entrances to the palace on the north side is provided by a stepped ramp leading up from a pillared hall past a raised portico. On the wall of the portico was found a fresco-relief depicting a charging bull. This portion may have stood out from the wreck of the palace after 1400 BC and given rise to the legend of the Minotaur

63 The settled and peaceful nature of Minoan civilization is reflected in this wine press that was found *in situ* in a Minoan villa at Vathypetro near Arkhanes on Crete. The pithos sunk into the floor on the left of the group received the grape juice from a shallow, clay vat. Behind the pithos is an overflow runnel of a type often found in the magazines of the great palaces

64 The large fallen blocks here seen lying immediately below the south wall of the palace of Knossos (in the foreground were judged by Evans to have been dislodged from the palace walls in the severe earthquake of c. 1570 BC. Their size and weight were such that they were not replaced in position in subsequent rebuilding. Beside them was a small shrine containing the horns of sacrificed bulls, perhaps a propitiation to Poseidon the Earth-Shaker

65 Elaborately constructed plumbing systems are a feature of all the Minoan palaces, a point which is emphasized about the ancient royal palace in the metropolis of Atlantis. There was an underground system of jointed terracotta pipes at Knossos and also overground runnels carved in stone to channel away rainwater

66 At the north-east corner of the palace is a particularly elaborate system to bring water down to a large stone trough which may have been a washing place. Narrow channels with parabolic curves to slow the water on the descent following the turns of the cut stone staircase. The water passes through two small square settling tanks before reaching the large lower tank

67 A Late Minoan bath-tub, decorated with fish on the inside and with an outflow hole. It was found at Pachyammos near Gournia where it had been used as a sarcophagus. Baths of this type were often used for burials

68 This beautifully embossed gold cup from a plundered tholos tomb at
Vapheio near Sparta is a masterpiece of Minoan toreutic art. The scene
forms a connected sequence and shows the decoying and capture of wild
bulls in a rural setting. In this scene one bull is entangled in a mesh of
ropes secured to two trees and another has escaped and is galloping away
to the right. It is noteworthy that only ropes are being used in this
scene, a fact which finds a parallel in the capture of bulls as described in
the Atlantis legend

69 Egypt was attacked c. 1190 BC by a coalition of 'Sea Peoples', 'northerners from all lands', who came in a great expedition down the Palestine coast. They were decisively defeated by the fleet and army of Ramesses III, who commemorated his victory on the walls of his temple at Medinet Habu. The scene shows the invaders with their typical feathered head-dresses falling from their galleys before the Egyptian onslaught. These invaders included the Peleset (Phillistines), the Shekelesh, and the Denyen (?Danaoi or Greeks)

70 Over the main entrance gate to the citadel of Mycenae is a carved limestone relief showing two lions (lionesses?) in heraldic pose flanking a Minoan pillar (*cf.* Plate 51).

71, 72 Evidence of a two-way trade between Crete and Middle Kingdom Egypt is provided by this Egyptian scarab found at Knossos, inscribed with a 'good luck' greeting on the base

73 The handsome Kamares two-handled and spouted jug was found in an undisturbed grave at Abydos. The grave is securely dated to the Middle Kingdom by the style of its contents and by cylinder seals of Senusret III and Amenemhet III, and the jug itself has exact parallels in Crete from the Kamares cave

74, 75 Several Egyptian tomb paintings of the fifteenth century BC depict men of Keftiu (Crete) bringing tribute. The most elaborate of these scenes is in the tomb of Rekhmire, visier to Tuthmosis III (*above*). The figures were originally painted wearing cut-away kilts and codpieces but were subsequently repainted to show a longer and more decorous type of kilt which can be paralleled from mainland Greece. Traces of the original design may be seen in figures 2, 3, and 4. They carry a rhyton and vases of typical Cretan form; one has an ox-hide copper ingot on his shoulder. A detail from the tomb of Menkheperresoneb, son of Rekhmire (*below*), shows a mixed group of figures, one, typically Cretan, carrying a bull's head rhyton on a platter. The figure prostrating himself on the left, although of Syrian type, has written above him the title 'Prince of Keftiu'

76, 77 Egyptian contacts with Crete are seen in these objects *(above and next page)* from the Middle Kingdom, Second Intermediate Period and New Kingdom respectively. The broken statue of User *(bottom)* was found at Knossos, leading one to suppose that he dedicated it there; *top,* an alabastron lid, also from Knossos, has the cartouche of the Hyksos pharaoh Khian of the XVII Dynasty

78 This fine alabaster jar was found in a Warrior Grave at Katsamba and carries the name and titles of Tuthmosis III. It was this same grave that produced the fine pithos seen in Plate 47

6) Rhodes

Diodorus reports some traditions about a great flood in Rhodes.[107] There was heavy loss of life when it occurred, and only a few survivors managed to escape into the higher portions of the interior. The low-lying parts of the island became marshy as a result of excessive rainfall. The city of Cyrbê was devastated and obliterated by a great 'flood-tide' – a very unusual term in these reports pointing perhaps to a sound local tradition. After its destruction Lindos, Ialysos, and Cameirus divided the land and each founded a city bearing his name. This account can be related to archaeological data on the destruction of Minoan Trianda, for which see p. 109 f.

7) Samothrace

Diodorus reports that in his own time the Samothracians were still sacrificing on altars which had been set up in a circle round the island to mark the flood-line of a great inundation from the sea.[108]

The Argonauts and Thera

So much for memories of tidal waves and torrential rainfall perhaps associated with the Thera eruption. Is there any legendary memory of the volcano itself? None can be certainly identified in Greek history or mythology. This is not altogether surprising. The eruption occurred in a pre-literate period, so far as mainland Greece was concerned, and at a time when Mycenaean civilization was only at an early formative stage. It is not likely that any Greeks were living on Thera at the time of its obliteration. And after the final cataclysm the volcano ceased to exist. The tidal waves were apparently remembered – they actually reached Greece – but it is hardly surprising that there seems to be no clear and certain memory of the volcano itself.

There are, however, some curious incidents in the Argonaut saga which occur at or near Thera, and which may preserve an oblique memory of volcanic phenomena.[109] The Argonauts in the final stages of their voyage crossed Lake Tritonis (identified with Shatt el Jerid in Tunisia), and made their way back into the Mediterranean. On their way through Lake Tritonis they encountered a local god called Triton who presented them with a clod of earth. One of them later dropped this clod into the sea to the north of Crete where it formed the island of Thera. Triton instructed them how to cross the 'Minoan Sea', and they coasted along the North Africa shore as far as Libya, and then made their way to Karpathos. Next they turned back to Crete, and were about to land at the 'Dictaean roadstead'. But here they were confronted by the formidable figure of Talos, a bronze giant, who prevented them from landing by throwing fragments of stone at them. Talos had been given to Europa by Zeus (or to Minos by Hephaestus, in another account) to be the 'watcher of the island', and he patrolled round it, moving swiftly on his brazen legs. He was made entirely of invincible bronze except for a vein near his ankle covered by a thin membrane. In terror of his missiles the Argonauts backed away from the shore, and were about to sail on when Medea announced that she could overcome the giant. She cast a spell on him which had the effect of dimming his vision, and as he was levering up a great boulder to hurl at them, he grazed his ankle on a rocky pinnacle. 'Then the ichor flowed out like molten lead', and, losing strength rapidly, he fell from his rocky crag 'with a terrible crash'.

Such is the story as told by Apollonius Rhodius writing in the third century BC. But the Argonaut saga goes back to the earliest stages of Greek epic poetry, and has often been supposed to reflect early Mycenaean voyages of exploration. Some have thought that the Talos episode is a late addition to the saga, but there is no strong reason for supposing so, and one indication I have noticed points in the other direction. The Talos episode is located at the 'Dictaean roadstead', a harbour in Crete which would be entered by a ship coming from Karpathos to the east. On the east coast of Crete ancient ships certainly used the well-sheltered beaches of Itanos, Palaikastro and Kato Zakro (Plate 28). Can any of these be identified with the 'Dictaean roadstead'? Now Professor G. Huxley has recently argued, without mentioning this passage of Apollonius Rhodius, that the Minoan name for Kato Zakro may have been Dikta.[110] If he is correct, it looks as though Apollonius may have recorded a Minoan harbour name in eastern Crete not otherwise clearly remembered even in antiquity. This lends support to the view that his account of Talos is based on a good and ancient tradition.

To return to Talos: what can one make of this bronze warder

who hurls rocks at ships trying to sail to Crete? Is he simply a figure of folk-tale and imagination? Or can he be rationalized? Talos has been explained as the Minoan sun-god, and the all-seeing sun always makes a good watchman. But other features, such as the stone-throwing, the ankle vein, and the collapse and death of the giant are not at all appropriate to a solar myth. A quite different and very ingenious explanation was advanced by J. Schoo.[111] Schoo suggested that the figure of Talos embodies an early Greek memory of the Thera volcano. Thera 'guards' the northern approaches to Crete which would have been used by the early Mycenaean sailors. His frame of 'unbreakable bronze' represents the wall of the newly formed crater on the mountain peak of Thera as it then was. The rocks which he throws are the 'bombs' shot from the vent of the volcano. His 'heel' is a subsidiary volcano on the coast of the island, like Cape Kolumbo or Cape Mavrorachidi. He collapses and becomes quiescent when all his ichor has flowed out like 'molten lead' – a reminiscence of the cooling off of lava streams after the end of an eruption. Finally, like the Cyclops (another stone-thrower), he is left with a great blind eye when the caldera has formed.

This delightfully ingenious suggestion won the approval of Hennig, who thought that the influence of volcanic and seismic phenomena on Greek mythology had been generally under-estimated.[112] The Talos legend could have been formed in the twenty or thirty years between the awakening of the volcano *c.* 1500 and its final disintegration *c.* 1470. In this period Thera was probably deserted, and must have formed an object of awe-some speculation to the inhabitants of surrounding islands. If its central peak was really over 1500 m. high (as some geologists think), it would have been clearly visible from Crete. The people of Knossos may well have watched with apprehension this strange aggressive 'watcher' which the gods had sent them – a mountain giant glowing like a bronze furnace after its age-long period of quiescence. If any of the former inhabitants tried to sail back in the hope of recovering some of their possessions, they may well have been turned back in dismay by the ejection of volcanic debris.

This explanation of Talos gives remarkable point to Simonides' description of him as 'wrought by Hephaestus'. And there is one final detail in this legend, not given by Apollonius, which seems to suggest that he was indeed in origin a personification of the Thera volcano. He is credited with a son called Leukos, who drove out the lawful king of Crete, destroyed ten Cretan cities, and murdered his fiancée, the king's daughter.[113] By a strange coincidence – or is it coincidence? – the fiancée's name is Kleisithera, 'Key of Thera'. Leukos' own name means 'White One'. Could this be a memory of the very heavy fall-out of white ash which covered the cities and fields of Crete after the 'death' of Talos himself? I like to think it was.

After the overthrow of Talos, the Argonauts sailed north from Crete, and the next incident in their voyage could also be interpreted as a memory of one of the after-effects of the Thera eruption. The strongly worded description of Apollonius speaks for itself:[114]

And then straightaway, as they moved swiftly over the great Cretan deep, night terrified them, the night which they call 'the pall of darkness'. No stars nor moonbeams pierced this deadly darkness. It was black chaos coming down from the sky, or some other darkness rising from the inmost recesses of the earth. They did not in the least know whether they were voyaging on the water or in Hades. Helplessly they entrusted their safe return to the sea, to carry them whither it would.

In this extremity Jason prayed to Apollo, and the god guided them with the glint of his bow to Anaphi, east of Thera, where they landed and sacrificed in sunshine once again.

Could this be a memory of the time when the paroxysmal eruption of Thera turned day into night over a wide area of the Aegean? At the AD 79 eruption of Vesuvius a darkness descended described by Pliny as 'not the darkness of a moonless or cloudy night, but the total blackness of an enclosed space when lights have been extinguished'.[115] The same thing happened at the Krakatoa eruption. The darkness which shrouded and terrified the Argonauts is strangely unexplained. It was not due to an eclipse or to a storm. A volcanic cloud of dust and vapour might well be called 'black chaos descending from the sky, or another darkness rising from the depths of the earth'. At least the Argonauts were in the right place to enter such a cloud – the deep and open sea between Thera and Anaphi.

It might be objected that no boat could survive the tidal waves in the vicinity of Thera, but the experience of Krakatoa contradicts this objection. There were several European ships in the Sunda Strait at the climax of the eruption. The British ship *Charles Bal* was tacking about only 20 km. from Krakatoa for most of the night of 26–27 August, and was probably less than 50 km. on when the worst explosion and wave occurred at 10 a.m. on the 27th. The *Norham Castle* and the *Sir Robert Sale* were in the narrows farther to the east at this time. The *Gouverneur-General Loudon* had just dropped anchor 40 km. from the volcano. There were no casualties on any of these ships. Apparently the only fatalities at sea were four people drowned on the Dutch barque *Marie* which was at anchor close to Telok Betong. Yet 36,380 people were killed by the waves in the coastal regions.

These are significant facts. The great tidal waves formed rounded ridges of water which moved swiftly and silently under the ships in the open, and reared up into devastating breakers only when they reached land. None of the ships noted any particularly large waves. All they noticed was a confused sea with heavy squalls from different directions. They noted also the darkness lit only by flashes of lightning, and a heavy rain of mud and pumice – truly a 'black chaos'.

To return to the Argonauts: on the above evidence, it seems that a ship could have survived on the open sea quite close to Thera even at the moment of a paroxysmal eruption. Tidal waves which proved extremely destructive on reaching Crete could have passed unnoticed. The crew might not even have heard very much of the eruption. It was noticed at Krakatoa that, after the big explosion, the volcanic cloud became so thick that it blanketed out all further noise; subsequent explosions were not even heard by those who still survived on the nearer shores of the Sunda Strait. Did a Greek ship really pass close to Thera in eruption about 1470 BC and bring back an account of the resulting darkness? Did such an account become part of the repertoire of Mycenaean bards? Was it then handed down in each re-telling of the Argonaut saga until finally the tradition reached Apollonius? Some may feel that it is not even worth asking such questions. But I think it is worth raising them, and it does seem to me that conceivably the answer in each case could be 'Yes'. Is it not perhaps too much of a coincidence that the 'pall of darkness' incident, if invented, should be so carefully located on a route passing close to Thera?

After making their landfall at Anaphi in sunshine once more, the Argonauts sacrificed to Apollo, and then came the final incident on their homeward voyage.[116] As they sailed on calm weather Euphemus threw overboard the clod of earth he had received from Triton, and from it rose up the island of Kallistê which was later colonized and called Thera by Euphemus' descendant, Theras.

Possibly this curious tale embodies some distant memories of the changes in the topography of Thera caused by the eruption. If ships sailed past Thera soon afterwards they would have noticed that much of the old island had vanished, and that 'new' islands – really the fragments of the old one – had been formed. Such reports could have formed the basis for the story of Kallistê rising up in the wake of the Argo. Similar reports could have percolated to Egypt, and become incorporated in the story of the disappearance of 'Atlantis'. The final detail in the Atlantis legend is that after the disappearance of the island the sea in the area became unnavigable, being blocked up by shoals of mud left behind after the subsidence. Reports brought back by the first ships to visit Krakatoa after the 1883 eruption read remarkably like this statement. It was reported that two-thirds of the island had disappeared, and that the Sebesi channel to the north was completely blocked by banks of debris. The debris included masses of still smoking pumice floating in such thick masses that no vessel could force a way through. In a final flicker of activity on 10 October the volcano ejected large quantities of black mud.

Floating islands

After the Thera eruption masses of floating pumice must have littered the Aegean for many months. They must have been reported by sailors as unexpected apparitions on their familiar routes. Such reports could underlie Greek legends about the early history of Delos. Callimachus tells us that before Apollo came to Delos (the Minoan period?) the island was called Asteriê, 'star island', and that it floated round the Aegean, and was seen in various places.[117] Some details of specific sightings are given. It was often seen by ships in the Saronic gulf coming from Troezen to Corinth, and on their return journey they were astonished to find it no longer there. Other sightings were reported from the Euripus between Euboea and the mainland, from off Cape Sunium, and from near Chios and Samos. But after Apollo had been born on the island, the island put down roots, and became a clearly marked place, so the sailors called it Delos, the 'clear' island.

Ship reports after the Krakatoa eruption speak of banks of floating pumice up to 40 km. long (see p. 68). This is far bigger than Delos, which is a very small island. Obviously the nineteenth-century captains and crews were very intrigued by these 'floating islands' which were appearing in the middle of the Indian Ocean. It is easy to imagine that similar reports were brought back by the mariners of the fifteenth century BC. They could have told quite sensational stories of the new white islands which had fallen from the sky 'like stars', and now lay dipping and twinkling along the old sea-lanes. Such stories could have passed into the matrix of early Greek tradition later to become specifically attached to the saga of Delos.

Some confirmation of this suggestion is provided by Callimachus' account of how Asteriê came to be floating around in the first place. His actual words are:

In the beginning a great god striking the mountains with a triple-tongued blade, which the Telchines had wrought for him, fashioned islands in the deep. He heaved and levered them up from the depths and rolled them into the sea. Some he rooted fast but you [*i.e.* Asteriê-Delos] sailed freely over the sea.

The 'great god' is reminiscent of Poseidon with his trident. The Telchines are closely connected with Crete, and suggest that 'in the beginning' may refer to the Minoan period. Thera certainly was fashioned into three islands after its mountain had been struck a fearsome blow. Finally, many 'floating islands' of pumice were launched from its side like ships into the surrounding waters giving rise to the various legends.

Asteriê-Delos was not the only floating island of Greek legend. The island of Aeolus, king of the winds, is described by Homer in the *Odyssey*.[118] It too was a floating island with sheer cliffs and a wall of bronze all round it. Aeolus' island has often been identified with one of the Lipari islands, then, as now, a volcanic area. There is evidence that the Mycenaeans were trading to the Lipari islands as early as the fifteenth century BC. The sheer encircling cliffs of 'unbreakable bronze' could be interpreted as a poetical description of a crater. In certain lights the walls of the Thera caldera certainly have a very bronze look.

The Egyptians also had a 'floating island' called Chemmis. They showed it to Herodotus when he visited them, but he remarks: 'I never saw it moving.'[119] It was at Buto in the Delta, a region where Greek and Egyptian mythology had become curiously intertwined by the time of Herodotus' visit. Herodotus picked up a complicated tradition about the island – a tradition which linked it with the mythology of Delos through Leto and Apollo. The tradition demands fuller treatment than can be attempted here. I shall comment on one detail only, an interesting detail which suggests that Egyptian legend had undergone some impregnation by Aegean vulcanism. The Egyptians told Herodotus that the island had formerly been fixed, and that it began to float at the time when the dread monster Typhon came looking for the child of Osiris (=Apollo) who had been hidden there by Leto. Does the intrusion of Typhon embody a memory of a Thera *tsunami* which once inundated the Delta and washed around the sacred island at Buto? Typhon has affinities with Tiamat, the Babylonian dragon of the deep. If their sacred island was inundated as a direct result of the Thera eruption, the priests may well have put about the story that Typhon-Tiamat had come looking for the baby Horus.

In this connection we may note an obscure tradition, which probably goes back at least to Pindar, that the gods once fled to Egypt to escape from the rage of Typhon.[120] This myth could embody a vague memory of the Thera eruption, and the flight of Minoan refugees to Egypt.

There is a passage in Hesiod's *Theogony* which describes tidal waves resulting from the battle between Zeus and Typhoeus (=Typhon). I quote from the point where battle is joined between them:[121]

And the heat from them both gripped the purple sea, the heat of thunder and lightning and of fire from such a monster, the heat of fiery storm-winds and flaming thunderbolt. And the whole earth and firmament and sea boiled. And long waves spreading out in circles went seething over the headlands, and unquenchable earthquakes broke out.

This passage could be interpreted as a classic description of a volcanic eruption complete with electrical storms, earthquakes, and tidal waves. But it must be admitted that there is nothing to locate it on Thera. Homer puts Typhoeus at Arima, an unknown place; Pindar and Aeschylus put him under Mt Aetna.[122] At least the latter writers associate him with an active volcano. Enceladus, another earth-born giant, was also believed to have been imprisoned under Aetna after his defeat by the gods. Polybotes was located under the little volcanic islet of Nisyra near Kos. Generally speaking, the imagery of Greek mythological descriptions of battles between Gods and Giants owes something to volcanic phenomena. As H. J. Rose remarks, the Giants were 'not exactly personifications of volcanic forces and other formidable phenomena of nature, but anciently-conceived spirits supposed to be responsible for such things.'[123] Hesiod was heir to the ancient poetic traditions of Boeotia, and it seems just possible that his description of the Zeus-Typhoeus contest owes something to a memory of the Thera eruption. The picture of the long waves radiating outwards from a central point, and washing over promontories, has a distinctly factual ring about it.

The fate of the Phaeacians

This round-up of possible memories of the Thera eruption in Greek literature may fittingly conclude with a glance at Homer. Following the suggestion of Drerup early in this century, many writers have at least noticed the possibility that Homer's picture of the gay, enterprising Phaeacians, who dwell in a remote sea-girt island, may owe something to distant memories of life in Minoan Crete. The description of the gardens of Alcinous, the fondness of the Phaeacians for dancing, and their love of hot baths (Plate 67) and comfortable beds, all lend some colour to this theory. Even more significant, perhaps, is their noted seamanship, and their expertise in conveying goods and passengers in speed and comfort to the most distant destinations. Odysseus benefits from their skill when they convey him and his treasures back to Ithaca, and this exploit moves Poseidon to anger.[124] He feels that the Phaeacians, though his descendants, have flouted his wishes by giving his enemy Odysseus such a good passage, and he threatens to turn their ship into stone on its return voyage, and also to 'cover up their city with a great mountain'.

Zeus dissuades him from the more drastic punishment, but the returning ship is duly turned to stone in full view of the astonished Phaeacians. Thereupon king Alcinous bethinks him of an 'ancient oracle' heard from his father that Poseidon would one day become jealous of the Phaeacians because they were 'trouble-free conveyors of all and sundry', and that he would petrify one of their ships and 'shut in' the city with a mountain. Since half of the prophecy has already been fulfilled he quickly orders a propitiatory sacrifice of twelve choice bulls in an attempt to avert the destruction of the city. At this point in the *Odyssey* the story moves away from Phaeacia, and we are never told whether the remedy was successful.

In this connection we may recall a tradition in the Orphic *Argonautica* that Poseidon once 'struck the Lyctonian land' with his trident, and 'scattered it' so that it became 'islands in the boundless ocean which men named Sardo, Euboea and Cyprus'. This is a particularly interesting reference since the epithet 'Lyctonian' points to Crete, where the important city of Lyctus was said to have been founded by Lyctus son of Lycaeon. The passage also has some common ground with the passage from Pindar's Fourth Paean discussed above (p. 108), in that in both the destruction results from a quarrel or battle between Poseidon and Zeus. I suggested that the Pindar passage contains a memory of the formation of the Thera caldera. It is also possible that the present passage preserves a remote tradition of seismic or volcano devastation in Crete followed by a wide dispersal of population, not only to Greece, but also to the far west (Sardinia ?), and eastwards to Cyprus.[125]

When excavating just to the south of the palace at Knossos, Evans found the horns of sacrificial bulls in a small shrine (Plate 64).[126] Near by were great fallen blocks which he judged to have been dislodged from the palace walls by an earthquake shock. In relation to this find he aptly quoted the Homeric line: 'The earth-shaker delighteth in bulls'. In Alcinous' propitiatory sacrifice of bulls to Poseidon there may well be an Homeric echo of an old Minoan rite. The precise nature of Poseidon's threat to the Phaeacians is not very clear. To destroy their city by an earthquake would be understandable, but it is hardly the same thing as 'covering it round', or 'shutting it in' with a mountain. Prophesies are often composed *post eventum*. Possibly the 'ancient oracle' remembered by Alcinous was really a Greek explanation devised soon after the Thera cataclysm to account for the terrible disaster suffered by Minoan Crete. It would be plausible to suggest that they had offended their sea-god by over-confidence in their navigational prowess, and therefore had to suffer from his wrath. The blanket of ash and the blocking of their harbours by floating pumice could both be covered by the terms of Poseidon's threat. Certainly a visit to Thera makes one very conscious of what happens when the forces of nature 'cover up a city with a large mountain'.

The Minoan 'diaspora'

I have argued that the final paroxysmal eruption of Thera about 1470 BC destroyed all the Minoan palaces except Knossos, and covered all the plains and valleys of Crete east of Mt Ida with a thick blanket of ash. All shipping in northern and eastern harbours would have been lost, and many thousands drowned in the resulting tidal waves. Colonies in the Cyclades and as far as Rhodes would have been badly hit, and communications generally disrupted. The first major political result of the disaster was the occupation of Knossos by a Greek-speaking dynasty. Simultaneously came a great westward displacement of the surviving population in search of cultivable land. New sites were occupied in western Crete, and former ones enlarged. The refugees did not stop there. An exodus now took place to parts of Greece, particularly the western Peloponnese, which had been much less seriously affected by the eruption. Cretan artists and architects emigrated to find work in the service of Mycenaean chieftains. We may suppose that the remnants of the Minoan nobility gathered what shipping and retainers they could muster, and set sail to find new homes. They would have followed the old sea routes with which their captains and sailors were familiar: westwards to southern Italy and Sicily, northwards to the Cyclades and Attica; eastwards to Rhodes, Cyprus and the Levant, southwards to Egypt. But they sailed no longer as masters of the sea, and chief traders of the eastern Mediterranean. They were now exporting themselves, not their goods.

A remnant of this Minoan dispersion may have settled as far away as Tunisia where a tribe of 'Atlantes' was known in the classical period (see p. 32). A remnant certainly went eastwards, and settled in the coastal strip of southern Palestine, and were later known as Philistines. The prophet Amos (c. 800 BC) refers to this migration, and, interestingly enough, links the event with a description of vulcanism and inundations:[127]

And the Lord God of hosts is he that toucheth the land, and it shall melt, and all that dwell therein shall mourn: and it shall rise up wholly like a flood; and shall be drowned as by the flood of Egypt.

It is he ... that calleth for the waters of the sea, and poureth them out upon the face of the earth ... Have not I brought up Israel out of the land of Egypt? And the Philistines from Caphtor, and the Syrians from Kir?

This type of prophetic literature, with its *dies irae* and 'saved remnant' motifs, may trace back continuously through written documents to fifteenth-century Canaan at least. There could be genuine memories of Thera embedded in it. The coincidence of Crete (Caphtor), melting lands, inundated plains, and possibly even of a sediment on the fields, is certainly striking.

Amos implies that the Cretan exodus from Caphtor followed the same pattern as the Jewish exodus from Egypt. An attempt has recently been made to link the Jewish exodus chronologically with the Thera eruption, with the suggestion that there was some causal relationship between the ten plagues of Egypt and Theran vulcanism.[128] Only in two respects does this suggestion seem at all plausible. The temporary retreat of seawater, and darkness 'which could be felt' lasting for three days, can be rationally explained as seismic and volcanic phenomena. But if the date proposed in this book for the final Thera eruption, *i.e. c.* 1470, is accepted, it seems out of the question to synchronize the exodus with it. Egypt was then united under Tuthmosis III and carrying aggressive war far north into Syria, and these are just not the conditions under which a mass migration of 'Asiatics' out of Egypt can be pictured. The Jewish occupation of Palestine was a complicated business, probably the result of several waves of immigration from different directions. There may have been some influx from the east as early as the fifteenth century, but on balance it seems more likely that the historic exodus from Egypt took place much later, *c.* 1250. This is not to say that the *language* in which that exodus is described is not indebted to earlier happenings.

Because of previous trade links with Egypt (Plates 71–8) one would expect that some Minoan refugees made their way there after 1470. Their reports of the disaster could have formed the nucleus of the tradition which found its way to Solon nearly 900 years later. Egyptian references to Keftiu do not continue after the reign of Amenophis II (1444–1412 BC). After 1400 BC Mycenaean pottery begins to appear in Egypt, and Egyptian objects at Mycenae. In Rhodes, towards the end of the fifteenth century, the Minoan colony at Trianda was destroyed, and replaced by a Mycenaean outpost (see p. 109 f.). After 1400 a vigorous expansion of Mycenaean trade is clear all along the route from Crete to Syria. After the destruction of the palace at Knossos c. 1400, symbol of the final extinction of Minoan power, we may presume there was a fresh wave of emigration. Did Cretans come with the Mycenaean pottery to the short-lived new city of the heretical Akhenaten? It is tempting to speculate that some of them may have found refuge there, and even more tempting to suppose that some of the impetus for Akhenaten's reforms in art and religion may have derived from Minoan culture.

The dispersion of the Minoans into western Crete and on to the Peloponnese, and to Messenia in particular, is archaeologically well documented. Marinatos has summarized the evidence for this movement in a recent paper.[129] As he remarks, the evidence is an outline guide for further investigation, and will be further tested by excavations, particularly in western Crete and the south-western Peloponnese. The main points are as follows:

1) Kydonia in western Crete (Khania), traditionally founded by Minos, increased greatly in importance from the mid-fifteenth century onwards, and became one of the leading centres in Crete. The inference, which will be tested by projected excavation, is that a strong influx of refugees came from farther east.

2) Pottery from the Pylos area and Kakovatos in Elis shows the influence of east Crete styles, particularly those of Gournia and Kato Zakro.

3) A large tomb at Peristeria (Moira) north of Pylos has a façade of limestone which may be regarded as a Minoan innovation in the architecture of tholos tombs on the mainland. Two Minoan masons' marks are on the doorpost at the left of the entrance.

Works of art of distinctively Minoan character have been found in the same neighbourhood, and Marinatos thinks it possible that some of the local dynasts may have been of Minoan descent.

Marinatos draws an interesting parallel here. Many recent innovations in Greek life, in arts and crafts, music, and even diet, can be traced back to the influx of one and a half million refugees from Turkey after 1922. We seem to see the same sort of thing taking place in Bronze Age Greece in the fifteenth century BC. A remarkable interpenetration of Minoan and Mycenaean culture results. *Mutatis mutandis,* it was true that *Creta capta ferum victorem cepit, et artes intulit.* . . . Greek tradition records that the daughters of Atlas married local rulers throughout the Peloponnese.[130] Minoan religion left a lasting impress on Greek polytheism. Perhaps the most potent symbol of the cultural conquest is still to be seen in the great relief over the Lion Gate at Mycenae. There the royal lions of the house of Atreus support themselves against a Minoan pillar standing on a Minoan altar base (Plate 70).

6 Atlantis Reviewed

Much of the evidence, new and old, which bears on the Atlantis problem has now been presented, and a summing-up must be attempted. Let us imagine that Plato is in the dock, and that a case is to be decided as follows: The Atlantis story – fiction or history?

The advocate of the former alternative might argue thus: We know that the writing of Utopias and historical romances was quite well developed as a Greek literary genre by the end of the fourth century BC. Aristophanes portrayed Cloud-cuckoo-land before 400 BC and Plato sketched an ideal 'Republic', probably between 380 and 370 BC. A generation later Theopompus was writing his imaginary account of the 'never-never-land' of Meropis. When Plato was asked by Dionysius I to write something for a literary 'festival' in Syracuse, he planned the trilogy *Timaeus-Critias-Hermocrates* with a West Greek colouring. The major political fact of West Greek life was the power of Carthage, which controlled much of the Mediterranean and the coasts and islands west to Gibraltar and out into the Atlantic. This gave Plato the idea of inventing an ancient 'Atlantic' power, and bringing it into conflict with prehistoric Greeks. He decided to treat this fiction on an epic scale, describing in detail the numbers and resources of the protagonists, and introducing the usual divine machinery of Zeus and the other gods. The fiction bears all the marks of a 'noble lie' – a device recommended in the *Republic* as useful for propaganda purposes in the interests of national solidarity. The Greeks of Southern Italy and Sicily needed to be reminded of the desirability of unity in the face of the Carthaginian menace. Plato wanted to strengthen their morale by describing how a great invasion from the west had been repulsed by their ancestors. So he invented his ancient Atlantean empire with its expansionist designs. This piece of pseudo-history was also useful for moral purposes. It enabled him to expatiate on the moral corruption introduced by wealth and impiety into the highly civilized commonwealth of Atlantis. He could also praise his own ancestors for their outstanding courage and leadership in his fictitious crisis. In their organization these proto-Athenians mirror the three classes of the ideal state. There are only 20,000 of them, but they repel the vast hordes of Atlantis as successfully as the men of Marathon beat back the Persians. Plato had previously expressed his intention of showing his ideal community in the stress of actual conflict, and this is the fulfilment of his earlier design.

This ambitious historical romance was to be made as convincing as possible by explicit location in time and space, by mentions of places his audience would know, such as Tyrrhenia and Gadeira, and by graphic description of harbours, palaces, and so on. But he did not get far with it. The plot is announced in the *Timaeus,* and the scene is set in the *Critias,* but Plato never finished it. He was interrupted by the death of Dionysius I in 367, and his subsequent involvement in Sicilian politics left him neither time nor inclination for romancing. He did, however, look far enough ahead in planning his work to anticipate the question: Where is Atlantis now ? As Aristotle said : 'The man who dreamed it up made it disappear.' Hence the reference in the *Timaeus* to the sudden catastrophe which marked the end of Atlantis. This would have been described with much more imaginative detail had he completed the *Critias.*

So much in the Atlantis story is totally improbable, our hypothetical advocate proceeds. Plato doesn't even take his own dates seriously. In the *Timaeus* he gives the foundation date of Athens as 9000 years ago; the foundation of Saïs, where the story of its great exploits was supposed to be preserved, is said to be 8000 years ago. But then in the *Critias* he dates the Atlantean invasion 9000 years ago, seemingly overlooking that Athens was only just founded then. Could one have clearer proof that the whole thing is mere fiction from start to finish ?

Details like a plain divided into 60,000 equal lots, and surrounded by an irrigation ditch nearly 1800 km. long are obviously absurd. In any case how does this square with the

generally mountainous character of the island which is emphasized elsewhere in the account? How did herds of elephants
come to be out on an island in the Atlantic?

Further rhetorical questions are unnecessary. The whole
thing is as fictional as Lilliput or Brobdingnag. Plato, like Swift,
was artist enough to embroider some realistic details on his
canvas. He also put the romance in a plausible setting by representing it as a tradition deriving from Egypt, where historical
records were much more ancient than anything in Greece. But
can we really suppose that this tale, with its strong Hellenic
interest, survived all those years at Saïs, and was never apparently noted or acquired by anyone else except Solon, who very
conveniently happened to be an ancestor of Plato himself? Plato
has imposed upon our credulity with a bogus story, and, as
Jowett judiciously concluded, 'the world, like a child, has
readily, and for the most part unhesitatingly, accepted the tale'.

So much for the prosecution's case. How is this hard-headed
attack on Plato's credibility to be answered?

Counsel for the defence begins by pointing out that he is not
attempting to prove the contrary of what the prosecution has
asserted. It will be sufficient if he can show that there is some
truth in his client's story.

The prosecution has alleged that the empire of Atlantis is
entirely fictional. But surely the picture of an island-centred
empire dominating other islands and parts of a continent is a
very unlikely fiction for a romancer to have devised, especially in
a Utopian context? When it is realized that the picture is a
startlingly accurate sketch of the Minoan empire in the sixteenth
century BC, does this not create the presumption that there must
be some historical tradition at the core of the legend? The
prosecution has itself pointed out that Plato's dates for the
Atlantis conflict cannot be taken seriously. Plato was also misled
by his informants as to the precise location of the empire of
Atlantis. He was told that it lay in the 'far west'. Now obviously
such a description is relative to the perspective of the person
using it. Plato put Atlantis in the Ocean beyond the Pillars of
Heracles, which was the extreme western limit of the world for
him and his contemporaries. For us, such a location no longer
seems in the west at all.

We must use our historical imaginations, and ask ourselves a crucial question: What was 'far west' to those who first recorded the Atlantis legend? The first recorders of the tradition were the Egyptians of the Bronze Age, and their geographical horizons were exceedingly limited by our standards. They had trade links with Minoan Crete, but this was literally the western limit of their horizon. Crete, which lay 720 km. away across the 'Great Green' with no intervening islands, was literally to them an island in the 'far west'. They probably knew it was very mountainous, and so they regarded it as one of the 'four pillars of heaven', holding up the sky at the western limits of the world. And yet they knew that Crete was no barbaric and backward place, for it produced exquisite metal-work and pottery (Plate 76). Any merchants who visited it brought back marvellous accounts of the complexity and beauty of its great palaces, the luxury of its mansions, and the expertise of its engineers and seamen. Crete must have become something of an El Dorado to the ancient Egyptians. In view of the trade links they must have known something about its network of island bases and its connection with the Greek mainland beyond. Indeed, by the beginning of the fifteenth century they were beginning to draw some distinctions between Keftiu and the islands and coasts beyond it. The Mycenaeans were beginning to impinge on their consciousness as well as the Minoans.

Then, quite suddenly, the whole situation in the Aegean changed. While Tuthmosis III was campaigning in Canaan, and using ports frequented by Minoan traders, a great and terrible disaster overwhelmed Keftiu and its island dependencies. The Egyptians must have heard about the cataclysm from refugees and sailors. They probably recorded something about the physical disappearance of a large part of Thera, and the shrouding of Crete in darkness and dust. They must also have known about the change of regime at Knossos. Rekhmire, as foreign minister, took official cognizance of this at some date between 1460 and 1450, and there must have been some notice in the archives. But even at the time the Egyptians may not have realized at all clearly how the Minoan collapse occurred. They probably thought in terms of an invasion with the cataclysm as a concomitant, not the cause, of the overthrow.

By the XX Dynasty Egypt was on the defensive and had suffered from attacks by peoples whom they called 'peoples of the sea' or 'northerners from all lands.' These invaders probably included Greek tribes. There is a good deal of repetition in the monuments of the XIX and XX Dynasties. Later Pharaohs did not scruple to borrow extensively from the victory hymn of Tuthmosis III (see above, p. 40 f.), even though he was a successful conqueror, and they were much more on the defensive. It would not be at all surprising if the Saïte priests put rather a confused and garbled picture of Late Bronze Age history before Solon. Mycenaeans were partly involved in the downfall of Keftiu, and then, occupying the island, proceeded later to use it as a base for attacks on Egypt. There may have been enough detail in the records for the priests to be able to tell Solon that his 'ancestors' broke the power of Keftiu. In actual fact, we do not know where the new Greek dynasty at Knossos came from. One would tend to suppose they were from the Argolid, but Attica had just as close links with Crete in the LM I period, and was probably even more dominated by Minoan sea power from bases like Keos and Mina off Megara. Attic tradition preserved memories of oppressive tribute levied by Minos, and of a period of tension between the two countries. Historically speaking, there is nothing impossible in the supposition that a Mycenaean prince from Attica took advantage of the confusion and prostration of Crete after the eruption to install himself in power at Knossos.

Solon, of course, would not have connected his Egyptian information with the Theseus legend. To him Keftiu can never have had anything to do with Crete. It must have seemed to him, as it did to the Egyptians of the XVIII Dynasty, a remote and mysterious island. He would have been intrigued by the dramatic possibilities of the story of its sudden and catastrophic 'disappearance'. The priests may even have told him that its ancient civilization fell before the anger of the Earth-shaker. If he asked what 'Keftiu' meant, he may have received an indication that it was an island with a pillar which held up the sky. From Homer Solon would have remembered the account of the remote western island of Kalypso the 'concealer', daughter of Atlas who 'knows the deep places of the sea and guards the lofty pillars which hold earth and sky asunder'. This may have seemed to him the nearest equivalent from his own reading for Keftiu, the Egyptian pillar island which became hidden in the sea. So he may have decided to call it 'Atlantis, the daughter of Atlas', and to place it under the patronage of Poseidon the Earth-shaker. He could then go on to work out the 'plot' of his epic: the rise to power of Atlantis, the growing insolence of its rulers, the anger of Poseidon, and the terrible 'act of god' which laid it low. On this framework he could work in some of the historical information gained from the Saïte priests, in particular the early struggles between the mainland Greeks and 'Atlantis', and the aggression of the 'sea peoples' against Egypt.

The overall case is that Solon acquired in Egypt a genuine, if somewhat garbled, tradition of Minoan Crete; that he did not appreciate the connection of the tradition with the Crete which he knew; that he saw great poetical possibilities in the story; and that he set down its outlines on his return to Athens, giving Greek equivalents for the Egyptian names, *e.g.* Atlantis for Keftiu, and embellishing his 'western island' with some of the historical and topographical information that he had received. Solon's account, and possibly also a Solonian manuscript, then descended to Plato by the route he indicates within his own family. This would explain why it was a genuine historical tradition, and yet not a part of current Greek mythology.

Plato, like Solon, realized the great dramatic possibilities of the Keftiu-Atlantis story. His imagination got to work on the details. He gilded the palace architecture with touches of oriental splendour from his readings in Herodotus and Ctesias. He filled the upland pastures with herds of African elephants. The square allotments and the great irrigation ditches owe much to Egypt (which he had seen) and Babylon (which he had not). The great naval arsenal could be an idealized version of Syracuse with a touch of Carthage. Unconsciously perhaps, he may have introduced something of the luxury of Homer's Phaeacia, itself in part a memory of Minoan Crete. Above all he made Atlantis very large, and put it far back in time and far away in space.

Solon, or the priests, could have mistakenly multiplied some actual dates and linear measurements by ten.[131] If the oblong plain round the palace was only 300 by 200 *stadia* (not 3000 by 2000), it would fit the actual dimensions of the Messara plain near Phaistos. The Messara region is the earliest part of Crete to show Egyptian influence, and is also the largest plain in Crete. If the priests were working with a date 900 years before (not 9000), the disappearance of Atlantis falls about 1490 BC.

These are interesting coincidences, but could be no more than that. However, there are a number of other circumstantial details which cumulatively strengthen the case for identifying Atlantis with Minoan Crete. These are as follows:

1) Atlantis 'was the way to other islands, and from these you might pass to the whole of the opposite continent' (*Timaeus*, 25 a). From the Egyptian point of view this is an accurate description of Crete as the gateway to the Cyclades and mainland Greece.

2) The site of the primeval 'earthborn' dwellers in Atlantis was on a low hill about 50 *stadia* inland, near a very fertile plain, and half-way along the coast of the island (*Critias*, 113 c). The hill was five *stadia* in diameter (*Critias*, 116 a). Here the Atlantians built their palace 'in the habitation of the god and their ancestors, which they continued to ornament in successive generations, every king surpassing the one who went before him to the utmost of his power, until they made the building a marvel to behold for size and beauty' (*Critias*, 115 c–d).

The figures are quite out of proportion with the vast size of Atlantis as imagined by Plato, but very appropriate to the actual site of Knossos, which is on the low mound of Kephala, a hill about 4 *stadia* across and about 5 km. distant from Katsamba and rather farther from Amnisos. The coastal plain here is very rich and fertile, and lies about half-way along the north coast of Crete. There was a neolithic settlement at Knossos going back to the fifth millennium B.C. About 2000 BC the top of the mound was levelled for the building of the first palace. During the next six centuries the palace was frequently rebuilt and enlarged until it covered an area of about 20,000 sq. m. It was, and to some extent still is, 'a marvel to behold for size and beauty.'

3) 'And now I must endeavour to represent to you the nature and arrangement of the rest of the land. The whole country was said by him [Solon] to be very lofty and precipitous on the side of the sea, but the country immediately about and surrounding the city was a level plain, itself surrounded by mountains which descended towards the sea; it was smooth and even, and of an oblong shape, extending in one direction three thousand *stadia*, but across the centre inland it was two thousand *stadia*. This part of the island looked towards the south, and was sheltered from the north. The surrounding mountains were celebrated for

their number and size and beauty, far beyond any which still exist, having in them also many wealthy villages of country folk, and rivers, and lakes, and meadows supplying food enough for every animal, wild or tame, and much wood of various sorts, abundant for each and every kind of work' (*Critias*, 117e–118b).

This is a good description of the southern coast of Crete, which would have been the most familiar part to the ancient Egyptians. Crete is the most mountainous of all the Aegean islands with three great mountain massifs in west, centre, and east. To the west of Phaistos the coastline for 100 km. is an almost unbroken line of mountains coming sheer down to the sea, and eastwards the coast is also steep in many places. The largest plain in Crete forms the hinterland to Phaistos. It is distinctly oblong with the shorter dimension from north to south (see above, p. 140). In ancient times all cultivable parts of the island were thickly covered with a network of villages, farms and manor houses. The forest cover was much greater than it is now. Crete is still well supplied with rivers and springs by Mediterranean standards.

4) 'There were bulls who had the range of the temple of Poseidon; and the ten kings, being left alone in the temple, after they had offered prayers to the god that they might capture the victim which was acceptable to him, hunted the bulls, without weapons, but with staves and nooses' (*Critias*, 119 d–e).

A feature of the bull-ring at Knossos, which distinguishes it from all other bull 'fights' (if we except certain forms of American rodeo) was that the toreadors were completely unarmed. It is also thought that, originally at any rate, they were of royal rank. The Vapheio cups show the hunting of wild bulls 'with nooses'.

5) 'They constructed buildings about them [*i.e.* the hot and cold springs near the palace] and planted suitable trees; also they made cisterns, some open to the heavens, others roofed over, to be used in winter as warm baths; there were the kings' baths and the baths of private persons, which were kept apart; and there were separate baths for women, and for horses and cattle, and to each of them they gave as much adornment as was suitable. Of the water which ran off they carried some to the grove of Poseidon . . .' (*Critias*, 117 a–b).

The excellence and 'modernity' of the plumbing and drainage system of the palace of Minos (Plates 65, 67) has always excited admiring comment. The queen's *megaron* had its own separate bathroom and toilet. On the north-east corner of the palace an elaborate series of runnels with parabolic curves to slow the water and prevent it overflowing at the turns carried the run-off of rain-water through two small settling tanks to a large cistern.

These details taken together seem to provide quite strong circumstantial evidence for identifying Atlantis with Crete. Point 3 suits better the hinterland of Phaistos, but, given the transmission of the legend via Egypt, this amount of garbling is understandable. It is probably easier to believe that Plato was utilizing a genuine tradition of the topography and customs of Crete than to suppose that all the parallels are the result of mere coincidence.

Some other minor details may be added to the list, though there is nothing so distinctive in them as in the list above:

A) 'The island was divided into ten relatively independent administrative districts under the primacy of the royal metropolis' (*Critias*, 119 c–d and 120 c–d). Three other palaces, not much inferior in size and splendour to Knossos, have already been found, and also a number of large mansions or villas.

B) 'The laws were engraved on a pillar in the main palace at the temple of Poseidon' (*Critias*, 119 c–d). This custom can be paralleled from Babylonia. Our copy of Hammurabi's law code is carved on a pillar with a relief of him receiving it from the sun god Shamash. His dates are 1728–1686 BC, and there is evidence that Crete was in contact with Mesopotamia at this period.

C) 'The kings of the ten districts gathered at the main palace for a grand assize in the fourth and ninth years of each nine-year period' (*Critias*, 119 d, adapted to our way of counting such intervals). Homer associates a period of nine years in some way with the rule of Minos (*Odyssey*, 19, 179). Curiously enough, Plato refers to this passage of Homer at the start of the *Laws*, and interprets it as referring to a consultation with Zeus every nine years prior to revision of the laws.

D) Before giving judgment the kings put on 'most beautiful azure robes' (*Critias*, 120 b). This could be a memory of the Minoan *murex* industry.

E) 'Also whatever fragrant things there now are in the earth,

143

whether roots, or herbage, or woods, or essences which distil from fruit and flower, grew and thrived in that land' (*Critias*, 115 a). Crete is still noted for the number and excellence of its aromatic plants and herbs. The export of Cretan lichens to Egypt, possibly for perfumery, has already been noted (see p. 114).

F) 'The stone which was used in the work they quarried from underneath the centre island, and from underneath the zones, on the outer as well as the inner side. One kind was white, another black, and a third red' (*Critias*, 116 a). On Thera and Therasia today the dominant colour scheme of the cliffs is red, black, and white (Plate VI). I do not press this point. These colours can probably be found in combination on most volcanic islands, and in other regions too. But it is, I think, just conceivable that this detail in the Atlantis legend goes back to an observation of Thera soon after the eruption. The new cliffs would look like the rock faces of giant quarries, and the colours of the freshly exposed lavas topped with the banks of dazzling pumice would have seemed even more strange and striking than they do today.

G) 'Moreover there were a great number of elephants in the island' (*Critias*, 114 e). This can never have been true of Crete in the Bronze Age, but nevertheless one of the envoys of Keftiu in the Rekhmire painting is shown carrying an elephant tusk (Plate 74). Elephant tusks have also been found in the palace at Kato Zakro, and are now on display in the Herakleion museum. The Egyptians may well have believed, and told Solon, that ivory came from Keftiu. Evans has suggested that the Minoans hunted elephants on the North African coast opposite Crete.[132] They could also have traded in ivory with Syria which had elephants in the time of Tuthmosis III.

After drawing attention to all these details counsel for the defence of Plato's veracity then proceeds to review the evidence for contacts between Crete and Egypt. Egyptian stone vases were imported into Crete and imitated there by Cretan craftsmen perhaps as early as 2500 BC. Before 2000 BC the influence of Cretan spiral motifs had made itself felt in Egypt. The Ipuwer papyrus reference to the disruption of Keftiu contacts could relate to the First Intermediate Period, *c*. 2181–2040 BC (see above p. 115). Scattered finds of pottery and other objects like scarabs indicate that trade contacts continued all through the first half of the second millennium, though there is not enough evidence to prove that such contacts were very close or frequent. Minoan master masons assisted at the building of the pyramid of Sesostris II. The dedication at Knossos of a statuette by an Egyptian named User (Plate 76) is thought to show that he lived for a time in Crete. By the time of the XVIII Dynasty Egyptian schoolboys were being taught to take an interest in Keftiu (see above p. 42). The important series of pictures of Keftiu envoys (Plates 74, XIV) confirms that there was fairly close contact during the reign of Tuthmosis III, that is to say, precisely at the time when the Thera disaster occurred (see p. 115 f.).

In general, the name Keftiu does not appear very often in Egyptian records and surprisingly little Minoan pottery has been found in Egypt. Crete, it seems, always remained something of a land of mystery, and could be written off as 'missing, presumed sunk' when its power was broken by the eruption and part of its realm literally sank into the sea. But there had clearly been enough contact before this for the sort of particulars to be noted which we find in Plato's account. Egyptian shrines in the Delta at cities like Saïs and Buto had a continuous existence from the XVIII to the XXVI Dynasty when Solon's visit took place. There is nothing improbable in the picture of Solon discussing with priestly antiquarians the history of Greece and Egypt in the Late Bronze Age. Nor is it unreasonable to suppose that some detailed, but not well understood, information about the fabled land of Keftiu and its sudden 'disappearance' was in fact transmitted to Solon. Details from the closing decades of the LM I period (1500–1470) may well have been intermingled with accounts based on the Merenptah and Rameses III inscriptions detailing the great invasions of Egypt between 1225 and 1190 BC. Solon was without any coherent chronological framework for the Late Bronze Age, and could not have detected that the picture was composite. His Egyptian informants may not even have realized it themselves. For them, these old records were all part of the story of relations between Europe and Egypt, culminating in a massive invasion attempt by 'sea peoples and Libyans and northerners from all lands'. The information may even have contained some data about Bronze Age Attica. The priests were priests of the goddess Neith, who had a real affinity with Athena, as Evans has pointed out.

In this way Solon acquired a picture, garbled in dating and incident, but basically reliable in outline and some of the details, of some very important events of the Late Bronze Age. In preparation for his epic poems he worked his information into a 'plot', with the main theme of aggression by an island empire of the west against ancient Greece and Egypt.

This was the shape in which the material was inherited by Plato, partly as an oral tradition from his family circle, partly in the form of a Solonian manuscript with Grecianized forms of the Egyptian proper names, including the crucial one, Atlantis, which Solon substituted for Keftiu. By the time of Herodotus people called Atlantes had been located in Tunisia near a lofty mountain. Herodotus is also the first to name the western ocean the Atlantic. It was therefore quite reasonable and natural for Plato, inheriting the name Atlantis, to imagine the island as a large land mass beyond the Pillars of Heracles. It was he who made it out to be 'larger than Libya and Asia' with a total area of about two and a half million square kilometres. And we can still detect that this inflation was done by Plato from the fact that the overall size of Atlantis is so vastly out of proportion with the size of its metropolis on a hill 1 km. in diameter. A possible explanation of this discrepancy is that the data about the metropolis came from the Solonian tradition and derived ultimately from actual conditions at Knossos.

Counsel now submits that there is sufficient evidence to establish the truth of the following six propositions with reasonable certainty:

1) There was sufficient contact between Crete and Egypt (Plates 71–8) during the Middle and New Kingdoms for the Egyptians to have received reliable and fairly detailed information about the nature and extent of the Minoan empire and its sudden collapse about 1470 BC.

2) This information was recorded and preserved, and a somewhat garbled version made available to Solon on his visit to Egypt, c. 590 BC.

3) Solon assimilated the information to the best of his ability, and re-cast it in the form of notes for an epic poem, with an outline plot, and some Grecianized forms of the names he had been given.

4) Solon did not realize that the information related to Minoan Crete.

5) The information in the form that Solon imposed upon it was transmitted to Plato, either orally or in manuscript form, and was the basis for his account of Atlantis.

6) Plato exaggerated the size and antiquity of Atlantis, and embellished the account with various details gathered from his own reading or personal experience.

At this point in the proceedings we may imagine that Plato himself agrees to submit to cross-examination about his attitude to defence counsel's six basic propositions. He agrees at once with 5 and 6, which are within his own personal knowledge. He also states that he believes 2 and 3 to be true, with the reservation that he never felt sure how much imaginative detail Solon himself had contributed to the account, and how much of the information of the priests was itself reliable or fictitious.

'I always felt', says Plato,

that the Atlantis story, strange though it was, could be basically true, and no mere fiction. Some of the details had an authentic ring about them. However, I thought that some distortion and falsification must have crept in along the long transmission route. Another of my difficulties in handling it arose from the fact that I could not relate the story to anything in my own picture of the Aegean world in the two hundred years or so before the Trojan War. You will remember that even Thucydides could only produce a very sketchy and inferential outline of that epoch. To forestall criticism I therefore took the precaution of locating Atlantis a long way back in time, and a long way off in space. When in Sicily, I had heard talk about the difficulties of navigation outside the Pillars together with sailors' stories of delectable but mountainous islands a long way west of the Libyan coast. It seemed to me, on weighing up all the available evidence, that I would be quite safe in locating Atlantis out there, and in making it the size I did. Its disappearance was a convenient part of the tradition making it difficult if not impossible for anyone to prove me wrong. Just in case anyone did sail out and find traces of the lost land, you will remember that I allowed some reefs and shoals to remain. Finally, may I say that your propositions 1 and 4 surprise and interest me. I recollect now that Thucydides attributes a thalassocracy to the eldest Minos, but it never occurred to me that such an empire located on Crete and the Cyclades could have had anything to do with Atlantis. I must confess that what you say about Solon in 4 applies to me also. Can you give me any evidence for the advanced civilization which you attribute to Minoan Crete?

At this point, with counsel handing up a copy of *The Palace of Minos* to the witness box, I drop the fiction of a judicial enquiry, and present the rest of my conclusions in the conventional way.

Atlantis studies have always tended to become, in the words of Paul Couissin, an 'archipelago of hypotheses'. My first main hypothesis is that a fragment of Bronze Age history is embedded in Plato's account of Atlantis. My second main hypothesis is that the power of Minoan Crete was shattered by a cataclysmic explosion centred on Thera about 1470 BC. I believe that this volcanic destruction of Crete is part of the history embedded in the Atlantis legend. But the two hypotheses can be taken in isolation. It would not be illogical to reject the first and accept the second. Acceptance of the first hypothesis involves acceptance of the existence and reliability of a long and tenuous chain of human testimony. The identification of Crete with Atlantis depends on the sifting and assessment of a mass of circumstantial evidence. The second hypothesis is supported by direct scientific and archaeological evidence in a way in which the first can never be. It also explains a major problem in Aegean history – the collapse of the Minoan empire.

There is no doubt that Thera did erupt violently in the earlier half of the fifteenth century BC. The case for the destructive effects of the eruption on Minoan Crete rests on an assessment of the intensity of the eruption. There are two main points to be considered in such an assessment: first, the analogy of the 1883 Krakatoa eruption; secondly, the evidence of Thera tephra in deep-sea cores.

In the considered opinion of vulcanologists who have studied Thera it is reasonably certain that the Late Bronze Age eruption was of the same paroxysmal type as the 1883 Krakatoa eruption. There are indications that the history of the two volcanoes, in the Late Quaternary period at least *(Fig. 9)*, has followed the same pattern – a cyclical pattern of the build-up of a large volcanic cone, which is then undermined by a series of shattering explosions and collapses, leading to the formation of a large sea-filled caldera. The caldera is then gradually filled in by materials extruded from a vent or vents on the sea floor, and the whole cycle repeats itself. The evidence of the 'lower' tephra in the deep-sea cores puts the previous paroxysmal eruption of Thera in the Würm period about 23000 BC. Both volcanoes are now islands consisting of disconnected fragments of rock and tuff round an enlarging central volcanic dome. In general dimensions, plan and profile they are not at all dissimilar.

In the course of two days, 26–27 August 1883, 23 sq. km. of Krakatoa disappeared as the result of a series of violent explosions. The biggest explosion, at 10 a.m. on the 27th, was heard from Alice Springs in Australia to Martinique, and from Ceylon to Northern Malaya. Atmospheric shock waves from it travelled three and a half times round the globe. The blast caused serious damage to houses up to 160 km. away. Tidal waves were associated with the explosions, and that associated with the biggest explosion was reliably reported as 17 m. high at Vlakke Hoek lighthouse 88 km. away from Krakatoa. The waves destroyed nearly 300 towns and villages on the surrounding coasts of Java and Sumatra, and a large proportion of the coastal population, amounting to over 36,000 people, was drowned. A pall of darkness spread east and west up to 240 km. in each direction, and caused extreme distress in the towns of Batavia and Buitenzorg 180 km. away. A rain of fine ash fell on ships up to 1600 km. distant. Masses of floating pumice blocked harbours and filled the sea in the Sunda Strait for a considerable time, and for many months afterwards ships over a wide area of the Indian Ocean reported pumice in considerable quantities.

The Krakatoa tephra, white in colour, was found by analysis to consist of 95 per cent fine volcanic glass. The Thera tephra is also white, and consists of 97 per cent fine volcanic glass. Both this colour and texture are associated with paroxysmal eruptions after a long period of quiescence. Further evidence for the paroxysmal nature of the Thera eruption is provided by the distribution pattern of the fine tephra. This tephra was ejected high into the upper atmosphere, and was carried by high-altitude winds of the Etesian or summer pattern mainly in a south-easterly direction. It was deposited in detectable amounts over an area of 300,000 sq. km. The deposit in one of the deep-sea cores, 212 cm. thick, is by far the largest deposit of this type known to science. The deposit in the core nearest to north-east Crete is 78 cm. thick.

After thousands of years of erosion Thera is still blanketed by layers of tephra in some places over 60 m. thick, and in many places between 20 and 30 m. These massive deposits (Plate II) are in the main the product of the final stages of the eruption when violent explosions exhausted the magma chamber, and a large part of the centre of the island subsided, forming the caldera. The depth of the submarine trenches, in some places up to 400 m. in the caldera, gives some indication of the force of the explosions. Thera lost an estimated 83 sq. km. of its surface, almost four times as much as Krakatoa. It cannot be inferred that the Thera explosion was four times as powerful, but there is a strong probability that it was at least as powerful, and quite possibly considerably more so. One may therefore reasonably think in terms of an explosion heard from one end of the Mediterranean to the other. One may suppose that the blast damaged houses on Crete and the surrounding islands over a radius of at least 150 km., and possibly much farther. A thick pall of darkness, possibly aggravated by choking dust and vapours, would have spread outwards up to 250 km. at least. The eruption is likely to have been accompanied by violent electrical storms and torrential rain. Next, one must think of the devastating effect of huge tidal waves associated with the final paroxysmal outburst. There is only one direct indication of the size of these waves: a bank of pumice 5 m. thick resting at the head of a valley on the neighbouring island of Anaphi at a height of 250 m. But in historical times all violent seismic and volcanic activity at Thera has been accompanied by destructive *tsunamis* in the Aegean. It is virtually certain that the convulsions attending the formation of the caldera must have been accompanied by an enormous displacement of water. The sea around Thera is deep, particularly in the direction of Crete. It is possible to think in terms of vast mountains of water, perhaps 60 to 100 m. high, moving shoreward at velocities of up to 160 km. per hour. The thickly populated northern coast of Crete, with its many important settlements lying on or near the shore, is likely to have suffered most severely. East coast ports like Palaikastro and Kato Zakro were also very vulnerable. Devastating inundations may also have occurred on all the islands and coasts of the central Aegean. The effect of the waves may have been felt as far as Sicily in the west, and east to the Syrian coast and the Egyptian delta. Finally, one must consider the effects of the ash fall-out, especially on central and eastern Crete. When the darkness cleared, the surviving Minoans would have found their fields and orchards choked and blanketed with a thick covering of acid tephra. A conservative estimate puts this covering at not less than 10 cm. thick. It may have been much thicker, up to 75 cm. or more – a thickness which can kill trees and destroy buildings. Evidence from Iceland and elsewhere shows that such a fall-out is very destructive to vegetation, and a deposit of 10 cm. is enough to put fields out of action for several seasons. It is a reasonable assumption that famine and disease in Crete and other islands destroyed at least as many lives as the tidal waves.

This reconstruction of the Thera disaster is confirmed at many points by archaeological evidence. First, and most obviously, there are the remains of settlements at various points on Thera proper (Plates VI–XIII) and Therasia which were hastily evacuated by their inhabitants and then buried under pumice and ash. The evidence of pottery, and of other finds such as fresco fragments and an inlaid dagger blade (Plate 31), shows that the settlements were Cycladic in type, but strongly under the influence of Minoan culture. Next there is the evidence of widespread and simultaneous destruction of palaces, manor houses, towns and villages, at many points in Crete. At Knossos the palace apparently survived, but at least one substantial building in the vicinity was totally destroyed and not rebuilt. From outside Crete there is evidence of destruction in Minoan colonies at Ayia Irini on Keos (Plate 56), and at Trianda on Rhodes. At the same time Minoan overseas bases like Kythera were abandoned.

When was this time? The chronology of the eruption has been discussed in an earlier section (pp. 50ff.). The accepted framework of Early, Middle and Late Minoan periods based largely on pottery styles and synchronized with absolute dates in Egyptian history is indispensable in any discussion, but has its limitations in this problem. All the indications are that the disaster occurred in the Late Minoan I period, but further refinement as between LM IA and LM IB becomes difficult. There seems to have been a considerable amount of overlap between LM IA and LM IB styles, especially outside Knossos and Crete itself. At Knossos, until the 1961 finds, there was no evidence at all of LM IB pottery as a distinct period. There is also some disagreement over the LM II style and its chronological relationship to LM I pottery. I assume that the LM II style ('Palace Style') came later than LM IB at Knossos, that it represents the products of the Palace pottery under the first Greek dynasty at Knossos, and that it lasted as a style down to about 1400 BC, when it was succeeded generally through Crete by the LM III style.

It is surely a significant fact that no LM II pottery has been found on any of the sites which were destroyed and abandoned over such a wide area. On all such sites the pottery is either LM IA or LM IB or a mixture of the two styles. The most obvious explanation is that the destruction came towards the end, or at the end, of the LM IB period. One can perhaps assume that no fine painted pottery was produced anywhere in Crete except Knossos for quite a long time after the disaster. The date of the final eruption will then be the date of the end of LM IB. Evans, who did not believe in the Thera theory at all, dated this to 1450. Schachermeyr, who is not convinced by the Thera theory, puts it twenty years earlier in 1470. Hood appears to put it about 1460. I favour the earliest of these three dates. I base this opinion, not on the pottery evidence, but on the volcanic evidence. I feel that the evidence points to a shorter rather than a longer period between the initial outbreak and the final paroxysm. Therefore I want to bring the final date back as far as possible in the fifteenth century because, on present evidence, the initial outbreak occurred not far from 1500. I regard the evidence of overpainting in the Keftiu pictures in Rekhmire's tomb as very significant for the chronology (see p. 116). This is said to have taken place between 1460 and 1450. I agree with the view which finds in it a recognition of a new and Greek regime at Knossos. I would also argue that the change of regime was a consequence of the volcanic disaster. If the Rekhmire date is firm, then a date c. 1470 for the final paroxysm cannot, in my opinion, be very far from the mark.

If the eruption culminated in 1470 when did it start? If we follow the analogy of Krakatoa here we would have to posit only a few months from initial outbreak to climax. But the gap is generally thought to have been much longer than this. The date of the initial outbreak is obviously fixed by the latest datable object found under the bottom pumice layer. One expert takes this to be a jug, the pattern of which has affinities with a fifteenth-century Mycenaean piece (Plates 18, 19) from Lachish (see p. 53). On the other hand Marinatos has always supported a date c. 1520, though, as a result of his 1967 excavations at Akrotiri, he is prepared to come down as low as 1500. So far nothing distinctively

LM IB has been found on Thera. If this is still the case after further extensive excavation Marinatos' view will have been considerably strengthened. The preferred carbon-14 date for the Phira tree (1967) is 1559 BC±44 years, which gives a lower limit of 1516 BC. But it is doubtful if the method is accurate enough for 1516 BC to be taken as an absolute lower limit for the first outbreak.

The geological evidence indicates that there was some time gap between the first and final stages of the eruption. The lower layers of pumice are well stratified, and there is some erosion on the surface of layers below the fine white ash (Plate 12). The evidence of core 50 with its three distinct layers is also relevant to this question, but unfortunately its interpretation is by no means certain (see p. 73). Fouqué and Reck both imply that the gap was measured in years rather than months, but neither commits himself to a definite figure. Further examination of the tephra layers on Thera, and further deep-sea cores might well produce a solution of this problem.

Some data from the 1967 Thera excavation also bear on the problem. Marinatos found a massive wall (Plate 37) apparently resting on top of the pumice layer laid down in the first outbreak. This led him to wonder whether people may have returned to Thera and re-occupied it before the final paroxysm. He also noted brown patches on the surface of the coarser pumice which were later covered up by fresh fine tephra. The inference is that mud-brick walls protruding above the debris of the first outbreak had time to decay before the concluding stages of the eruption (see p. 96).

Pending further information from Thera, or other sources, one can only note that a gap of 25 to 30 years would fit neatly with the 1961 evidence from Knossos (for which see pp. 56–60). LM IA pottery was there sealed under a floor, and some time later developed LM IB pottery formed a new and separate deposit above the floor. It seems reasonable to postulate about 25 to 30 years to allow for the development of the new style. The LM IA deposit can then be synchronized with the first outbreak on Thera, and the LM IB deposit with the final paroxysm. The first outbreak will be *c.* 1500 and the final paroxysm *c.* 1470 BC.

I now proceed to give a brief synopsis of the scattered passages from Greek history, poetry, and mythology which I have quoted as possibly containing memories of the Thera eruption and its effects on Aegean life.

First, there is the tradition preserved in Herodotus that Crete was 'depopulated' a considerable time before the Trojan War, and re-occupied by Greeks among others (see above, p. 111ff.). The tradition came from the Praisians who were 'genuine' Cretans, and who maintained their independence and continued to speak a non-Greek language well into the Hellenistic period. No reason for the depopulation is given, but in view of the source from which it comes this tradition could very well embody a genuine memory of the loss of life caused by the tidal waves, and the displacement of population resulting from the tephra fall-out.

I agree with the suggestion that Homer's picture of the Phaeacians contains some features drawn from life in Minoan Crete before the cataclysm (see above, p. 129f.). I therefore view as significant the passage in the *Odyssey* (13, 177) recording an obscurely worded prophecy that Poseidon would 'shroud' or 'shut in' the city of the Phaeacians with a mountain. This could be a remote and not clearly understood memory of some of the consequences of the Thera eruption: the obliteration of a Minoan settlement on Thera, for example, or the blocking of Minoan harbours with floating pumice, or possibly even the ash fall-out on Crete.

The saga of the Argonauts is an ancient part of the Greek epic tradition, and has often been supposed to contain memories of the first voyagings of the Mycenaean Greeks, especially in the Black Sea area. It would not therefore be out of the question for some of its material to go back to the fifteenth century. I have suggested that this is in fact the case with regard to Apollonius' account of a mysterious and chaotic darkness which enveloped Jason and his crew as they were sailing from Crete to Anaphi (see above, p. 124). I have argued that this is a memory of the pall of darkness which spread out from Thera after the final eruption. The evidence from Krakatoa shows that ships survived even quite close to the volcano and were not affected by the tidal waves which passed under them almost unnoticed. The location of this strange and unexplained incident does suggest quite strongly that it is in fact a genuine tradition of one of the eruption phenomena.

The interpretation of the Talos episode is admittedly more speculative, but at least the story makes sense if taken as a volcano myth (see above, p. 123). According to some accounts Talos was given to Minos by Hephaestus, the god of fire. He was the watcher of Crete. He stood on a mountain peak, and was made of 'unbreakable bronze'. He hurled stones (volcanic 'bombs'?) at passing ships, and didn't become 'quiescent' until the ichor flowed out of his heel (lava from a peripheral vent?). Talos had a son called Leukos who was said to have betrayed the king of Knossos, murdered his wife and children, including a daughter Kleisithera to whom he had been betrothed, and destroyed ten cities in Crete. There are certainly some intriguing points here, particularly the occurrence of 'thera' in the girl's name, and the fact that Leukos means 'the white one'. It rounds off the volcanic interpretation of Talos neatly enough to regard his 'white' son as a personification of the destructive fall-out of tephra.

The myth of Typhoeus (see above, pp. 128-9) probably reeds further investigation in relation to the Thera eruption. From Aeschylus and Pindar onwards Typhoeus was often associated with active volcanoes. In Hesiod's account of his battle with Zeus there is a vivid description of the tidal waves which spread outwards from the scene of the 'conflict' (wherever precisely that was). I have suggested that there may be a connection here with the tradition picked up by Herodotus at Buto in Egypt that Typhon once came looking for Horus there (see above, p. 128). This could be a memory of an inundation of the Delta by *tsunamis* associated with the Thera eruption.

The historicity of Greek accounts of floating islands, *e.g.* the island of Aeolus, and Asteriê-Delos, may be seen in a new light if viewed in relation to the masses of floating pumice which must have littered the Aegean for many months after the Thera explosion. For a considerable time after the Krakatoa eruption, ships in the Indian Ocean recorded sighting banks of pumice, in one case up to 40 km. long. Some such tradition could underlie the legend of Asteriê-Delos told with much circumstantial detail by Callimachus. Especially notable are the splitting of a mountain by a god armed with a Minoan trident, the levering-up and rolling forth of islands, the detail that Asteriê-Delos fell from heaven like a star, and the various sightings of it by ships in the

Saronic gulf and elsewhere in the central Aegean (see above, pp. 126–7).

Greek myth-history supplies a number of references to the flooding of coastal plains on both sides of the Aegean. These references cannot be firmly dated, and there is no certainty that they all refer to the same event. Nevertheless as a group they may add up to a genuine memory of the Thera *tsunamis c.* 1470 BC. They come from Attica, the Saronic gulf, and Argolid, Rhodes, Lycia, the hinterland of Smyrna, the Troad, and Samothrace. In the Rhodian tradition there is mention of the Heliadae whom Myres equated with the Minoan colonists on Rhodes[133] (see above, pp. 119–21).

The connection of Deucalion's flood with these traditions is more problematical. The historical basis for the Deucalion story is probably to be sought in Boeotia, where the Copaic lake certainly inundated some settlements in the second millennium. The inundation could have been brought on by excessive rainfall, and by the blockage of natural and artificial outlets by earthquakes, and both these events could be synchronous with stages in the Thera eruption. It is interesting that Manetho apparently dated Deucalion's flood to the reign of Tuthmosis III (see above, p. 118).

My main historical thesis of the shift of power from Crete to Mycenaean Greece as directly caused by the Thera eruption is at least not contradicted by Thucydides. He records that the eldest Minos 'ruled the Cyclades and controlled piracy with the aid of a fleet' (I, 4). This is the clearest and strongest statement that we have from ancient Greece about the Minoan thalassocracy in what I take to be the sixteenth and early fifteenth centuries. As a result of this Minoan control, Thucydides continues, sea-borne commerce prospered, leading to the growth of rich and strongly fortified power centres on the Greek mainland which dominated 'the lesser cities'. This was the political set-up in Greece at the time of the Trojan War (I, 8). Without mentioning Thera, of course, Thucydides has here given us the essentials of Late Bronze Age history in the Aegean with the *Pax Minoica* giving way to the Mycenaean military ascendancy.

Many of my readers may feel that if the Thera disaster was really so important in early Greek history it would have been remembered more clearly. The evidence just reviewed must seem devious, sketchy, and often very problematical. Two points may be made in reply to this objection. First, the Greeks remembered very little at all about the fifteenth century BC. Their national consciousness was then only in an early formative stage. Their main saga cycles date from the thirteenth century when, under the leadership of Mycenae, they had become a major power in the eastern Mediterranean. Secondly, even the Mycenaean world as a whole was only dimly remembered by the later Greeks. Epic poetry was the main bridge on which their thoughts went back across the gulf of four dark centuries when the art of writing was completely lost in Greek lands. With the aid of aristocratic pedigrees their chronographers managed to produce a reasonably accurate date for the siege of Troy, but for events further back than that they had little or no data to go on. It is not, therefore, altogether surprising that there was no clear memory of the circumstances under which the Minoan empire collapsed. The legend of Theseus and the Minotaur comes closest to being such a memory. But it contains no hint of the Thera disaster, except possibly in the statement attributed to Pherecydes that Theseus 'stove in the bottoms of the Cretan ships and thus prevented them from pursuing him' when he was abducting Ariadne from Knossos.[134] One might speculate that this 'scuttling' of the Minoan navy was really done by the Thera *tsunamis*. The legend of Atlantis, on the other hand, does attribute the disappearance of a great civilization to a natural disaster. But there, because of the circumstances under which the legend came back from Egypt to Greece, there was no recognition that the lost island civilization was that of pre-Mycenaean Crete. The suggestion that Atlantis reflected Minoan Crete was not made, and could not have been made, until the archaeological discoveries of this century revealed once more the achievements of Minoan art and technology.

I interpret the 'disappearance' of Atlantis to mean the end of Minoan dominance in the Aegean world. Admittedly parts of Thera literally disappeared under the sea, a strange and portentous occurrence which was probably recorded in Egyptian annals, and perhaps also left some mark on the Argonaut saga. But I do not look for the lost Atlantis under the surface of Thera bay. Thera was in no sense the metropolis of Crete, and cannot be identified with the metropolis of Atlantis.[135] Thera was simply a Minoan dependency like Kythera, Keos, and half a dozen more. For me 'lost Atlantis' is a historical rather than a geographical concept. The volcano obliterated settlements on Thera and wrecked the island, and what it did to Thera may still be seen and studied in detail, and forms the strongest testimony to the destructiveness of the eruption. But what it did to Thera is comparatively unimportant in comparison with what it did to the Minoanized archipelago surrounding it, and to the Minoan heartland to the south. A brilliant and refined culture foundered under the brutal impact of Theran vulcanism. The tidal waves were the real 'bull from the sea' which was sent to plague the rulers of Knossos.

The Egyptians had long known and wondered at the Minoan world of sea-borne commerce and gracious living. It was a world that was very remote and different from their own and they recorded, I believe, some details of its organization, and of the bizarre fate which overtook it. In a confused and garbled form this record descended to the time of Solon, and formed the basis of the Atlantis legend that he recorded and passed on to Plato.

The Greeks were too young to remember the Thera cataclysm at all clearly, but there can be little doubt that their Mycenaean world benefited greatly from the Minoan dispersion. After the eruption, when Crete was devastated and depopulated, a stream of refugees went to the western Peloponnese, and doubtless to other parts of Greece too. Minoan princesses, the 'daughters of Atlas', married into the houses of Mycenaean war-lords. Minoan architects designed the mainland palaces, and Minoan painters adorned them with frescoes. Greek first became a written language in the hands of Minoan scribes. Minoan folklore, I believe, acted like a leaven in the Greek imagination. Minoan religion did much to mould the forms of the Greek gods.

Much of this cultural heritage was lost in the break-up of the Mycenaean world at the end of the Bronze Age. But something, undoubtedly, was carried across the dark centuries, and went to enrich the culture of the classical period. To my eyes the spirit of Ionia is already astir in the stately palace of the Neleids at Pylos. The later Greeks, as they looked back proudly to their heroic age, did not consciously or coherently remember what they owed to Minoan culture. They had legends with a Cretan flavour – Minos as judge in Hades, Rhadamanthys in Elysium, the birth and death of Zeus. But this last legend in particular served only to brand all Cretans as liars. The historical realities of the Minoan world had passed into limbo, and they recognized no trace of it in the Atlantis legend.

Yet, in a sense, they never quite forgot that far-off world. They vaguely knew that there had been eras of great peace and prosperity in the remote past, and they distilled this consciousness into the potent myth of the golden and silver ages which came before the more warlike generations of bronze and iron. In Minoan Crete, if anywhere, there had been 'peace within the walls and plenteousness within the palaces.' A dim memory of this persisted, I believe, all through antiquity, and coloured the Greeks' attitude to the past with a certain nostalgia. We too, as we look back at the fine flowering of Minoan culture, may feel a touch of sadness at its sudden obliteration. Minoan civilization did not wither and decay. It was snapped and broken off short at a high point in its growth. Its delicate superstructure could not stand up to the storm which struck it. We may borrow for its epitaph the sad question of Shakespeare:

> How with this rage shall beauty hold a plea
> Whose action is no stronger than a flower?

But not everything was lost. Like a fire-ravaged olive tree, Minoan culture went dormant for a time, and then sent up fresh shoots in the shade of the Mycenaean citadels. It is probably no accident that Dorian Crete in the Archaic Period was noted for the excellence of its laws and institutions. The stock that had been tended so lovingly through the long peaceful centuries was not to be easily eradicated. Grafts from the same stock were transplanted to Greece itself, and took root and flourished there too. And down the years, as the wind whispered gently over the golden corn-fields and through the silvery branches of the olive groves, the Greeks still caught a faint echo of the happy generations who had lived in peace and plenty in their sea-girt island before the bronze of imperialism and the iron of nationalism had come to bruise and break the peoples of the Mediterranean world.

Appendix

Here follow translations of passages from Plato's *Timaeus* and *Critias* relevant to the Atlantis legend.

1) *In the first extract* (Timaeus 20 d–27 a) *Critias explains how Solon acquired the legend in Egypt, and gives a brief summary of it.*

Crit. Then listen, Socrates, to a tale which, though strange, is certainly true, having been attested by Solon, who was the wisest of the seven sages. He was a relative and a dear friend of my great-grandfather, Dropides, as he himself says in many passages of his poems; and he told e the story to Critias, my grandfather, who remembered and repeated it to us. There were of old, he said, great and marvellous actions of the 21 Athenian city, which have passed into oblivion through lapse of time and the destruction of mankind, and one in particular, greater than all the rest. This we will now rehearse. It will be a fitting monument of our gratitude to you, and a hymn of praise true and worthy of the goddess, on this her day of festival.

Soc. Very good. And what is this ancient famous action of the Athenians, which Critias declared, on the authority of Solon, to be not a mere legend, but an actual fact?

Crit. I will tell an old-world story which I heard from an aged man; for Critias, at the time of telling it, was, as he said, nearly ninety years of age, and I was about ten. Now the day was that day of the Apaturia b which is called the Registration of Youth, at which, according to custom, our parents gave prizes for recitations, and the poems of several poets were recited by us boys, and many of us sang the poems of Solon, which at that time had not gone out of fashion. One of our tribe, either because he thought so or to please Critias, said that in his judgement Solon was not only the wisest of men, but also the noblest of poets. The old man, c as I very well remember, brightened up at hearing this and said, smiling: Yes, Amynander, if Solon had only, like other poets, made poetry the business of his life, and had completed the tale which he brought with him from Egypt, and had not been compelled, by reason of the factions and troubles which he found stirring in his own country when he came home, to attend to other matters, in my opinion he would have been as d famous as Homer or Hesiod, or any poet.

And what was the tale about, Critias? said Amynander.

About the greatest action which the Athenians ever did, and which ought to have been the most famous, but, through the lapse of time and the destruction of the actors, it has not come down to us.

Tell us, said the other, the whole story, and how and from whom Solon heard this veritable tradition.

He replied: In the Egyptian Delta, at the head of which the river e Nile divides, there is a certain district which is called the district of Sais, and the great city of the district is also called Sais, and is the city from which King Amasis came. The citizens have a deity for their foundress; she is called in the Egyptian tongue Neith, and is asserted by them to be the same whom the Hellenes call Athene; they are great lovers of the Athenians, and say that they are in some way related to them. To this city came Solon, and was received there with great honour; he asked the 22 priests who were most skilful in such matters, about antiquity, and made the discovery that neither he nor any other Hellene knew anything worth mentioning about the times of old. On one occasion, wishing to draw them on to speak of antiquity, he began to tell about the most ancient things in our part of the world – about Phoroneus, who is called 'the first man', and about Niobe; and after the Deluge, of the survival of Deucalion and Pyrrha; and he traced the genealogy of their descendants, b and reckoning up the dates, tried to compute how many years ago the events of which he was speaking happened. Thereupon one of the priests, who was of a very great age, said: O Solon, Solon, you Hellenes are never anything but children, and there is not an old man among you. Solon in return asked him what he meant. I mean to say, he replied, that in mind you are all young; there is no old opinion handed down among you by ancient tradition, nor any science which is hoary with age. And I will tell you why. There have been, and will be again, many destruc- c tions of mankind arising out of many causes; the greatest have been brought about by the agencies of fire and water, and other lesser ones by innumerable other causes. There is a story, which even you have pre- served, that once upon a time Phaëthon, the son of Helios, having yoked the steeds in his father's chariot, because he was not able to drive them in the path of his father, burnt up all that was upon the earth, and was himself destroyed by a thunderbolt. Now this has the form of a myth, but really signifies a declination of the bodies moving in the heavens around the earth, and a great conflagration of things upon the earth, d which recurs after long intervals; at such times those who live upon the mountains and in dry and lofty places are more liable to destruction than those who dwell by rivers or on the sea-shore. And from this calamity we are preserved by the liberation of the Nile, who is our never-failing saviour. When, on the other hand, the gods purge the earth with a deluge of water, the survivors in your country are herdsmen and shepherds who dwell on the mountains, but those who, like you, live in cities are carried by the rivers into the sea. Whereas in this land, neither then nor at any e other time, does the water come down from above on the fields, having always a tendency to come up from below; for which reason the tradi- tions preserved here are the most ancient. The fact is, that wherever the extremity of winter frost or of summer sun does not prevent, mankind exist, sometimes in greater, sometimes in lesser numbers. And whatever happened either in your country or in ours, or in any other region of 23 which we are informed – if there were any actions noble or great or in any other way remarkable, they have all been written down by us of old, and are preserved in our temples. Whereas just when you and other nations are beginning to be provided with letters and the other requisites of civilized life, after the usual interval, the stream from heaven, like a pestilence, comes pouring down, and leaves only those of you who are destitute of letters and education; and so you have to begin all over again b like children, and know nothing of what happened in ancient times, either among us or among yourselves. As for those genealogies of yours which you just now recounted to us, Solon, they are no better than the tales of children. In the first place you remember a single deluge only, but there were many previous ones; in the next place, you do not know that there formerly dwelt in your land the fairest and noblest race of men which ever lived, and that you and your whole city are descended from a c small seed or remnant of them which survived. And this was unknown to you, because, for many generations, the survivors of that destruction died, leaving no written word. For there was a time, Solon, before the great deluge of all, when the city which now is Athens was first in war and in every way the best governed of all cities, and is said to have performed the noblest deeds and to have had the fairest constitution of any of which tradition tells, under the face of heaven. Solon marvelled at d his words, and earnestly requested the priests to inform him exactly and in order about these former citizens. You are welcome to hear about them, Solon, said the priest, both for your own sake and for that of your city, and above all, for the sake of the goddess who is the common patron and parent and educator of both our cities. She founded your city a thousand years before ours, receiving from the Earth and Hephaestus e the seed of your race, and afterwards she founded ours, of which the constitution is recorded in our sacred registers to be 8,000 years old. As touching your citizens of 9,000 years ago, I will briefly inform you of 24 their laws and of their most famous action; the exact particulars of the whole we will hereafter go through at our leisure in the sacred registers themselves. If you compare these very laws with ours you will find that many of ours are the counterpart of yours as they were in the olden time. In the first place, there is the caste of priests, which is separated from all the others; next, there are the artificers, who ply their several crafts by themselves and do not intermix; and also there is the class of shepherds and of hunters, as well as that of husbandmen; and you will observe, too, b that the warriors in Egypt are distinct from all the other classes, and are commanded by the law to devote themselves solely to military pursuits; moreover, the weapons which they carry are shields and spears, a style of equipment which the goddess taught of Asiatics first to us, as in your part of the world first to you. Then as to wisdom, do you observe how our law from the very first made a study of the whole order of things, extending even to prophecy and medicine which gives health; out of these divine c elements deriving what was needful for human life, and adding every sort of knowledge which was akin to them. All this order and arrangement the goddess first imparted to you when establishing your city; and she chose the spot of earth in which you were born, because she saw that the happy temperament of the seasons in that land would produce the wisest of men. Wherefore the goddess, who was a lover both of war and of wisdom, selected and first of all settled that spot which was the most likely to produce men most like herself. And there you dwelt, having such laws as these and still better ones, and excelled all mankind in all virtue, as became the children and disciples of the gods.

Here follows the extract quoted above, pp. 19-20

I have told you briefly, Socrates, what the aged Critias heard from e Solon and related to us. And when you were speaking yesterday about your city and citizens, the tale which I have just been repeating to you came into my mind, and I remarked with astonishment how, by some mysterious coincidence, you agreed in almost every particular with the narrative of Solon; but I did not like to speak at the moment. For a long time had elapsed, and I had forgotten too much; I thought that I must **26** first of all run over the narrative in my own mind, and then I would speak. And so I readily assented to your request yesterday, considering that in all such cases the chief difficulty is to find a tale suitable to our purpose, and that with such a tale we should be fairly well provided.

And therefore, as Hermocrates has told you, on my way home yesterday I at once communicated the tale to my companions as I remembered **b** it; and after I left them, during the night by thinking I recovered nearly the whole of it. Truly, as is often said, the lessons of our childhood make a wonderful impression on our memories; for I am not sure that I could remember all the discourse of yesterday, but I should be much surprised if I forgot any of these things which I have heard very long ago. I listened at the time with child-like interest to the old man's narrative; he was **c** very ready to teach me, and I asked him again and again to repeat his words, so that like an indelible picture they were branded into my mind. As soon as the day broke, I rehearsed them as he spoke them to my companions, that they, as well as myself, might have something to say. And now, Socrates, to make an end of my preface, I am ready to tell you the whole tale. I will give you not only the general heads, but the particulars, as they were told to me. The city and citizens, which you yesterday described to us in fiction, we will now transfer to the world of reality. **d** It shall be the ancient city of Athens, and we will suppose that the citizens whom you imagined, were our veritable ancestors, of whom the priest spoke; they will perfectly harmonize and there will be no inconsistency in saying that the citizens of your republic are these ancient Athenians. Let us divide the subject among us, and all endeavour according to our ability gracefully to execute the task which you have imposed upon us. Consider then, Socrates, if this narrative is suited to the purpose, or whether we should seek for some other instead. **e**

Soc. And what other, Critias, can we find that will be better than this, which is natural and suitable to the festival of the goddess, and has the very great advantage of being a fact and not a fiction? How or where shall we find another if we abandon this? We cannot, and therefore you must tell the tale, and good luck to you; and I in return for my yester- **27** day's discourse will now rest and be a listener.

2) *In the second extract* (Critias *108 c–109 a and 113 a–end*) *Critias recounts the Atlantis legend in greater detail.*

Crit. Friend Hermocrates, you, who are stationed last and have another in front of you, have not lost heart as yet; the gravity of the situation will soon be revealed to you; meanwhile I accept your exhortations and encouragements. But besides the gods and goddesses whom **d** you have mentioned, I would specially invoke Mnemosyne; for all the important part of my discourse is dependent on her favour, and if I can recollect and recite enough of what was said by the priests and brought hither by Solon, I doubt not that I shall satisfy the requirements of this theatre. And now, making no more excuses, I will proceed.

Let me begin by observing first of all, that nine thousand was the sum **e** of years which had elapsed since the war which was said to have taken place between those who dwelt outside the pillars of Heracles and all who dwelt within them; this war I am going to describe. Of the combatants on the one side, the city of Athens was reported to have been the leader and to have fought out the war; the combatants on the other side were commanded by the kings of Atlantis, which, as I have said, once existed, greater in extent than Libya and Asia, and afterwards when sunk by an earthquake, became an impassable barrier of mud to those voyagers from hence who attempt to cross the ocean which lies beyond. The progress of the history will unfold the various nations of barbarians and 109 families of Hellenes which then existed, as they successively appear on the scene; but I must describe first of all the Athenians of that day, and their enemies who fought with them, and then the respective powers and governments of the two kingdoms. Let us give the precedence to Athens.

Critias next gives a detailed account of prehistoric Athens and Attica, here omitted as only marginally relevant to the identification of Atlantis. He then introduces the 'Solonian' account of Atlantis, as follows:

Yet, before proceeding further in the narrative, I ought to warn you, 113 that you must not be surprised if you should perhaps hear Hellenic names given to foreigners. I will tell you the reason of this: Solon, who was intending to use the tale for his poem, enquired into the meaning of names, and found that the early Egyptians in writing them down had translated them into their own language, and he recovered the meaning of the several names and when copying them out again translated them into our language. My grandfather had the original writing, which is b still in my possession, and was carefully studied by me when I was a child. Therefore if you hear names such as are used in this country, you must not be surprised, for I have told you how they came to be introduced. The tale, which was of great length, began as follows:

I have before remarked in speaking of the allotments of the gods, that they distributed the whole earth into portions differing in extent, and made for themselves temples and instituted sacrifices. And Poseidon, c receiving for his lot the island of Atlantis, begat children by a mortal woman, and settled them in a part of the island, which I will describe. Towards the sea, half-way down the length of the whole island, there was a plain which is said to have been the fairest of all plains and very fertile. Near the plain again, and also in the centre of the island at a distance of about fifty stadia, there was a mountain not very high on any side. In this mountain there dwelt one of the earth-born primeval men of that country, whose name was Evenor, and he had a wife named Leucippe, d and they had an only daughter who was called Cleito. The maiden had already reached womanhood, when her father and mother died; Poseidon fell in love with her and had intercourse with her, and breaking the ground, inclosed the hill in which she dwelt all round, making alternate zones of sea and land larger and smaller, encircling one another; there were two of land and three of water, which he turned as with a lathe, each having its circumference equidistant every way from the centre, so that no man could get to the island, for ships and voyages were e not as yet. He himself, being a god, found no difficulty in making special arrangements for the centre island, bringing up two springs of water from beneath the earth, one of warm water and the other of cold, and making every variety of food to spring up abundantly from the soil. He also begat and brought up five pairs of twin male children; and dividing

the island of Atlantis into ten portions, he gave to the first-born of the 114
eldest pair his mother's dwelling and the surrounding allotment, which
was the largest and best, and made him king over the rest; the others he
made princes, and gave them rule over many men, and a large territory.
And he named them all; the eldest, who was the first king, he named
Atlas, and after him the whole island and the ocean were called Atlantis. b
To his twin brother, who was born after him, and obtained as his lot the
extremity of the island towards the pillars of Heracles, facing the country
which is now called the region of Gades in that part of the world, he
gave the name which in the Hellenic language is Eumelus, in the language of the country which is named after him, Gadeirus. Of the second
pair of twins he called one Ampheres, and the other Evaemon. To the
elder of the third pair of twins he gave the name Mneseus, and
Autochthon to the one who followed him. Of the fourth pair of twins he c
called the elder Elasippus, and the younger Mestor. And of the fifth pair
he gave to the elder the name of Azaes, and to the younger that of
Diaprepes. All these and their descendants for many generations were
the inhabitants and rulers of divers islands in the open sea; and also, as
has been already said, they held sway in our direction over the country
within the pillars as far as Egypt and Tyrrhenia. Now Atlas had a
numerous and honourable family, and they retained the kingdom, the d
eldest son handing it on to his eldest for many generations; and they had
such an amount of wealth as was never before possessed by kings and
potentates, and is not likely ever to be again, and they were furnished
with everything which they needed, both in the city and country. For
because of the greatness of their empire many things were brought to
them from foreign countries, and the island itself provided most of what e
was required by them for the uses of life. In the first place, they dug out
of the earth whatever was to be found there, solid as well as fusile, and
that which is now only a name and was then something more than a
name, orichalcum, was dug out of the earth in many parts of the island,
being more precious in those days than anything except gold. There was
an abundance of wood for carpenters' work, and sufficient maintenance
for tame and wild animals. Moreover, there were a great number of 115
elephants in the island; for as there was provision for all sorts of animals,
both for those which live in lakes and marshes and rivers, and also for
those which live in mountains and on plains, so there was for the animal
which is the largest and most voracious of all. Also whatever fragrant
things there now are in the earth, whether roots, or herbage, or woods, or
essences which distil from fruit and flower, grew and thrived in that
land; also the fruit which admits cultivation, both the dry sort, which is
given us for nourishment, and any other which we use for food – we call
them all by the common name of pulse, and the fruits having a hard rind, b
affording drinks and meats and ointments, and good store of chestnuts
and the like, which furnish pleasure and amusement, and are fruits which
spoil with keeping, and the pleasant kinds of dessert, with which we
console ourselves after dinner, when we are tired of eating – all these that
sacred island which then beheld the light of the sun, brought forth fair
and wondrous and in infinite abundance. With such blessings the earth
freely furnished them; meanwhile they went on constructing their
temples and palaces and harbours and docks. And they arranged the
whole country in the following manner:

First of all they bridged over the zones of sea which surrounded the ancient metropolis, making a road to and from the royal palace. And at the very beginning they built the palace in the habitation of the god and of their ancestors, which they continued to ornament in successive generations, every king surpassing the one who went before him to the utmost of his power, until they made the building a marvel to behold for d size and for beauty. And beginning from the sea they bored a canal of three hundred feet in width and one hundred feet in depth and fifty stadia in length, which they carried through to the outermost zone, making a passage from the sea up to this, which became a harbour, and leaving an opening sufficient to enable the largest vessels to find ingress. Moreover, e they divided at the bridges the zones of land which parted the zones of sea, leaving room for a single trireme to pass out of one zone into another, and they covered over the channels so as to leave a way underneath for the ships; for the banks were raised considerably above the water. Now the largest of the zones into which a passage was cut from the sea was three stadia in breadth, and the zone of land which came next of equal breadth; but the next two zones, the one of water, the other of land, were two stadia, and the one which surrounded the central island was a stadium only in width. The island in which the palace was 116 situated had a diameter of five stadia. All this including the zones and the bridge, which was the sixth part of a stadium in width, they surrounded by a stone wall on every side, placing towers and gates on the bridges where the sea passed in. The stone which was used in the work they quarried from underneath the centre island, and from underneath the zones, on the outer as well as the inner side. One kind was white, another black, and a third red, and as they quarried, they at the same time hollowed out docks double within, having roofs formed out of the b native rock. Some of their buildings were simple, but in others they put together different stones, varying the colour to please the eye, and to be a natural source of delight. The entire circuit of the wall, which went round the outermost zone, they covered with a coating of brass, and the circuit of the next wall they coated with tin, and the third, which encompassed the citadel, flashed with the red light of orichalchum. The c palaces in the interior of the citadel were constructed on this wise: In the centre was a holy temple dedicated to Cleito and Poseidon, which remained inaccessible, and was surrounded by an enclosure of gold; this was the spot where the family of the ten princes was conceived and saw the light, and thither the people annually brought the fruits of the earth in their season from all the ten portions, to be an offering to each of the ten. Here was Poseidon's own temple which was a stadium in length, and d half a stadium in width, and of a proportionate height having a strange barbaric appearance. All the outside of the temple, with the exception of the pinnacles, they covered with silver, and the pinnacles with gold. In the interior of the temple the roof was of ivory, curiously wrought everywhere with gold and silver and orichalcum; and all the other parts, the walls and pillars and floor, they coated with orichalcum. In the temple they placed statues of gold: there was the god himself standing in a chariot – the charioteer of six winged horses – and of such a size that he e touched the roof of the building with his head; around him there were a hundred Nereids riding on dolphins, for such was thought to be the number of them by the men of those days. There were also in the interior of the temple other images which had been dedicated by private persons. And around the temple on the outside were placed statues of gold of all who had been numbered among the ten kings, both them and their wives, and there were many other great offerings of kings and of private persons, coming both from the city itself and from the foreign cities over which they held sway. There was an altar too, which in size and workmanship corresponded to this magnificence, and the palaces, in like manner, answered to the greatness of the kingdom and the glory of the temple.   117

In the next place, they had fountains, one of cold and another of hot water, in gracious plenty flowing; and they were wonderfully adapted for use by reason of the pleasantness and excellence of their waters. They constructed buildings about them and planted suitable trees; also they made cisterns, some open to the heaven, others roofed over, to be used in b winter as warm baths; there were the kings' baths, and the baths of private persons, which were kept apart; and there were separate baths for women, and for horses and cattle, and to each of them they gave as much adornment as was suitable. Of the water which ran off they carried some to the grove of Poseidon, where were growing all manner of trees of wonderful height and beauty, owing to the excellence of the soil, while the remainder was conveyed by aqueducts along the bridges to the outer circles; and there were many temples built and dedicated to many gods; also gardens and places of exercise, some for men, and others for c horses in both of the two islands formed by the zones; and in the centre of the larger of the two there was set apart a race-course of a stadium in width, and in length allowed to extend all round the island, for horses to race in. Also there were guard-houses at intervals for the main body of guards, whilst the more trusted of them were appointed to keep watch in the lesser zone, which was nearer the Acropolis; while the most d trusted of all had houses given them within the citadel, near the persons of the kings. The docks were full of triremes and naval stores, and all things were quite ready for use. Enough of the plan of the royal palace.

Leaving the palace and passing out across the three harbours, you came e to a wall which began at the sea and went all round: this was everywhere distant fifty stadia from the largest zone or harbour, and enclosed the whole, the ends meeting at the mouth of the channel which led to the sea. The entire area was densely crowded with habitations; and the canal and the largest of the harbours were full of vessels and merchants coming from all parts, who, from their numbers, kept up a multitudinous sound of human voices, and din and clatter of all sorts night and day.

I have described the city and the environs of the ancient palace nearly in the words of Solon, and now I must endeavour to represent to you the nature and arrangement of the rest of the land. The whole country was 118 said by him to be very lofty and precipitous on the side of the sea, but the country immediately about and surrounding the city was a level plain, itself surrounded by mountains which descended towards the sea; it was smooth and even, and of an oblong shape, extending in one direction three thousand stadia, but across the centre inland it was two thousand stadia. This part of the island looked towards the south, and was b sheltered from the north. The surrounding mountains were celebrated for their number and size and beauty, far beyond any which still exist, having in them also many wealthy villages of country folk, and rivers, and lakes, and meadows supplying food enough for every animal, wild or tame, and much wood of various sorts, abundant for each and every kind of work.

I will now describe the plain, as it was fashioned by nature and by the labours of many generations of kings through long ages. It was naturally c for the most part rectangular and oblong, and where falling out of the straight line had been made regular by the surrounding ditch. The depth, and width, and length of this ditch were incredible, and gave the impression that a work of such extent, in addition to so many others, could never have been artificial. Nevertheless I must say what I was told. It was excavated to the depth of a hundred feet, and its breadth was a stadium everywhere; it was carried round the whole of the plain, and d was ten thousand stadia in length. It received the streams which came down from the mountains, and winding round the plain and meeting at the city, was there let off into the sea. Farther inland, likewise, straight canals of a hundred feet in width were cut from it through the plain, and again let off into the ditch leading to the sea: these canals were at intervals of a hundred stadia, and by them they brought down the wood from the mountains to the city, and conveyed the fruits of the earth in ships, cutting transverse passages from one canal into another, and to the city. Twice in the year they gathered the fruits of the earth – in winter having the benefit of the rains of heaven, and in summer the water which the land supplied, when they introduced streams from the canals.

As to the population, each of the lots in the plain had to find a leader a 119 for the men who were fit for military service, and the size of a lot was a square of ten stadia each way, and the total number of all the lots was sixty thousand. And of the inhabitants of the mountains and of the rest of the country there was also a vast multitude, which was distributed among the lots and had leaders assigned to them according to their districts and villages. The leader was required to furnish for the war the sixth portion of a war-chariot, so as to make up a total of ten thousand chariots; also two horses and riders for them, and a pair of chariot- b horses without a car, accompanied by a horseman who could fight on foot carrying a small shield, and having a charioteer who stood behind the man-at-arms to guide the two horses; also, he was bound to furnish two heavy-armed soldiers, two archers, two slingers, three stone-shooters and three javelin-men, who were light-armed, and four sailors to make up the complement of twelve hundred ships. Such was the military order of the royal city – the order of the other nine governments varied, and it would be wearisome to recount their several differences.

As to offices and honours, the following was the arrangement from the c first. Each of the ten kings in his own division and in his own city had the absolute control of the citizens, and, in most cases, of the laws, punishing and slaying whomsoever he would. Now the order of precedence among them and their mutual relations were regulated by the commands of Poseidon which the law had handed down. These were inscribed by the first kings on a pillar of orichalchum, which was situated d in the middle of the island, at the temple of Poseidon, whither the kings were gathered together every fifth and every sixth year alternately, thus giving equal honour to the odd and to the even number. And when they were gathered together they consulted about their common interests, and enquired if any one had transgressed in anything, and passed judgement, and before they passed judgement they gave their pledges to one another on this wise: There were bulls who had the range of the temple of Poseidon; and the ten kings, being left alone in the temple, after they had offered prayers to the god that they might capture the victim which

was acceptable to him, hunted the bulls, without weapons, but with e
staves and nooses; and the bull which they caught they led up to the pillar
and cut its throat over the top of it so that the blood fell upon the sacred
inscription. Now on the pillar, besides the laws, there was inscribed an
oath invoking mighty curses on the disobedient. When therefore, after
slaying the bull in the accustomed manner, they proceeded to burn its 120
limbs, they filled a bowl of wine and cast in a clot of blood for each of
them; the rest of the victim they put in the fire, after having purified the
column all round. They they drew from the bowl in golden cups, and
pouring a libation on the fire, they swore that they would judge according to the laws on the pillar, and would punish him who in any point had
already trangressed them, and that for the future they would not, if they
could help, offend against the writing on the pillar, and would neither
command others, nor obey any ruler who commanded them, to act b
otherwise than according to the laws of their father Poseidon. This was
the prayer which each of them offered up for himself and for his
descendants, at the same time drinking and dedicating the cup out of
which he drank in the temple of the god; and after they had supped and
satisfied their needs, when darkness came on, and the fire about the
sacrifice was cool, all of them put on most beautiful azure robes, and,
sitting on the ground, at night, over the embers of the sacrifices by c
which they had sworn, and extinguishing all the fire about the temple,
they received and gave judgement, if any of them had an accusation to
bring against any one; and when they had given judgement, at daybreak
they wrote down their sentences on a golden tablet, and dedicated it
together with their robes to be a memorial.

There were many special laws affecting the several kings inscribed
about the temples; but the most important was the following: They
were not to take up arms against one another, and they were all to come
to the rescue if any one in any of their cities attempted to overthrow the
royal house; like their ancestors, they were to deliberate in common d
about war and other matters, giving the supremacy to the descendants of
Atlas. And the king was not to have the power of life and death over any
of his kinsmen unless he had the assent of the majority of the ten.

Such was the vast power which the god settled in the lost island of
Atlantis; and this he afterwards directed against our land for the following reasons, as tradition tells: For many generations, as long as the
divine nature lasted in them, they were obedient to the laws, and well- e
affectioned towards the god, whose seed they were; for they possessed
true and in every way great spirits, uniting gentleness with wisdom in the
various chances of life, and in their intercourse with one another. They
despised everything but virtue, caring little for their present state of life,
and thinking lightly of the possession of gold and other property, which
seemed only a burden to them; neither were they intoxicated by luxury;
nor did wealth deprive them of their self-control; but they were sober,
and saw clearly that all these goods are increased by virtue and friendship 121
with one another, whereas by too great regard and respect for them they
are lost, and virtue with them. By such reflections and by the continu-
ance in them of a divine nature, the qualities which we have described
grew and increased among them; but when the divine portion began to
fade slowly, and became diluted too often and too much with the mortal
admixture, and the human nature got the upper hand, they then, being b
unable to bear their fortune, behaved unseemly, and to him who had an

eye to see grew visibly debased, for they were losing the fairest of their precious gifts; but to those who had no eye to see the true happiness, they appeared glorious and blessed at the very time when they were becoming tainted with unrighteous ambition and power. Zeus, the god of gods, who rules according to law, and is able to see into such things, c perceiving that an honourable race was in a woeful plight, and wanting to inflict punishment on them that they might be chastened and improve, collected all the gods into their most holy habitation, which, being placed in the centre of the world, beholds all created things. And when he had called them together, he spake as follows:

At this point the unfinished Critias *breaks off.*

Notes

References Bibl. *are to the numbered list in the Bibliography*, p. 176

CHAPTER I

1 Aristotle's view is inferred from two passages in Strabo, II, 102 and XIII, 598. *Cf.* Proclus in *Timaeum* 61a (Diehl I, p. 197).
2 Proclus, in *Timaeum* 24a-b (Diehl I, p. 76).
3 J. O. Thomson, *A History of Ancient Geography*, New York, 1964, 91.
4 B. Jowett, *The Dialogues of Plato* (3rd ed.), Oxford, 1892, vol. 3, 519: (from introduction to *Critias*): 'Hence we may safely conclude that the entire narrative is due to the imagination of Plato ...', F. M. Cornford, *Plato's Cosmology*, New York, 1957, 8: 'all this elaborate romance about the invasion from Atlantis ...' A. E. Taylor, *Plato, The Man and his Work*, London, 1926, 439. W. W. Hyde, *Ancient Greek Mariners*, Oxford, 1947, 158. T. G. Rosenmeyer, *Classical Philology 44*, 118.
5 M. P. Nilsson, *The Mycenaean Origin of Greek Mythology*, New York, 1932.
6 Site at Tris Langadas on the north slope of Polis Bay: *Annual of the British School at Athens 40*, 10. Cave shrine of the Nymphs, *ibid. 35*, 45ff.; *39*, 1ff.; *Antiquity 10*, 358ff.
7 Homer, *Odyssey* 3, *passim*; bath: 464-8, wine: 391.
8 Nestor's Palace: first reported in *American Journal of Archaeology 43*, 557ff. For a concise description see *A Guide to the Palace of Nestor*, University of Cincinnati, 1962.
9 Thera, the ancient name of the island, has been officially revived. The alternative name Santorin (Santorini) derives from the Venetian occupation after the Fourth Crusade. 'Thera' derives from Theras, the leader of the Dorian colonists who occupied the island in the Geometric period. 'Santorin' is a corruption of the name of the island's patron saint, St Irene.
10 Diehl, *Anth. Lyr. Graec.* fr. 6. The line is quoted in Plutarch, *Solon* 26, with the information that Psenophis of Heliopolis and Sonchis of Sais were Solon's mentors during his stay in Egypt.
11 For a survey of the evidence see J. Boardman, *The Greeks Overseas*, Harmondsworth, 1964, 133-50.
12 *Timaeus*, 20d-22b. See Appendix, p. 160.
13 *Critias*, 113a-b. See Appendix p. 164.
14 Posidonius in Strabo II, 102.

15 A stade=600 Greek feet, or 606¾ English feet; 9 stadia (approx.) = 1 mile; 6 stadia (approx.)=1 kilometre.

16 Plutarch, *Solon* 32.

CHAPTER 2

17 *Bibl.* 2.

18 E. T. Berlioux, *Les Atlantides*, Paris, 1885. L. Frobenius, *The Voice of Africa*, London, 1913, vol. I, 319–49. J. Spannuth, *Atlantis – the mystery unravelled*, London, 1956. For the Tartessus theory see, for example, A. Schulten, Atlantis, *Rheinische Museum 88*, 326–46.

19 L. Spence, *The Problem of Atlantis*, London, 1924, *Atlantis in America*, London, 1925, *The History of Atlantis*, London, 1926.

20 See the *National Geographic Magazine* Map Supplement, 'The Atlantic Ocean Floor', vol. 133, June 1968.

21 For a Boeotian location of Atlantis see the local tradition recorded by Pausanias, IX, 120, 3, and also note (daughters of Atlas).

22 Herodotus I, 202; IV, 42; IV, 185. *Cf.* Diodorus III, 54.

23 P. B. S. Andrews, Larger than Africa and Asia?, *Greece and Rome 14*, 76–9.

24 *Phaedo*, 109a–b; *Timaeus*, 25a quoted p. 19, where see diagram.

25 In the later article, *Journal of Hellenic Studies 33*, 189 ff., Frost acknowledges his authorship of *The Times* article (though wrongly dating it 19 January, 1909). It was submitted, the editor of the *Times* archives tells me, c/o Professor P. Gardner.

26 The placing of Keftiu in Cilicia was first suggested by G. A. Wainwright, *Liverpool Annals of Archaeology and Anthropology 6*, 24ff. For a criticism of Wainwright, see H. R. Hall, Keftiu, in *Essays in Aegean Archaeology presented to Sir A. Evans* (S. Casson, ed.), Oxford, 1927, 31–41. Schachermeyr comes out firmly in support of the Keftiu-Crete identification, *Bibl.* 19, 109–15 with notes. A. H. Sayce, *Essays* (*op. cit.*), 107–8, argues that the identification of Keftiu with the Biblical Caphtor is made certain by the Sargon of Akkad tablet which refers to Kap-ta-ra as lying 'beyond the Upper Sea'. Biblical passages connecting the Philistines with Caphtor are: *Genesis* 10, 14 (which should read 'and the Caphtorim whence came the Philistines'); *Amos* 9, 7; *Jeremiah* 47, 4; For Kerēthim (?Cretans) see *Ezekiel* 25, 16, *Zephaniah* 2, 5.

27 Keftiu does appear in lists of tribute countries under Amenophis III (1405–1367) and Rameses II (1304–1237), but J. A. Wilson suspects these later lists as 'having a strong fictional colouring', and as merely repeating for propaganda purposes the genuine entries of Tuthmosis III's lists. See *Bibl.* 12, 242.

28 *Bibl.* 13, 127–34.

29 Full texts in translation in *Bibl.* 8, vol. 2, 262–6 and *Bibl.* 12, 373–5.

30 For a definitive study of the Ipuwer papyrus, see A. H. Gardiner, *The Admonitions of an Egyptian Sage*, Leipzig, 1909. J. van Seters, *Journal of Egyptian Archaeology 50*, 13ff. favours a late XIII Dynasty date for it. *Cf.* C. Aldred, *The Egyptians*, London, 1961, 102.

31 See A. J. Evans, *Early Nilotic, Libyan and Egyptian Relations with Minoan Crete*, London, 1925, 22.

32 T. E. Peet, The Egyptian Writing Board BM 5647 bearing Keftiu names, in *Essays in Aegean Archaeology presented to Sir A. Evans* (S. Casson, ed.), Oxford, 1927, 90–99.

33 H. R. Hall in *Essays* (*op. cit.*), 32.

34 For a detailed study, with many illustrations, of the significance of pillars in Minoan religion, see A. J. Evans, Mycenean tree and pillar cult, *Journal of Hellenic Studies 21*, 99–204.

35 *Odyssey* 1, 48–54.

36 *Bibl.* 3. Bramwell, *Bibl.* 1, 75–90, argued against Frost's theory. Pendlebury, *Bibl.* 18, 286, gave it a brief word of approval. It was not really revived in earnest until the early 1950's, *e.g.* by C. Seltman in *History Today*, 1952, 332–43, and by S. Marinatos, On the myth of Atlantis (in Greek), *Kretika Chronika 2*, 1950, 195–213.

37 S. Marinatos, Amnisos, die Hafenstadt des Minos, *Forschungen und Fortschritte 10*, 341–43.

CHAPTER 3

38 The meaning of the term is fully discussed by H. Williams, *Bibl.* 32, 239ff. 'Caldera' is Spanish for 'kettle', 'cauldron'. A caldera is not to be confused with a crater, which is always an eruptive vent, typical of the active growing period of a volcano. The presence of a caldera is a sign that the volcano has run through a complete life-cycle. The caldera is a large steep-sided basin formed by subsidence and engulfment after an eruption or series of eruptions. After vast quantities of pumice have been ejected, the roof over the magma chamber collapses, and a caldera is formed. Both Thera and Krakatoa are classified by Williams as *explosive* calderas since they were formed by endogenous forces, but he points out that other factors operated in their formation besides a mere explosion decapitating a cone. Calderas formed purely by an explosion are never above 2½ to 3 km. in diameter.

38a The word 'tephra' (Greek for 'ashes') has recently been given scientific currency by Dr Thorarinsson (see note 60) as a general term for the lighter materials ejected during an eruption. These include dust, ashes, pumice, and cinders (*scoriae*), and are characteristic of the first phase of an eruption, which is often an explosive phase preceding the outflow of lava. These lighter *ejecta* are varied forms of the lava whose structure has been altered by the explosive disengagement of vapour. Pumice is, in effect, 'aerated' lava.

39 *Bibl.* 24: quarrying methods, 7; carbon-14 date, 56.

40 A. G. Galanopoulos, Zur Bestimmung des Alters der Santorin-Kaldera, *Neues Jb. f. Geol. und Paläeont. 9*, 419–20.

41 H. Baker, in *The Scientist and Archaeology*, E. Pyddoke, ed. London, 1963, 123–35.

42 *Bibl.* 25.

43 *Bibl.* 20.

44 *Bibl.* 24, 55.

45 *Bibl.* 26, 35.

46 F. H. Stubbings, *Mycenaean Pottery from the Levant*, Cambridge, 1951, 56 and Plate xiv, 1. The cup was found close to the altar in the sanctuary of the Fosse temple at Lachish.

47 *Bibl.* 30, vol. 1, 122–3.

48 *Bibl.* 27, 292–4.

49 *Archaeological Reports* 1961/2, 25–7 and *Illustrated London News*, Archaeological Section No. 2080, 17 Feb. 1962.

50 N. A. Critikos, Sur des phénomènes sismiques produits avant et depuis l'éruption du volcan de Santorin, *Annls. Obs. nat. Athènes 8*, 56, 58; Sur la sismité des Cyclades et de la Crête, *ibid. 9*, 77–109.

51 A. Alexiou, New materials for late Aegean chronology and history, (in Greek), *Kretika Chronika 6*, 9–41. For a summary of the article by R. W. Hutchinson see *Antiquity*, 1954, 183ff. See also *Bibl.* 11, 29.

52 For full details of the Krakatoa eruption see *Bibl.* 31. Also, R. D. M. Verbeek, *Krakatav*, Batavia, 1886.

53 Pliny, *Epistles*, VI 20, 18, uses the same comparison to describe the scene after the eruption of Vesuvius in AD 79: *omnia alto cinere tanquam nive obducta.*

54 *Cf.* Pliny, *Epistles*, VI 16, 5.

55 *Bibl.* 32, 257.

56 *Bibl.* 29. See also *Nature 213*, Feb. 11, 1967, 582–4, by same authors.

57 G. Marinos and N. Melidonis, On the amplitude of the tsunami originating in the prehistoric eruption of Santorini, (in Greek), *Greek Geological Society, 4*, (1959–61), 210–18.

58 *Bibl.* 6, 434.

59 The evidence has been collected by Galanopoulos, *Bibl.* 28.

60 K. Eldjarn, Two Mediaeval Farm Sites in Iceland and some remarks on tephrochronology, in *The Fourth Viking Congress*, A. Small, ed., 1965.

61 *Bibl.* 14, 167.

62 Dr G. Walker of the Geological Department, Imperial College, London, has very kindly allowed me to see an unpublished graph which he has compiled confirming this point.

63 Strabo, I, 57.

64 Philostratus, *Vita Apollonii* section 175=Bk. IV, 34.

65 P. Dekigalla (de Cigala), *Diary of the 1866 volcanic eruption at the Kameni islands*, (in Greek), Syra, 1881.

CHAPTER 4

66 Fouqué, *Premier Rapport sur une mission scientifique à l'ile de Santorin* Paris, 1867 and *Bibl.* 27, 104–31.

67 *Bibl.* 22, vol. 3, 40f.

68 *Bibl.* 20.

69 *Bibl.* 26, 26 and 38.

70 Illustrated in G. Perrot and C. Chipiez, *History of Art in Primitive Greece*, London, 1894, vol. 2, 450, fig. 541.

71 *Bibl.* 24, *passim.*

CHAPTER 5

72 *Bibl.* 26, 39.

73 Thucydides, I, 4.

74 *Archaeological Reports* 1963/4, 25–6.

75 *Odyssey* 7, 321–4.

76 *Bibl.* 26, 31.

77 *Iliad* 2, 108.

78 *Bibl.* 11, 29; *Bibl.* 18, 228; *Bibl.* 15, vol. IV, 885; A. Furumark, *The Chronology of Mycenaean Pottery*, Stockholm 1941, 82.

79 *Bibl.* 18, 229.

80 Apollodorus, *Bibliotheca* III, 15, 7–8.

81 *Bibl.* 11, 46.

82 *Cf.* Plutarch, *Theseus* 19.

83 *Bill.* 18, 289.

84 See reports by J. L. Caskey in *Hesperia 31, 33, 35*, especially vol. 33.

85 *Bacchylides*, 1, 2–17 (Jebb). See also J. M. Edmonds, *Lyra Graeca* III, 126–35.

85a Pindar, *Paen* IV, 27–44. In line 34 I follow Wilamowitz's emendation Ἐωοσιδα, (Pindaros, 475).

85b Pindar, *Isthmia* 27ff.

86 G. Monaco, *Clara Rhodos 10*, 41ff. F. H. Stubbings, *Mycenaean Pottery from the Levant*, Cambridge, 1951, 6–8. A. Furumark, *Opuscula archaeologica* VI, Lund, 1950, 150–271.

87 Herodotus, 7, 170–1.

88 Diodorus, IV, 79, 3.

89 O. R. Gurney, *The Hittites,* Harmondsworth, 1961, 47–9.

90 *Odyssey*, 7, 120–8.

91 *Bibl.* 8, vol. 3, 240–52, vol. 4, 18–68, especially 33–38. *Bibl.* 12, 262–3.

92 *Bibl.* 12, 441. See also note 30.

93 B. B. Baumann, The botanical aspects of ancient Egyptian embalming and burial, *Economic Botany 14.*

94 See note 30.

95 N. M. Davies and A. H. Gardiner, *Ancient Egyptian Paintings* I, Chicago, 1936, Pls. XXI–XXIV.
   N. de G. Davies, *The tomb of Rekhmire at Thebes,* Publications of the Metropolitan Museum of Art Egyptian Expedition, XI, New York, 1943.
   Bibl. 15, vol. 2, 736–48. *Bibl.* 19, 112–15.

96 *Bibl.* 19, 113.

97 Text and discussion conveniently in Waddell's *Manetho* (Loeb Classical Library) 112 and 86–7.

98 Apollodorus, *Bibliotheca* I, 7, 2.

99 J. Forsdyke, *Greece before Homer*, New York, 1957, 57–8.

100 See the genealogical table in J. L. Myres, *Who were the Greeks?* Berkeley, 1930, 344–5.

101 I am indebted to Marinatos, *Bibl.* 10, for most of the following references to flood traditions.

102 Apollodorus, *Bibliotheca,* III, 14, 1, with Frazer's notes *ad loc.* in the Loeb edition.

103 Pausanias II, 22, 4. A temple of Poseidon Proklystios (The Flooder) at Argos commemorated the event.

103a Pausanias, II, 30, 6 and 32, 8.

104 Euripides, *Hippolytus* 1198–1212.

105 Plutarch, *Moralia* 248a–b.

106 Strabo I, 58.

107 Diodorus V, 56–57.

108 Diodorus V, 47, 3–5.

109 Apollonius Rhodius, *Argonautica* 4, 1537–1764. Gift of the 'clod', 1552–3; formation of Thera, 1755–64.

110 G. L. Huxley, The Ancient Name of Zakro, *Greek, Roman and Byzantine Studies 8,* 85–7.

111 J. Schoo, Vulkanische und seismische Aktivitat des Agaischen Meeresbeckens im Spiegel der griechische Mythologie, *Mnemosyne* ser. III, vol. IV, 257–94.

112 R. Hennig, Altgriechische Lagengestalte als Personifikation von Erdfeuern und Vulkanischen Vorgangen. *Jb. d. Deutsch. Arch. Instituts 54,* 230–46.

113 Eustathius, *Commentaria ad Iliadem et Odysseam*, 1860, 59. Eustathius is commenting on *Odyssey* 19, 174–5 ('ninety cities in Crete') and the discrepancy with *Iliad* 2, 649 ('hundred-citied Crete'). He reports the theory that ten cities were destroyed in the struggle between Idomeneus king of Knossos and his treacherous son-in-law to be, Leukos. *Cf.* Apollodorus, *Epitome* VI, 10. Lycophron, *Alexandra* 1214–1224, introduces the legend with the ominous words: 'Great woe shall come to Knossos', and calls Leukos a 'viper in the bosom' for Crete. Idomeneus, son of Deucalion and Minos, is traditionally synchronised with the Trojan War, but in the Leukos story a tradition of earlier devastation in Crete could have become fused with the legends of a later period. Confusion could have arisen from the fact that Idomeneus is credited with a son named Lykus, and also from the genealogical duplication of Deucalion and Minos.

114 *Argonautica*, 4, 1694–1701.
115 Pliny, *Epistles* VI, 20, 14.
116 *Argonautica* 4. 1731–1764.
117 Callimachus, *Hymn* IV, 30–54.
118 *Odyssey* 10, 1–4.
119 Herodotus II, 156.
120 Pindar fr. 91 (Bergk). I owe this reference to W. B. Stanford.
121 Hesiod, *Theogony*, 844–49.
122 *Iliad* 2, 782–3. Pindar, *Pythia* 1, 17–20. Aeschylus, *PV*. 365.
123 H. J. Rose, *A Handbook of Greek Mythology*, 57. *Cf. ibid* 60 (of Typhon): 'the imagery clearly owes something to volcanic phenomena'.
124 *Odyssey* 13, 125ff. threat: 149–52.
125 'Orpheus', *Argonautica* 1268–80.
126 *Bibl.* 15, vol. 2, 301–3.
127 *Amos* 9, 5–7.
128 A. G. Galanopoulos, Die ägyptischen Plagen und der Auszug Israels aus geologischer Sicht, *Zeitschrift f.d. Kl. Altertum 10*, 131–7.
129 *Bibl.* 10.
130 Pauly-Wissowa *R.E. sv.* Atlas, cols. 2120–2122.

CHAPTER 6

131 Diodorus I, 26 is evidence for Egyptian 'years' which were really months, and led to a greatly inflated chronology.
132 *Bibl.* 15, vol. 2, 742–3.
133 J. L. Myres, *Who were the Greeks?*, Berkeley, 1930, 139–40. L. Farnell, *Cults of the Greek States*, New York, 1967, vol. V, 418–9.
134 Plutarch, *Theseus*, 19.
135 As is done by A. G. Galanopoulos. *Bibl. 5.*

Bibliography

The following list does not aim to do more than set out systematically the books and articles which have formed the main basis of the present study. Many of them will be found to give extensive guidance for further reading.

a) Surveys of Atlantis literature

1 BRAMWELL, J. *Lost Atlantis,* London, 1937.
2 MARTIN, T. H. *Etudes sur le Timée de Platon,* Paris, 1841, I, 257–332.

b) Atlantis as Minoan Crete

3 BRANDENSTEIN, W. *Atlantis,* 1951.
4 FROST, K. T. The *Critias* and Minoan Crete, *Journal of Hellenic Studies 33,* 189–206.
5 GALANOPOULOS, A. G. On the location and the size of Atlantis, (in Greek with English summary), *Praktika Akad. Ath. 35,* 401–18.
6 MARINATOS, S. The volcanic destruction of Minoan Crete, *Antiquity 13,* 425–39.
7 – On the Myth of Atlantis, (in Greek), *Kretika Chronika 2,* 195–213.

c) Records and historical background

8 BREASTED, J. H. *Ancient Records of Egypt,* 4 vols, Chicago, 1906.
9 HOOD, S. *The Home of the Heroes: The Aegean before the Greeks,* London, 1967.
10 MARINATOS, S. The volcano of Thera and the States of the Aegean, (in Greek), *Acta of the 2nd Cretological Congress (1967),* vol 1, Athens, 1968, 198–216.
11 MATZ, F. *Minoan Civilisation: Maturity and Zenith,* Cambridge Ancient History, rev. edn., vol. 2, chaps. IV (b) and XII (fasc. 12), 1962.
12 PRITCHARD, J. B. *Ancient Near Eastern Texts,* Princeton, 1955.
13 VERCOUTTER, J. *Essai sur les relations entre Egyptiens et Pré-hellénes,* Paris, 1954.

d) Ancient Crete

14 ALEXIOU, S., PLATON, N. and GUANELLA, H. *Ancient Crete*, London, 1968.
15 EVANS, Sir ARTHUR. *The Palace of Minos at Knossos*, London, 1921–36.
16 HUTCHINSON, R. W. *Prehistoric Crete*, Harmondsworth, 1962.
17 MARINATOS, S. *Crete and Mycenae*, London, 1960.
18 PENDLEBURY, J. D. S. *The Archaeology of Crete*, London, 1939.
19 SCHACHERMEYR, F. *Die minoische Kultur des alten Kreta*, Stuttgart, 1964.

e) Archaeology of Thera and the Cyclades

20 ÅBERG, N. *Bronzezeitliche und Früheisezeitliche Chronologie*, Stockholm, 1930, vol. iv, 127–37.
21 CASKEY, J. L. Investigations in Keos, *Hesperia 31, 33, 35*.
22 GAERTRINGEN, F. HILLER VON. *Thera*, 4 vols, Berlin, 1899–1909.
23 MAMET, H. *De Insula Thera*, Lille, 1874.
24 MARINATOS, S. *Excavations at Thera, First preliminary report (1967 season)*, Athens, 1968.
25 RENAUDIN, L. Vases préhelléniques de Théra, *Bulletin de Correspondance Hellénique 46*, 113–59.
26 SCHOLES, K. The Cyclades in the later Bronze Age: A synopsis, *Annual of the British School at Athens 51*, 9–40.

f) Thera Vulcanism : Krakatoa

27 FOUQUÉ, F. *Santorin et ses éruptions*, Paris, 1879.
28 GALANOPOULOS, A. G. Tsunamis observed on the coasts of Greece from antiquity to the present time, *Annali Geofisici 13*, 369–86.
29 NINKOVICH, D. and HEEZEN, B. C. Santorini Tephra, in *Submarine Geology and Geophysics*, Colston Papers, vol. 17, Bristol, 1965.
30 RECK, H. *Santorin: Der Werdegang eines Inselvulkans und sein Ausbruch 1925–28*. 3 vols, Berlin, 1936.
31 SYMONS, G. J. *The eruption of Krakatoa and subsequent phenomena*. The Report of The Krakatoa Committee of the Royal Society, London, 1888.
32 WILLIAMS, H. *Calderas and their origin*, University of California Publications in Geological Science 25, 239–346.

List of Illustrations

Unless otherwise acknowledged photographs are by the author

Colour Plates

Monochrome Plates

Figures   *drawn by Lucinda Rodd*

Index

ANTHROPOLOGY

THE CHILDREN OF THE DREAM Bruno Bettelheim 75p
The dream is the kibbutz, one of the most enduring modern attempts
to create a Utopian human society. Bruno Bettelheim examines the
products of that dream and goes on to examine the Western middle-
class ideal of family.

CLASS, CODES AND CONTROL Basil Bernstein 75p
The collected papers of one of the most genuinely creative minds in
British sociology today – the development of Bernstein's theories of
the 'restricted' and 'elaborated' codes of speech and of 'open' and
'closed' rule systems. Spoken language is a process and processing
phenomenon and is the major means by which an individual becomes
self-regulating.

HOMO HIERARCHICUS Louis Dumont 90p
Ostensibly, a study of the caste system in India; Louis Dumont sheds
new light on Western notions of equality and democracy: a classic of
Anthropology.

MAN AND BEAST Roy Willis 75p
Animals are man's best friends and deadliest foes, the object of his
worship, the victims of his abuse. Roy Willis shows how animals are
actually living symbols of man's innermost identity in a work that
vastly extends our knowledge of the human and animal within
ourselves.

STEPS TO AN ECOLOGY OF MIND Gregory Bateson £1·00
This book develops a new way of thinking about the nature of order
and organisation in living systems, a unified body of theory so
encompassing and inter-disciplinary that it illuminates all areas of
study of behaviour and biology.

ARCHAEOLOGY

THE ANCIENT SUN KINGDOMS OF THE AMERICAS
Victor W. Von Hagen £1–00
For centuries, the strange exotic civilisations of the Aztecs, Mayas,
and Incas, flowered in total separation from the rest of mankind.
Victor Von Hagen takes these people out of the flow of the purely
archaeological and puts them back into the human stream of life.
Illustrated.

BEFORE THE DELUGE Herbert Wendt 90p
Palaeontology sets out to find the point in the past when life began
to exist on our planet, how it developed, and when man first appeared.
This is the story of how palaeontology developed as a science and
what it now tells us about the planet on which we live. Illustrated.

THE BOG PEOPLE P. V. Glob 75p
In a peat bog in Schleswig, Denmark, the body of a fourteen–year–old
girl was found. It was almost 2,000 years–old and had been perfectly
preserved by the strange chemical properties of the peat. An
authoritative account of one of the most remarkable archaeological
finds ever. Illustrated.

THE DAWN OF EUROPEAN CIVILISATION V. Gordon Childe
£1–00
The last edition of the classic archaeological work that continues to
dominate all explanations of the growth of European prehistory.
Illustrated.

INDUSTRIAL ARCHAEOLOGY Arthur Raistrick 75p
The 'forgotten' aspect of archaeology; both an introduction and an
essential reference work from Britain's leading authority. Illustrated.

MYSTERIOUS BRITAIN Janet and Colin Bord £1–50
All over the British countryside, are totems and indications of lost
civilisations and knowledge, scattered in a rich profusion if only the
eye can see. This book looks into the past while suggesting some
startling research for the future. Illustrated.

THE PILTDOWN MEN Ronald Millar 75p
The case study of the most notorious hoax in the history of
archaeology. Illustrated.

HISTORY

MICROBES AND MORALS Theodor Rosebury £1-95
The strange social and medical history of attitudes towards venereal
disease.

THE MONKS OF WAR Desmond Seward £1-00
The courageous and often savagely brutal history of the military
religious orders; a compulsive epic of the Knights Templar, the
hospitallers and the Teutonic Knights. Illustrated.

THE MYTHOLOGY OF THE SECRET SOCIETIES
J. M. Roberts £1-50
A spectre haunted 18th and 19th century European history; that a
secret society would seize power. It was a false myth. "J. M. Roberts
has written an important and scholarly essay on the conspiracy theory
of history." *Sunday Telegraph.*

THE PURSUIT OF THE MILLENNIUM Norman Cohn 75p
Revolutionary millenarians and mystical anarchists in the Middle
Ages roamed Europe searching for redemption. A masterpiece of the
history of ideas. Illustrated.

THE QUEST FOR ARTHUR'S BRITAIN Geoffrey Ashe £1-00
The story of Arthur and the Knights of the Round Table, the chief
myth of Britain. How true is it? Illustrated.

THE ROSICRUCIAN ENLIGHTENMENT Frances A. Yates
£1-50
The Rosicrucians stood midway between the Dark Ages and the
scientific Renaissance: The Hermetic tradition of magic, alchemy
and the Kabbalah revealed.

RUSSIA IN REVOLUTION Lionel Kochan £1-00
A compact, readable and authoritative account of one of the
most important events in modern history.

HISTORY (cont.)

DECISIVE BATTLES OF THE WESTERN WORLD
VOLS. 1 & 2 J. F. C. Fuller £2–00
The most original and influential military thinker Britain has ever produced: His major work.

THE DREYFUS TRIALS Guy Chapman 90p
The classic exposition of one of the most scandalous political trials ever.

THE EXTENSION OF MAN J. D. Bernal 75p
The story of the development of Physics as part of man's attempt to control his environment and sustain his own life. Illustrated.

FOLK SONG IN ENGLAND A. L. Lloyd £1–50
The classic history of the natural expressions of the British people.

INDUSTRIAL ARCHAEOLOGY Arthur Raistrick 75p
The 'forgotten' aspect of archaeology; both an introduction and an essential reference work from Britain's leading authority. Illustrated.

MACHIAVELLI Sydney Anglo 60p
Was Machiavelli a devil incarnate or a political genius? "Altogether, this is the best introduction to Machiavelli one could hope for."
A. L. Rowse.